ADVANCE PRAISE FOR *Protecting the Prairies*

"*Protecting the Prairies* is an engaging overview of Saskatchewan's environmental policies and the contributions of Saskatchewan's most humble environmental advocate. Andrea Olive's book will help inspire a new generation of environmentalists and remotivate those of us who need it." —**CAROLYN GAUDET**, Manager of Saskatchewan Prairie Conservation Action Plan

"In this affectionate portrait, Andrea Olive brings humanity and warmth to the politics of conservation." —**CANDACE SAVAGE**, author of *A Geography of Blood*

"This is a wonderful story of a man who has given most of his life to protecting Saskatchewan's natural environment." —**KEN LUDWIG**, president of Nature Saskatchewan

"Combining the deep research of an experienced environmental policy scholar with first-hand interviews and an accessible narrative, Andrea Olive's *Protecting the Prairies* is an engaging political biography of renowned conservationist Lorne Scott. It is also a sweeping history of the last half-century of Saskatchewan wildlife/conservation policies and a meditation on the perennial prairie paradox: exploit or protect resources. Considering Scott's many accolades, awards, and roles, it is easy to see why Olive frames her subject as the province's most important wildlife protector.

A compelling, eloquent, and wise book, *Protecting the Prairies* is for any Saskatchewanian interested in their province's environmental past, present, and future—which should be everyone." —**DANIEL MACFARLANE**, Associate Professor, Institute of the Environment and Sustainability, Western Michigan University

"A captivating read serving as a testimonial to the lifelong work of conservationist, advocate, and farmer Lorne Scott, while drawing attention to the reality of ecosystems at risk, alerting us to the need for better stewardship practices to safeguard our natural heritage for future generations." —INGRID CAZAKOFF, CEO, Heritage Saskatchewan

"It would be my opinion that over the past 40+ years, if you have lived in Saskatchewan and care a whit about native prairie, grassland animals, or sustainable agriculture, you have been utterly unconscious if you have not spent at least some time in the presence of Lorne. His boundless energy and enthusiasm are justifiably legendary. In my opinion, he is a fascinating and driven (in the right way) human. I feel that a simple biography of him would have been well justified, but in effect using him as a means to making the points that this book does is simply a fabulous opportunity taken advantage of. I suspect Lorne is tickled that his story was used for this latter purpose and not just the former. I really hope that our politicians of all stripes will read and think about the messages in this book." —MARK BRIGHAM, Professor of Biology, University of Regina

PROTECTING THE PRAIRIES

LORNE SCOTT
and the Politics of Conservation

ANDREA OLIVE

Foreword by TREVOR HERRIOT

University of Regina Press

Printed and bound in Canada at Marquis. The text of this book is printed on 100%
post-consumer recycled paper with earth-friendly vegetable-based inks.

COVER AND TEXT DESIGN: Duncan Noel Campbell
COPY EDITOR: Dallas Harrison
PROOFREADER: Kelly Laycock
COVER IMAGE: "Mountain Bluebird." Adobe Stock

Library and Archives Canada Cataloguing in Publication

TITLE: Protecting the prairies : Lorne Scott and the politics of conservation / Andrea Olive.

OTHER TITLES: Lorne Scott and the politics of conservation

NAMES: Olive, Andrea, 1980- author.

DESCRIPTION: Includes bibliographical references and index.

IDENTIFIERS: Canadiana (print) 20230224555 | Canadiana (ebook) 20230224571 | ISBN
9780889779600 (softcover) | ISBN 9780889779631 (hardcover) | ISBN 9780889779617 (PDF) |
ISBN 9780889779624 (EPUB)

SUBJECTS: LCSH: Scott, Lorne. | LCSH: Environmentalists—Saskatchewan—Biography. |
LCSH: Naturalists—Saskatchewan—Biography. | LCSH: Farmers—Saskatchewan—Biography. |
LCSH: Environmentalism—Political aspects—Saskatchewan. | LCGFT: Biographies.

CLASSIFICATION: LCC GE56.S36 O45 2023 | DDC 333.72092—dc23

10 9 8 7 6 5 4 3 2 1

University of Regina Press

University of Regina, Regina, Saskatchewan, Canada, S4S 0A2
TEL: (306) 585-4758 FAX: (306) 585-4699 WEB: www.uofrpress.ca

University of Regina Press is located on Treaty 4 Territory, the traditional
lands of the nêhiyawak (Cree), Anihšinapêk (Saulteaux), Dakota, Lakota,
and Nakoda Nations, and the homeland of the Métis peoples.

We acknowledge the support of the Canada Council for the Arts for our publishing program.
We acknowledge the financial support of the Government of Canada. / Nous reconnaissons
l'appui financier du gouvernement du Canada. This publication was made possible with
support from Creative Saskatchewan's Book Publishing Production Grant Program.

This book is dedicated to the stewards of Saskatchewan:
past, present, and future.

CONTENTS

On our Saskatchewan prairie, the nearest neighbor was four miles away, and at night we saw only two lights on all the dark rounding earth. The earth was full of animals—field mice, ground squirrels, weasels, ferrets, badgers, coyotes, burrowing owls, snakes. I knew them as my little brothers, as fellow creatures, and I have never been able to look upon animals in any other way since. The sky in that country came clear down to the ground on every side, and it was full of great weathers, and clouds, and winds, and hawks. I hope I learned something from knowing intimately the creatures of the earth; I hope I learned something from looking a long way, from looking up, from being much alone. A prairie like that, one big enough to carry the eye clear to the sinking, rounding horizon, can be as lonely and grand and simple in its forms as the sea. It is as good a place as any for wilderness experience to happen; the vanishing prairie is as worth preserving for the wilderness idea as the alpine forest.

—WALLACE STEGNER

FOREWORD

This book details the career of one conservation-minded farmer, not merely as a biography but also as a way of bringing to light the environmental issues that the Canadian Plains, and Saskatchewan in particular, have faced during the past fifty years. At the same time, its author, Andrea Olive, has given us a portrait of a rural citizen fully awake to and engaged in the well-being of the community—human and more than human—in which he is embedded. And that, more than anything, makes *Protecting the Prairies* a book for our times.

As we discover that modern agricultural practices are driving both climate change and biodiversity collapse, places like Saskatchewan, with its millions of hectares of land used for crops and grazing, have the people and resources to lead the transformation of how we grow and distribute food. Part of that shift will be to find ways to leave more natural cover on and around land used to grow crops. The narrative that follows shows how Lorne Scott has done just that while at the same time fostering vital social connections and becoming a leading defender of wild creatures and places throughout farm country.

Poet and bioregionalist Gary Snyder once famously said that "the most radical thing you can do is stay at home." Lorne would not like me calling him a radical, but, in the original sense of the word (as *rootedness*), he is the most radical person I know. His farm is a few kilometres from where he was born. He knows where the grouse begin to dance as winter ends, where the orchids show up in June, and where the snow buntings will return in December. Every farmstead has a history he can recount. Farther away, along highways in every direction from his farm, he sees a landscape of familiar places, creatures, and people.

The experts tell us that communities adapting to the twin crises of climate change and biodiversity collapse need to give priority to the work of restoring lost social connections and fostering new ones. People like Lorne do that work without thinking. They know it in their bones.

That said, a farmer conservationist calling for reform in today's agricultural-industrial complex is standing at the margin of a margin. Western nations over the past century have sidelined the growing of food, and that marginalization is entangled with the environmental destruction seen on and around modern farms. Agricultural policy has cast the growing of food out to the hinterlands, where a relatively small number of rural people use increasingly complex, destructive, and fossil-fuel dependent technologies to "produce" the commodities that are then processed further into the items we purchase at grocery stores. In the Earth-destroying logic of global economics, the fewer people a nation has working in farming or fishing the more developed and "advanced" it is.

All farmers and rural people in Canada are living and working at the margins of a mainstream culture that too easily dismisses them as unsophisticated rednecks out of step with the world. And in a province like Saskatchewan, where we have lost tens of thousands of farmers in recent decades, the marginalization is driven by the corporate values of the agricultural-industrial complex itself. The few farmers who remain survive by financing their operations within an economically and ecologically unsustainable system that is more

about land investment and wealth generation than it is about growing healthy food and rural communities.

To stand among such farmers and declare that the system is broken, as Lorne has done, is to set yourself farther out on the margins
until you become the prophet unwelcome in your hometown. There
is only one reason to take such a precarious stand: love. To be a
conservation-minded farmer and activist is a courageous act of love
for the land, for heritage, and for all who will inherit the land—from
the bluebirds and meadowlarks to your neighbours down the road.

I have heard people tease Lorne about all the meetings he attends
in any given month. It is nothing for him to drive from a church par-
ish meeting in town to two more meetings in the city with producer
or conservation organizations during the afternoon and evening.
Theologian and back-to-the-land activist Peter Maurin once said,
"when you don't know what else to do, just keep going to meetings."
Every so often something really important happens at a meeting. It
was at meetings where Lorne and others in the movement discussed
and planned the actions and campaigns that this book recounts.

If you were to ask Lorne Scott how long he intends to keep up
the phone calls, the meetings, the fundraisers, the organizing, I know
what he would say. "For as long as it takes." If that isn't radical—the
rootedness that comes from loving where you live—then I don't
know what is.

TREVOR HERRIOT
Regina writer and naturalist

PREFACE

I am from the prairie ecosystem. It is the original homeland of the nêhiyawak (Cree), Anihšinapêk (Saulteaux), Dakota, Lakota, and Nakoda Nations, and the homeland of the Métis peoples. Before that, it was the land of the dinosaurs—a landscape that eventually gave rise to grassland bison and birds.

I grew up in Regina and went to the University of Calgary for an undergraduate degree in political science. During summer breaks from university, I worked for TransGas, the government-owned and -operated natural gas company in Saskatchewan. For three consecutive summers, my job, for the most part, was to drive around the southern part of the province fixing pipeline post markers. I explored the prairie and toured small towns. I became an expert of sorts in rural Saskatchewan Chinese food and dive bars. I was not an environmentalist and knew virtually nothing about prairie plants, birds, and animals. I had to leave the province before I became interested in all of that.

I completed my PhD in environmental policy at Purdue University in Indiana. Trading in wheat fields for corn fields, I felt more at home in Indiana than I had expected. My supervisor was the right mix of philosophy, environmentalism, and pragmatism. We spent a few years working together on a project about a brown bat and private landowners in rural Indiana. This work led me to other landowners and other rural spaces in North America—Ontario, Ohio, Utah, Nunavut, and Saskatchewan. It also led me to the work of Aldo Leopold, the American conservationist, philosopher, and ecologist.

A Sand County Almanac is his best-known book, and the often-quoted line is "a thing is right when it tends to preserve the integrity, stability, and beauty of the biotic community. It is wrong when it tends otherwise." This was his moral code. By "biotic community," Leopold meant everything—all life that together comprises a place. Soil, water, humans, bugs, air, rain, birds. The ecosystem and its functionality (or "beauty") are what matter, and when you are helping the ecosystem you are doing right on this Earth. This seems to be a relatively simple code by which to live. It is also aspirational.

So is his "land ethic" written about in *A Sand County Almanac*. Leopold says that, "in short, a land ethic changes the role of *Homo sapiens* from conqueror of the land-community to plain member and citizen of it. It implies respect for all fellow-members, and also respect for the community as such." Here Leopold is really suggesting a different value system in which human beings are not at the centre of the ecosystem. For him, a landowner can own private property but is responsible to the land and must steward it in such a way as to sustain the biotic community. Indeed, a landowner does the (morally) right thing by respecting all members of the community, such as birds, trees, and water.

Born in Iowa, Leopold married Estella Luna Otero Bergere, an American-born Spanish heiress to one of the great sheep empires in the west. They made a home in New Mexico, but Leopold was not a farmer or shepherd. Instead, with the support of his wife and family, he became a professor, a poet, and the founder of wildlife management as a science. However, he believed that farmers could be conservationists and uphold the land ethic in service to their biotic communities. In his mind, a farmer could put soil, animals, and wetlands ahead of economic profits. A farmer could value nature and in doing so be "rich." This all sounds pretty dreamy.

But such a farmer does exist. I was introduced to Lorne Scott, the main conservationist in this book, through Aldo Leopold. Not literally of course. Leopold died helping a neighbour fight a wildfire on a farm in Wisconsin in 1948. But in 2008 I was writing a book about how attitudes toward private property shape how individuals think and feel about land and stewardship. I read a lot of Leopold's writing and thought deeply about how an individual could possibly care for the land and the community the way that Leopold envisioned. It did not seem to be possible. There is no "farmer as conservationist." Not in real life.

It turned out that Lorne was the answer to the main puzzle in my book. As part of my book project, I toured his farm in 2008, and it was full of . . . nature. It was different from the surrounding farms, each of which cultivated every square metre. His property had trees! It had bluffs and wetlands! This meant that Lorne did not destroy all of the habitat on his land so that he could maximize crop production and economic profit.

He showed me where he spotted moose and his favourite place to sit and watch birds. He enjoyed his farm—not only the food aspect but also the nature aspect. As we were driving back to town, Lorne sighed aloud as he pointed to a road allowance that had been plowed. This is a practice that I never would have noticed or given any thought to, but it bothered Leopold too. In fact, he believed that such a practice was a "withering indictment of current public taste and morals." I never heard anyone talk like that until I met Lorne.

I almost did not believe at first what I had found. A farmer can love his land, farm it, and steward wildlife all at the same time? Was Lorne for real? Everything that I had read in the academic literature suggested that farmers would always maximize profit first and then consider conservation. Most landowners whom I spoke to in Ohio, Ontario, Indiana, and Utah said as much—they were concerned about wildlife but wanted to be left alone to manage their land as they saw fit. Private property provides no space for the government and, by extension, no space for the community. But Lorne was real—genuine proof that farmers can be conservationists, just like Leopold promised. And, maybe even more surprising, Lorne had been right there on the prairie all along. I didn't need to keep searching. And I certainly didn't need to be searching far and wide across North America.

🐦 🐦 🐦

THE PRAIRIES ARE MY HOME. And they feel like home. Like Wallace Stegner, the writer and conservationist, I was exposed to this landscape at the right age, and it has left an "imprint" on me for life. Indeed, the prairies "taught me identity" and will forever be the place that "my well-conditioned unconscious turns to like an old horse heading for the barn." Now that I live in Mississauga, I better understand why I love the prairies. First and foremost, the prairies offer space. Wide open space. But the prairies also require stewardship. As a scholar, I am attracted to endangered species and endangered spaces. I am a sucker for underdogs and seemingly lost causes. That is why I tend to focus on "non-charismatic" species like snakes and bats in my work. It is also why I focus on Saskatchewan.

However, it is important to understand that I don't believe in sacrifice zones. They are geographic areas that have been so badly damaged that they can never be healed or restored. Chernobyl is an extreme example. But the grasslands are starting to look like another example. And most people in Saskatchewan seem to be rather carefree on environmental issues. There is a certain lack of concern about and an appalling lack of engagement with issues related to wildlife and land that affect all of us. In some ways, I think that I care about the prairies because others don't. Or won't.

Like Leopold and Stegner, I am interested in stories about humans and nature (not humans *versus* nature but humans *and* nature). I like the contradictions and the surprises in such stories. But now these stories scare me. I find myself scared about the future. I worry about climate change. I worry more about biodiversity loss. Every day I worry about the future of the grasslands. I feel like we are playing a giant game of Jenga, and the grassland ecosystem block is about to be pulled from the game. I fear that everything on the Earth will come crashing down.

And I can't help but think that I walked away. I left Saskatchewan the first chance that I had. Barely eighteen, I packed up my Honda and headed west to the University of Calgary. From there, I headed to Dalhousie University and then landed a job in Washington, DC. After I completed my PhD in Indiana, I immediately took a job in Michigan. I married an American. And in 2012 we accepted jobs at the University of Toronto. Although most of my family still lives in Saskatchewan, and I do have a summer home there just south of the boreal forest, it is not a place that I have returned to on a permanent basis.

I am a political scientist and a human geographer. I am interested in environmental policy and in understanding how people see and value their relationship with nature. I learned from Trevor Herriot, the Saskatchewan writer and grassland activist, that I am a "grasslands obligate." I am a migratory species that must return to the grasslands for survival. So maybe I didn't really leave Saskatchewan behind. I'd like to believe that I have taken it with me. I am a direct descendant of the prairie peoples—those fighting a lost cause. Today my lost cause is the same as Lorne's: to protect the prairies. Trevor tells me that this is in my nature. I believe that it is a calling. And it is my honour. In writing this book, I am providing an analysis of conservation policies and politics—with one key man in the middle of the story. But I am also looking for what Trevor says in his book *Grass, Sky, Song* is "the deeper human wish we all share: to find out how we might belong to a place, to find a way home."

ACKNOWLEDGEMENTS

As a conservationist, all I ever write about is love. Indeed, this book is a love story. It is about my love of nature and my love of Saskatchewan. It is also about the community of people who have helped me to bring this story to life. First and foremost is Lorne Scott. We spent countless hours at the Indian Head Dairy Mart with a tape recorder and note pad. I'm so thankful for that time and for his patience in answering every email and phone call. He shared his life with me, and I will be forever grateful.

My editor, Karen Clark, was instrumental in bringing these words into print. When I met her at the Canadian Political Science Association conference in 2017, I pitched a book about resource development in Saskatchewan. In passing, I mentioned how I have always wanted to write a book about a farmer near Indian Head. Later that week she and I were sitting in the Wooden Nickel Saloon with Lorne discussing a possible project. Karen has been so supportive of my vision since the beginning. It was a joy to hold my first baby bird with her in Lorne's farmyard in the summer of 2018. At the University of Regina Press, I would also like to thank Shannon Parr and Kelly Laycock for their work in bringing this book into the world, and to Duncan Campbell for the beautiful cover design.

My family has created and fostered a life conducive to writing. More than anyone, my husband has given me space and time to write as well as company on important walks. His photographs of Saskatchewan's nature and wildlife have validated my belief that this place is worth saving. My parents, important parts of the New Democratic Party (NDP) movement in Saskatchewan in the 1970s–2000s, helped me with details big and small. My brother was a gamer in the 1990s, and our Nintendo, which we spent countless hours playing, would warn us at the end of each session that "everything not saved will be lost." No quotation has stuck closer to my heart than that warning.

This book was also aided by reviewers. Trevor Herriot read an early first draft and provided much-needed guidance about structure and story. His books, and his lived principles, have inspired me for decades. It was an honour to have him provide comments on the manuscript and write the foreword. The University of Regina Press also found three fabulous anonymous reviewers. For all academia's complaints about peer review and the dreaded "reviewer two," my experience was very positive. This book—in its current form—has been improved significantly by the expertise, patience, and honest feedback provided by experts.

I would also like to thank the Wallace Stegner House, and Ethel and Ken in Eastend, for hosting me during the month of April 2019. That writer-in-residence program gave me the opportunity to finish a complete first draft of the manuscript. Being surrounded by the sheer beauty of the prairie ecosystem while sitting in Stegner's old house was the inspiration that I needed to complete the story. I also want to thank Lorne's daughter, Heidi, and her family for their generosity while my husband and I were visiting Eastend.

Finally, I want to thank the University of Toronto Mississauga and my colleagues for their encouragement and support. I also want to thank the Social Sciences and Humanities Research Council (SSHRC) of Canada for its ongoing support of my research. At the time of writing, my SSHRC grant allowed me to study the political ecology of hydraulic fracturing in Saskatchewan and North Dakota. Between 2016 and 2019, I learned a great deal about oil development and the history of the Great Plains. In my study of the grasslands and the devastating impacts of successive waves of resource extraction—beginning with the bison and following through to unconventional oil—I found myself drawn to the implications for the grassland ecosystem. Not just the disappearing songbirds but also all of the disappearing family farms. And on numerous occasions my path crossed with that of Lorne Scott. His name continued to surface as I dug deeper into the story of environmentalism and conservation in the grasslands.

INTRODUCTION

That the situation is hopeless should not
prevent us from doing our best.
—ALDO LEOPOLD

No one alive today has seen the grasslands sprawl across southern Saskatchewan northward to the treeline. All that we have left are small patches. The native grasslands were broken and cultivated more than a century ago by settlers looking to make a life on the frontier. This makes it hard for people now to grasp all that has been lost, for they have never seen the prairies in all their original beauty and splendour.

Hundreds of prairie flowers and grasses rolled in every direction across the plains. Living under the huge sky was a vibrant wilderness. Proud and noble animals such as bison, elk, pronghorn, and wolves roamed immense territories. Underfoot, rodents such as gophers and prairie dogs scurried for food and safety. Birds narrated dawn and dusk. Meadowlarks, sparrows, hawks, grouse, and owls took part in the daily rituals of life on the open plains. You have to close your eyes to really imagine it. The pioneers saw it, and before them the European traders might have noticed it. Our best knowledge of it comes from oral history, for Indigenous Peoples thrived across the North American Great Plains for thousands of years.

Today the Saskatchewan prairie is on fire. Not literally but met-aphorically. Settler colonialism has revealed a slowly burning fire destroying land, water, and habitat for the past 150 years. Since the grasslands were tilled under and the maps drawn in with political boundaries, Saskatchewan's rectangular shape and rather flat topog-raphy lead people to false assumptions. From the vantage point of the Trans-Canada Highway or an airplane, which is how the vast majority of people experience the prairies, the place seems to be empty—void of wildlife, trees, people, and for some any value at all. Sure, it supports agriculture. It is the "breadbasket of Canada." But this reputation of farming and ranching is predicated on what author James Daschuk aptly referred to as "clearing the plains"—clearing bison, clearing wetlands, and, most alarming, clearing Indigenous Peoples from their homeland. It leads residents and visitors alike to guess that the environmental narrative of the prairies is rather flat and gloomy.

More recent policy doesn't help Saskatchewan's reputation. Nat-ural resource extraction has included fish and fur, uranium, potash, lumber, oil, natural gas, and coal. Saskatchewan is the home of soaring per capita carbon dioxide and methane emissions, and the province leads the charge *against* the federal climate plan. Academics studying the government and regulation of natural resources have referred to the place as "the wild west" of oil and gas development since no place is extracting as much with so little regulation. For example, until a few years ago, there were no methane emission regulations in place, so the oil industry just flared off natural gas brought to the surface during oil extraction. It was literally burned without a thought about the environment and air pollution.

This track record is devastating because native grasslands are one of the richest in biological diversity of all the Earth's ecosystems. In Saskatchewan, the grasslands include hundreds of plant and grass species as well as hundreds of insects, birds, and mammals. Luckily for human beings, especially those living on the prairies, this ecosys-tem also supports all life. It provides necessary services such as soil nutrient recycling, water filtration, pollination, habitat for livestock grazing, and climate regulation. The prairies can even absorb more carbon dioxide than a forest. People cannot live in southern Saskatchewan without the support of their grassland ecosystem.

Unfortunately, and largely as a result of policies on the prairies in the twentieth century, Canada has lost more than 40 percent of grassland species populations since the 1970s. Among species at risk, birds are the hardest hit. The World Wildlife Fund Canada reported that grassland bird populations dropped on average 55 percent from 1970 to 2014. But overall the grassland itself—literally the prairie grass—is in the most danger. By 1990, the grasslands had lost 70 percent of their historical abundance. Where there used to be native grass there are now highways, farms, oil rigs, potash mines, houses, and strip malls. The majority of the decline happened prior to 1930 because of agricultural conversion. But the decline continues with agriculture as well as other resources, such as potash and oil. Today it is estimated that less than 15 percent of Saskatchewan's native prairie remains.

The story of conservation policy in Saskatchewan fits rather neatly into the larger story of the west—that region beyond the 100th meridian. It is a place of frontiers and boom-bust cycles. A region whose history is characterized more by resource development than by resource conservation. Bernard DeVoto, an early American conservationist and public lands advocate, wrote that the "paradox" is that the west wants an economy that is "steady, sustained," with a "permanent yield," but the west is "simultaneously moving to destroy the natural resources forever." The resource economy functions in such a way that profits, or benefits of that development, are largely distributed outside the west—to benefit either the federal government in the east or foreign powers. For example, the first threshing machines (early combines) arrived in western Canada in the mid- to late 1920s, and this was really how the native grasslands were cultivated to the point of extinction. It was done in the name of nation building and largely in the service of the east (Ontario) and markets in Britain, the United States, and Western Europe. This is why DeVoto claimed that "we lack space to describe the system by which the East maintains the West as an economic fief." Yes, the west does reap short-term financial benefits, but it also risks incurring long-term costs borne solely by the region. In the 1950s, DeVoto left the question hanging as to whether the west can "defend itself against itself."

Understanding why successive governments have pursued quick and substantive exploitation of nature, from fur to land to minerals, is important background for conservation policy and any understanding of the west. From a political and policy perspective, an analysis of wildlife and land *conservation* in Saskatchewan is remarkably short. But the past seventy-five or so years suggest that Saskatchewan cannot make up its mind most of the time. If there has been any continuity in conservation and environmental policy across political parties in Saskatchewan, then it has come by way of a shared focus on agriculture and the need to diversify the economy to ease the boom-bust nature of farming in which the weather is fierce and farms are at the mercy of global forces. Thus, natural resource development has appealed to both the political left and the political right as a way to create revenue independent of wheat prices. Of course, the province quickly became dependent on the global economy and export markets for oil, gas, and potash. But it didn't matter—all governments embraced growth, development, expansion, and exploitation. The province is always open for business. Always waiting for the next boom.

Saskatchewan, therefore, seems to be an unlikely place to look for hope. From an environmental perspective, it has been all gloom and destruction. There are now dozens of endangered species, from buffalo grass to burrowing owls. There is also a growing oil industry and an expanding potash industry. Drainage woes have destroyed wetlands in every nook and cranny. It isn't hard to think that it is too late—that the grasslands are gone—so we should move on and try to save rainforests or whales or old-growth forests.

That narrative is incomplete, and it overlooks so much. Saskatchewan is caught in an economic paradox of wanting prosperity but destroying the foundation of that prosperity. But the province's lesser-known conservation story, the one that you can't see from a car window as you drive along the Trans-Canada, includes the country's first regulation to protect an endangered species and the country's first environmental assessment. Saskatchewan is home to the *Canadian Environmental Assessment Act,* the reintroduction of the Canada goose, the Idle No More movement, Grasslands National Park, and the Great Sand Hills Ecological Reserve.

Saskatchewan is also the home of Lorne Scott, one of the country's great conservationists and naturalists. At first glance, Lorne looks like a "tubby farmer," as a friend said, in his cowboy boots, plaid shirt, and jeans. His handshake is solid and genuine, and his smile is often huge. He has a rather unassuming presence. To look at him, you would be tempted to make some false assumptions about him. I mean, really, what can a farmer with only a twelfth-grade education living in the middle of nowhere possibly know about stewardship of wetlands, bluffs, birds, and communities? But just as people are often wrong about Saskatchewan's value and its environmental track record, so too they would be wrong to judge Lorne too quickly.

Although the remainder of the book will explain his life—both successes and failures—in detail, a brief overview of his conservation story here will give you some idea of this great naturalist. Before Lorne finished high school in the mid-1960s, he was already well on his way to establishing one of the longest bluebird trails in Canada. He worked at the Royal Saskatchewan Museum for a few years as a budding naturalist before he became Wascana Centre Authority's first park naturalist. At the age of twenty-one, he won his first conservation award—the Saskatchewan Natural History Society's Annual Conservation Award for his work with bluebirds. Before he turned thirty, he began farming near Indian Head with a cousin on rented land. He volunteered with conservation organizations and wrote a column for the *Purple Martin Capital News* published in Griggsville, Illinois. In 1978, Lorne was honoured with an Order of Canada as an outstanding young citizen. A few years later, in 1981, he received the first Governor General's Conservation Award sponsored by the Tourism Industry Association of Canada. And in 1983 he received the John and Nora Lane Bluebird Conservation Award from the North American Bluebird Society.

After serving as president of the Saskatchewan Wildlife Federation and director of the Canadian Wildlife Federation, Lorne helped to lead the charge against the Rafferty-Alameda dams in southern Saskatchewan. Although ultimately unsuccessful, the resulting court cases led the federal government to pass the *Canadian Environmental Assessment Act*, which today is one of the most important pieces of federal environmental legislation.

On the heels of that battle, Lorne ran for a seat in the Legislative Assembly of Saskatchewan. He served as an MLA for Indian Head–Wolseley for almost ten years and was the minister of environment and resource management for over four of those years. While minister, he oversaw the development of uranium mines in the north as well as changes to forestry policy, wildlife policy, conservation policy, and the development of the province's Representative Areas Network.

After leaving public office, Lorne served as executive director of the Saskatchewan Wildlife Federation. He was also director of Bird Studies Canada and Saskatchewan Region board member of the Nature Conservancy of Canada. In 2003, he was awarded the Jerome J. Pratt Whooping Crane Conservation Award from the Whooping Crane Conservation Association for his continued efforts to help bring back the whooping crane from extinction.

For over ten years, from 2004 to 2016, Lorne was the Reeve of the RM of Indian Head. He continued to farm and work tirelessly in the conservation community, receiving all kinds of conservation awards. In 2008, he was invested as a member of the Order of Canada, the country's highest civilian honour, for a lifetime commitment to wildlife and environmental conservation in Canada. And then, in 2009, he was invested into the Saskatchewan Order of Merit, the province's highest honour for a lifetime working to preserve the natural world and inspiring others to enjoy and care about the future of our natural environment. In 2012, he was recognized by Queen Elizabeth II with a Diamond Jubilee Medal.

More recently, Lorne has busied himself with the protection of public lands in the province and started a non-governmental organization with his friend Trevor Herriot. Public Pastures—Public Interest is an advocacy group working to retain and preserve the federal pastures that contain some of the last and best native grasslands in Saskatchewan. Lorne is also heavily involved in opposition efforts to stop future development in Wascana Park in Regina.

Despite all of these accomplishments, most Canadians, even those living in Saskatchewan, probably have never heard of Lorne Scott. His name probably wouldn't sound familiar to most people. How can that be? In part, it is because Lorne has been living on a 325-hectare farm in southern Saskatchewan for almost his entire life. Even while an MLA, Lorne lived on his farm outside Indian Head. And he farmed his farm. He spent his free time in the community, in his church, or in the field. City life and city dreams were for other people.

And in part you haven't heard of him because Lorne is as quiet as he is humble. He is never one to seek the limelight and often works behind the scenes to bring opposing parties to the table for a conversation and, often, a compromise. His government colleagues remember him as a "lone wolf," "a gentle soul," and an "extraordinary person." To his family and friends, he is just *Lorne*—the farmer driving around in an old van with the licence place "Nature." He is the guy with thousands of slides of birds who enjoys reading nature magazines and, as his aunt told me, "loves going to meetings."

His life is the perfect metaphor for conservation on the prairies. Lorne was born in the late 1940s and came of age during a wave of environmentalism—including growing consciousness of as well as radical protest about new government policy in response. But he isn't a radical tree hugger or an ardent socialist. He is like no one else whom I have ever met. Kind, warm, big-hearted, with an encyclopedic knowledge of birds. Lorne does not drink coffee or get up early. (What kind of farmer doesn't wake up early?) He is not shy, but he is humble. In the era of big ag, he is the little guy still there. He lives a good life, one rooted in community and place. He is true to his values and isn't motivated by material objects or financial gain. He is generous, open, and honest. He gives people time, the most precious thing that we have. In many ways, Lorne seems to be simple, but like Saskatchewan he is also full of contradictions and surprises.

Like all of us, Lorne is a product of his time and place. His formative years occurred on a farm in the 1950s when access to information was low but access to nature was high. His knowledge of plants and wildlife stems from his lived experiences on the land. Many of the views that he expressed to me in 2018–22 while being interviewed for the book have been shaped by lifelong learning. The regrets and mistakes that he expresses today can be judged by our own present-day standards, but that is an ahistorical approach. It is important to keep in mind the time frame. This is why the following chapters briefly overview what was happening nationally and globally during the different decades of the analysis. We must remember that in the 1990s—prior to the internet and the iPhone—information about climate change, for example, was sorely lacking. It is easy to see now that governments and ministers of the environment made policy mistakes. However, I try to illustrate how Lorne made decisions about conservation in real time based upon the values that he developed growing up as part of the grassland ecosystem.

Lorne is living proof that we can prevent losses on the prairies. His life demonstrates that conservation is for the common person. We don't need advanced degrees or expert knowledge. But we do need to roll up our sleeves and get to work. Lorne is also a reminder of the great lesson that we need to keep learning: connection is love. Conservationists across Canada, and the world, can achieve victories and prevent losses by rooting themselves in a community, hanging on to it for dear life, and continually showing up for the people, animals, plants, and issues that matter.

🐦 🐦 🐦

THE GOAL OF THIS BOOK is not a straightforward political biography of Lorne Scott. The book, instead, is a critical analysis of wildlife and land conservation in Saskatchewan told through the life story of its most important naturalist. This is not a history book. The issues and stories told in the following pages focus on those most closely tied to Lorne's passions and time in political office. Thus, it is not comprehensive and not intended to be. (If one is interested in history, then I suggest Bill Waiser's *A World We Have Lost: Saskatchewan before 1905* and *Saskatchewan: A New History* as well as Wayne Pepper's new book *Conserving the Legacy: Wildlife Conservation in Saskatchewan, 1905–2005*). More broadly, this book is a story of conservation in a place that we did not expect it. And by a hero whom we didn't anticipate: a farmer. To that end, it is a story about finding the writer-scientist Aldo Leopold and the farmer-philosopher Wendell Berry in a Canadian wheat field.

Indeed, I see Lorne's conservation comrades as Leopold, Stegner, and Berry. Unknown to Lorne, who has never read any of these authors' works, the conservation principles shared by these men are the same as his core principles. Patterns emerge. For readers familiar with Leopold, Stegner, and Berry, the connections will be obvious. For those hearing these names for the first time, or who know only vaguely of *A Sand County Almanac, Wolf Willow: A History, a Story, and a Memory of the Last Plains Frontier*, or *The Unsettling of America: Culture and Agriculture*, the themes will become apparent in time. Leopold, often considered the father of conservation, wrote about a land ethic rooted in community. There is no denying that Lorne is Leopold's farmer as conservationist. Stegner, the great writer of the west, understands place and the boom-bust cycle of the Great Plains as much as anyone ever has. And Berry and Lorne would be instant friends I think—bonding over shared attitudes toward "gadgetry," the mechanization of farming, the decline of rural communities, an animosity toward chemicals and genetically modified organisms, and the shared act of farming.

This book does provide a critical assessment of wildlife conservation policy between 1970 and 2020 in Saskatchewan, particularly in the prairie region, where settler colonialism puts nature in tension with human population and values. Anyone interested in this place and these issues will be interested in Lorne's life. As an ecosystem, Saskatchewan's grasslands are in dire trouble. And looking back at government policy during Lorne's life, it is easy to understand why. Successive governments saw only nature's resources where they should have seen nature. Governments have failed to realize that economic sustainability depends on environmental sustainability. Indeed, the environment is the economy. They have kept Saskatchewan in the western economic paradox of wanting to grow the economy while destroying the very things on which the economy depends.

Lorne is the farmer trying to defend the prairies. He is an answer to the economic paradoxes that history reveals. If you know Lorne, or if you flip to the end of the book, then you will know that he stays on his farm. Despite all the destruction, despite all the pessimism, he stays on the prairies. He hasn't given up. He hasn't walked away. He is rooted in place and approaches each day and each challenge with love and compassion. His life is worth reflecting on. It reminds us that we are the stewards of one of the Earth's great ecosystems. His journey prompts us to ask what will our story be?

CHAPTER I
HUMANITY FIRST

By most estimates, including most of the estimates of memory,
Saskatchewan can be a pretty depressing country.
—WALLACE STEGNER

Lorne Scott was born in 1947, and he grew up on a small family farm in rural southern Saskatchewan near Indian Head. At the time, Tommy Douglas had just been elected premier of the province, and his government was the first social democratic government in North America. The Co-operative Commonwealth Federation (CCF) was formed in 1932 in Calgary and held its first national convention in Regina in 1933. Emerging from that convention was the Regina Manifesto, which, among other things, called for the collective ownership of wealth and resources so that goods would be produced co-operatively and shared collectively. This was quite radical on paper. The manifesto implied government control over the development of natural resources. "Humanity First" was an early party slogan and gave needed attention to the plight of farmers and the province's dwindling rural population. In 1944, about 75 percent of the province's population was rural—living either on a farm or in a small town like Indian Head.

The town of Indian Head lies beside the Trans-Canada Highway and has been a long-standing agricultural hub in the province. Indeed, the district produced the most wheat of anywhere in the entire Northwest Territories in the early 1900s. And in 1901 the Territorial Grain Growers Association formed in Indian Head and lobbied, under its president, William Richard Motherwell, for improved access to train cars to move wheat east. Indian Head is the kind of place where the iconic "breadbasket of the world" imagery is created.

The town lies in the Qu'Appelle Valley region. The valley is an area that I know fairly well. My grandparents farmed in that valley, and we often visited them in my childhood. It is also the route that we take to our summer home. Since 1983, the summer that my parents built our family cabin, we have driven on that road on countless summer nights and cool fall weekends. I know the exact feeling of dipping down into the valley and anticipating the weather changes. Until 2020, my great-grandmother lived in the area—in the same senior care facility as Lorne's mom.

Indian Head is not in the valley itself but in the surrounding flatlands. That area was demarcated by soft rolling hills of prairie grass and poplar bluffs, but today it is predominantly wheat and canola fields with few trees or natural areas remaining. There are lots of deer and ducks along with other common prairie species such as ground squirrels and sparrows foraging about. Where once there were wetlands, now there are wheat fields. Where there was prairie grass, there are seemingly endless fields of canola.

The region was first settled by Scottish pioneers (mostly by way of Ontario) in the 1880s. Folklore suggests that pioneers arrived in an empty land with nothing but the shirts on their backs to spread civilization and grow food for the nation. The reality of Indian Head, or really anywhere else in Saskatchewan, doesn't map neatly onto that myth. The region was far from empty, even if you want to discount the vibrant Indigenous populations that lived nomadically on the prairies. Indian Head was founded as the railway advanced through the country. Land had been mapped and marked, and conditions for obtaining that land had been planned and were controlled by the Canadian dominion government. It also helped that the Immigration Branch of Canada's Department of the Interior promoted Saskatchewan and the west as a land of opportunity, free from malaria, with summer days nothing short of "delightfully invigorating." The village of Indian Head had a curling rink as early as 1889. (What is more Scottish than that?) It became a town in 1902.

As the colonial settlers moved in, they pushed the Cree, Saulteaux, and Nakota people out of the area. According to local folklore at the Indian Head Museum, First Nations used the hills south of the present-day town as a burial site, what they called "Many Skeletons Hills" or "Many Skulls Hills." In his definitive accounting of geographic names in Saskatchewan, Bill Barry says that the name is a translation of the Cree phrase *iyiniwistikwânaciy* (Indian head hill), and the Nakota refer to the area as *wjcapa gena* (skull mountainettes). This is because the Indigenous people were severely affected by the 1837–38 smallpox epidemic, such that their skeletons ("Indian heads") were spread across the area. (Barry's account is corroborated in Arok Wolvengrey's *Cree: Words*).

The colonial settlers called the area "Indian Head Hills." When the Canadian Pacific Railway came through and needed a name, the townspeople offered the Indigenous people a campsite close to town in exchange for using the name "Indian Head" for the town. Supposedly, the First Nation wanted an area close to town so that they could conduct trade there. Indian Head lies squarely within Treaty 4 territory and is the traditional homeland of these Indigenous Peoples. It was not outlandish to think that the First Nation deserved a campsite and some land in the area. Unfortunately, that campsite never materialized. Today the closest First Nation land to Indian Head is Carry the Kettle Reserve, about thirty kilometres away.

Lorne was born and grew up on his parents' farm just south of the townsite. His granddad, Graham Scott, came from Ottawa by way of southern Manitoba—Irish, English, and Scottish background. He arrived in 1915 to farm and raise a family. He was successful at both. The farm, not large by today's standards, was enough to keep him busy. And he had help from nine children, including Lorne's father, Reginald Scott, born in 1918. Reginald was the second youngest of those nine children and grew up farming with his dad.

Graham Scott made a deal with his son that, after he returned home safely from the Second World War, he could have the family farm. Reginald went overseas and served with the Canadian military in England, France, and Belgium. Like other veterans, he did not speak about this time in his life once he returned home. Lorne knows very little about his dad's experience in the war. But he knows that his grandfather kept his promise, and Reginald took over the family farm. His wife, Lorne's mom, Gertie Guest, was originally from the Indian Head area, having grown up on a farm southwest of town. Her parents, Bertram and Ethel Gibba Guest, were both from England, and their families had immigrated to Canada in 1906 and 1901 respectively. Gertie, the second youngest of five children, lived close to Indian Head her whole life. When I visited her in July 2018, she bristled with pride, telling me that "they don't come any better than Lorne."

He is the oldest of six children. At the time of his birth, the farm had no running water and no electricity. This was life on the farm in Saskatchewan. There was a shallow well for drinking water, and in the winter snow was melted for laundry and chores. For warmth, there was a wood stove and oil burner. When Lorne turned seven, electricity came to the farm, and it "was a big deal." That's what his mom told me. It certainly made life a little easier for her (and farm families across the prairies).

Not surprisingly, Lorne's earliest memories revolve around farm life. Lorne would feed and milk the cows and sometimes clean the barn before breakfast and school. He started milking cows at age six. The one-room schoolhouse was four kilometres away, and the Scott children rode there by horse and buggy. He recalls that, when he was young, his dad would take them, but as Lorne grew older that responsibility fell to him as the oldest. During these trips to school, he was mesmerized by birds and other wildlife. His schoolteacher, Mrs. Rose McLaughlin, would sometimes ask Lorne which birds he had seen that morning, and he was happy to report the species and number.

He also recalls hunting with his dad at an early age. His dad hunted ducks mainly and once, according to Lorne, shot a canvasback, which unknown to him was really rare at that time. His dad must have been lucky or a really good shot since canvasbacks are surprisingly swift birds that can fly more than 100 kilometres per hour. In his childhood (and perhaps even now), Lorne was better with a slingshot than a gun. On the way to school, he would sometimes try to pick off robins and other common birds. He wasn't opposed to aiming at ground squirrels or any other animal that presented itself. As Lorne told me, "I had a slingshot, and I was very efficient at hunting birds. Some of these would have been protected species." He also did some hunting, mostly ducks, when he was fourteen and old enough to handle his own gun.

Today Lorne regrets that he didn't have a softer approach to the natural world in childhood. Writing for the *Purple Martin Capital News*, he reflected that "children are often encouraged to experience their first taste of killing by trapping, snaring or shooting ground squirrels. Perhaps a far more valuable and meaningful philosophy of life can be instilled in children by encouraging them to respect life and attempt to understand it more fully by observing and preserving the world around them." Lorne wasn't talking about children in general so much as himself. Despite the rough roaring of his childhood, eventually he did trade his slingshot and rifle for a camera, capturing wildlife through a lens rather than the sights of a gun. He developed that meaningful philosophy of life that he yearned for in his early reflections on life and nature.

Lorne fondly recalls picking raspberries with his mom around the farm. That is where he learned a lot about plant life. His mom let him bite into a yellow lady's slipper when he was convinced that it was fruit. He hasn't forgotten that taste. Nor has he forgotten his mom's love of raspberries. He has always kept raspberry bushes on his farm close to a little garden. In the summer, he'd pick the ripe berries and take them to his mother regularly, until she died in 2019. His knowledge of prairie plants is extensive.

When Lorne was eleven, he had spinal meningitis and was taken to the hospital in Indian Head. Although not uncommon in children, spinal meningitis can be very serious and even fatal. Lorne spent several weeks in the hospital and missed school and farm chores as he recovered. His mom recalled that he was very ill and credited the excellent doctor in their small town for saving his life. Lorne only recalls being stuck inside for weeks. In "those days you were outside doing chores and outside going to school. Nature was just a part of life. You were always exposed to it." Unless you got sick and were hemmed in by walls, which could feel like a prison to a child used to roaming freely across the farm.

Lorne completed Grades 11 and 12 at the Indian Head school. He has no fond memories of school save one incident. One day a skunk was lurking on the school grounds, and he was called to solve the problem. Refusing to shoot the poor lost creature, Lorne decided to trap it and release it in the country. The plan worked smoothly until he got sprayed and the school refused to let him back in until he went home to shower and change. Lorne claims that he was a terrible student, and this skunk incident was rather emblematic of his time there—being called out as a farm kid who loved wildlife. Missing almost an entire day of school was a highlight for him. After high school, he worked as a farmhand for the summer and fall. He then left Regina and only came home to farm on weekends. It was almost ten years before Lorne returned to the farm full-time. He never returned to school and earned no degree or certificate beyond his Grade 12 diploma.

Growing up on the prairies meant that certain hardships had to be endured, such as cold winters and hot summers without the luxuries of electric heat and air conditioning. But it also granted children exceptional freedom and plenty of space in which to explore the natural world. That said, Lorne's early life was unremarkable. If anything, it was ordinary. Playing out like any childhood on the prairies. My father was born two towns over from Indian Head in 1948, and I could literally substitute his name for Lorne's in the above narrative, and, save the part about meningitis, no one would notice—even my dad or Lorne.

SASKATCHEWAN'S CONSERVATION STORY during this time is fairly ordinary as well, not that dissimilar to the story of Alberta or Manitoba. Prior to the formation of the provinces, the prairie landscape underwent massive changes with the arrival of permanent settlers in the nineteenth century. Indigenous Peoples had lived across the Great Plains and into northern Saskatchewan since time immemorial. The nomadic peoples included five linguistic groups: Cree, Dakota, Dene (Chipewyan), Nakota (Assiniboine), and Saulteaux. These peoples lived off the land and lakes, with plentiful bison and fish, and developed trade routes along the river systems and over the extensive prairie terrain. Using their lived experiences as knowledge bases, Indigenous Peoples survived harsh winters, floods, droughts, storms, grass fires, and scorching summers. Walk almost anywhere in southern Saskatchewan today, and you can come across stone tools, arrowheads, and teepee rings going back hundreds, if not thousands, of years. The prairies are a deeply lived-in place.

The first recorded European to travel through the Canadian prairies was Henry Kelsey in 1690. This trip is memorialized on the highway between Sturgis and Preeceville in eastern Saskatchewan. It is a road on which I have driven hundreds of times. But it was not until the summer of 2017 that I stopped to look at the historical marker designated by a road sign. This "point of interest" surprised me:

> Henry Kelsey 1667–1724. In the summers of 1690 91, Henry Kelsey, accompanying Cree and Assiniboine Indians, is now believed to have passed this spot. Trekking from the north down the Etomani-lilian valley corridor, across the nearby Assiniboine River and up onto the open plains he was the first European to see the Canadian prairies. Until the 1926 discovery of the Kelsey papers in an Irish castle, the location of Kelsey's route was only conjecture. The "papers" provided historians the opportunity to re-write history and to assert persuasively that Henry Kelsey was here.

Following up on this revelation, I was disappointed to hear that Kelsey was not much of a diary writer. I think that the Indigenous historical record would show that Cree and Nakota people guided this stranger across terrain and waterways familiar to them. But whatever Kelsey saw and thought and felt as he walked over prairie grasses is pretty much lost to us now. He wrote some poetry but nothing much descriptive. The first European to see the prairie landscape apparently had little to say about it.

Although French and English traders directed and controlled networks across Canada during the seventeenth century, it was not until 1774 that the Hudson's Bay Company (HBC) established the first European settlement on the prairies at Cumberland House in east-central Saskatchewan. Prior to that, between 1670 and 1774, First Nations traders had to make the trip from the prairies to Hudson Bay. It is interesting to note that during this time North America was colonized by the French, Spanish, and British. Although we commonly think of Canada as being either French or British, the very southern part of Saskatchewan (at the forty-ninth parallel) was actually part of Spanish Louisiana because of claims to the river basin until the 1802 Louisiana Purchase transferred from France to the United States the southern part of Alberta and Saskatchewan. Then in 1818 it was ceded to the United Kingdom. After that time, what we know as Saskatchewan today was part of Rupert's Land and controlled by the Hudson's Bay Company. It was not until 1870 that Canada acquired the HBC lands, and the territory of present-day Saskatchewan became part of the Northwest Territories.

The Hudson's Bay Company was in Saskatchewan for the fur trade. This was one of the first resources to be exploited in Saskatchewan by Europeans—the first of many frontier resources. The establishment of formal trading posts was then predicated on bison, whose herds eventually collapsed under the weight of colonialism and drought. I recently visited the Grasslands National Park. I wanted to see where the last Métis bison hunt in Saskatchewan took place. In the west block of the sprawling park, 70-Mile Butte is an important historical place. There is a sign that tells the story of the Métis hunters who gathered on foot and horseback in the area to participate in the last hunt. It was successful, and the group fed their families for some time before having to move on to new ways of existing on the Great Plains. My husband and I walked around the area, and I tried to imagine the hunt. Later we came across the park's herd of bison released in 2005. As they stood on the native prairie against the backdrop of a darkening, stormy sky, their image brought tears to my eyes.

I understood what James Daschuk meant in *Clearing the Plains: Disease, Politics of Starvation, and the Loss of Indigenous Life* when he wrote about the demise of the bison as the "single greatest environmental catastrophe" on the Great Plains. The bison story in itself is a tragedy. But, as Daschuk says, "without the herds, Indigenous communities could not maintain their freedom." Destroying the bison starved and weakened Indigenous Peoples. Those who did not die from disease, malnutrition, or starvation were forced into treaties and onto reserves.

The loss of the bison is the greatest wildlife loss to occur in the region. It is perhaps fitting that the first Canadian environmental law, one for species at risk, occurred in Saskatchewan at this time. In 1887, Lieutenant-Governor David Laird proclaimed An Ordinance for the Protection of the Buffalo in the Northwest Territories. The ordinance as decreed in 1887 was what Saskatchewan historian Bill Waiser called "an attempt to save one of the iconic creatures of the northern plains." Although it was the first Canadian law on record to protect a species threatened with extirpation and perhaps extinction, within a year the ordinance was rescinded because of difficulties enforcing it and its extreme unpopularity among hunters, especially Métis and First Nations hunters. The ordinance was too late anyway, for by 1879 the bison were pretty much gone from the prairies. The law was symbolic—of many things. It came too late and offered too little to protect the bison. It also illustrated an attitude preserved for decades—the regulation was developed without any Indigenous consultation. First Nations and Métis asked for protection of the bison, but they ended up with a regulation in which they had no influence or participation.

The closing of the bison frontier opened up others: ranching, coal, and agriculture. These "resources" created the necessary foundation for government programs and business opportunities. During Lorne Scott's childhood years and to the end of Tommy Douglas's time as premier in 1961, the main focus of the government was health care and quality of (human) life. If anything, the development of natural resources was seen as the funding mechanism of the CCF platform. Since natural resources are publicly owned, their financial bene- fits should flow back through Crown corporations and royalties to the people. So, under the leadership of Minister Joseph Phelps, the Department of Natural Resources grew significantly and expanded its mandate through the creation of numerous Crown corporations and the exploration of Saskatchewan's resources.

Phelps carried the collective mindset into office as he set upon developing fur, fish, and timber resources across the province—and especially in the north. Until this time, resources were "underde- veloped" in the province, and wheat had been the main commod- ity. The problem was not just that wheat was not as productive as it once had been but also that revenue was required for the social pro- grams planned by the Douglas government. It was a government that campaigned on increased old-age pensions; disability care; medical, dental, and hospital services; education, and debt *reduction*. The only plausible way to pay for all those public services and not increase taxes was to boost the economy in Saskatchewan through natural resource development. In service to themselves and to distant mar- kets, settlers have since layered oil and gas, potash, uranium, inten- sive game (elk) farming, and hydraulic fracturing upon the prairies. Indeed, natural resources have been the foundation of settler life on the prairies. The landscape has been forever altered.

CHAPTER 2

THE 1960s – 70s: BIRDS FIRST

The bluebird carries the sky on his back.

—HENRY DAVID THOREAU

The 1960s and 1970s are known as "the environmental era" in North America. For the first time in human history, average people got to see the Earth from outer space. In 1968, astronauts aboard Apollo 8 snapped a colour photo of the Earth rising over the moon. The photo, dubbed *Earthrise*, became the most famous picture from the Apollo 8 mission, whose sole photographic purpose was to capture high-resolution pictures of the moon. Seeing the Earth from space changed how humans saw both their home and themselves. Earth is a closed system and the only planet that we know of capable of sustaining human life.

Technically, environmental historians note that the "first wave" of the environmental movement in North America was the creation of national parks in Canada and the United States during the late nineteenth century and early twentieth century. But Rachel Carson's famous book *Silent Spring* is often credited as starting the "second wave" of environmentalism. It was published in 1962, and with it North American momentum on environmental issues built through the 1960s. Carson's book was about pesticides. And it was written by a woman dying of cancer. Powerful stuff. The take-away was that people were poisoning nature, and in turn nature was poisoning people. If we didn't do something to stop chemical pollution, then we would destroy both the Earth and ourselves. It was a wake-up call for Americans and, importantly, their political leaders.

In Canada, there was growing awareness of chemicals, pollution, and the larger environmental realm. Groups such as Pollution Probe and Ecology Action Centre came into existence. In the conservation realm, the Canadian Parks and Wilderness Society formed in 1963, and World Wildlife Fund Canada formed in 1967. But otherwise the 1960s were rather quiet across Canada on conservation issues. And in the prairies, things were exceedingly dull.

Federally, the Co-operative Commonwealth Federation (CCF) and the Canadian Labour Congress (CLC) merged to form the National Committee for the New Party, the precursor to the New Democratic Party (NDP). Tommy Douglas was elected as the party leader, and his departure left a void in Saskatchewan. Woodrow Lloyd, a former school teacher and a cabinet minister under Douglas, became leader of the Saskatchewan NDP and premier of the province in 1961 after Douglas stepped down. During his time in office, Lloyd's government created no conservation policy of note.

Lloyd did undertake, however, an expansive and thorough tour of Saskatchewan's northern district. He never believed that the federal government should have authority over Indigenous Peoples in Saskatchewan, and he advocated that Indian Affairs, the federal department, be transferred to the province. After taking copious field notes on the state of education, rural infrastructure, health care, and environmental conditions in the north, Lloyd returned to Regina and set in motion new funding initiatives. The goal was to improve living conditions for Indigenous people in the north, and as such it was deeply related to environmental factors such as hunting and fishing. However, this program and its funding were short-lived. After only three years, Lloyd lost the government to Ross Thatcher's Liberal Party. This was largely because an extended doctors' strike and medical care turmoil soured voters on the CCF/NDP.

Thatcher, born in Neville, Saskatchewan, had joined the CCF in the early 1940s and been elected as a member of Parliament in 1945. However, the issue of corporate taxes had caused him to part ways with the Cooperative Commonwealth Federation, and he had become an independent MP. He then ran for the federal Liberal Party in 1957 and lost. But Thatcher was still able to become the leader of the Saskatchewan Liberal Party in 1959 after winning at the party convention. His government certainly did not sweep into office, winning only 0.1 percent more of the popular vote in 1964 and thirty-two of the fifty-eight seats in the legislature.

Once in office, Thatcher immediately started to sell off existing Crown corporations and encouraged private investment in natural resources, mainly potash. His government was re-elected in 1967 but introduced many unpopular austerity measures, including taxes and fees on some medical procedures. These measures contributed to his government's defeat in the next election. It would be the last time that the Liberal Party formed the government in the province.

Wildlife or land conservation (or even the environment) was not a focus for the government. However, it is important to acknowledge that the Wildcat Hill Wilderness Area, the province's first such area, was created during Thatcher's tenure. And the Wildlife Development Fund was created via significant lobbying from conservation groups such as the Saskatchewan Wildlife Federation, which formed in 1929 to ensure sustainable long-term game populations. It did take the threat of a lawsuit to become functional (under the later government of Allan Blakeney), but it was nevertheless a significant conservation accomplishment. In contrast, though, these achievements seem to be meagre relative to the dawn of a significant environmental movement in the United States and some parts of Canada.

🐦 🐦 🐦

DURING THE ENVIRONMENTAL ERA, Lorne Scott got his start in the conservation world with bluebirds. As honest a beginning as any, I suppose. Standing in an old structure on his farm in the summer of

2018, Lorne held up a wooden hand-made bird box for me to see and declared that the only thing he shoots these days are "raccoons and stray cats." He laughed and said "maybe don't put that in the book." The building that we are standing in, an old barn or farm shop, is full of boxes, boards, nails, and random materials organized into piles. It smells a bit like freshly cut wood. Those boxes are meant to house nesting bluebirds. Recently, Lorne started to put wire fencing around the mouth of the box; although it is aesthetically unpleasing, it keeps prey (raccoons and cats) from getting too close to the bird's little home.

In 1962, at the age of fifteen, Lorne began building nest boxes for birds. When I asked him why bluebirds, he smiled and admitted "because it was something that I could do." He liked being able to build bird boxes as a boy. Bluebirds and tree swallows use boxes, unlike many other birds that will not make a nest in a human-made structure. "At first, I put the boxes up around the farmyard, and I just got sparrows, but I was quite happy to just get sparrows." Lorne didn't have access to bird books or field guides, but he did have a teacher who would ask the students each morning to report on bird sightings. This led him to keep track of birds returning to Saskatchewan each spring since 1962.

There are three species of bluebirds in North America: mountain bluebirds (*Sialia currucoides*), eastern bluebirds (*Sialia sialis*), and western bluebirds (*Sialia mexicana*). On the prairies, it is often the mountain bluebird that is seen since its range stretches from eastern Manitoba to British Columbia and from the Gulf of Mexico to the Yukon. However, the eastern bluebird has been found as far west as Saskatchewan—in fact, Lorne has had several pairs nest near his farm. Bluebirds are about twelve centimetres long, and both the female and the male have blue colouring. But the males have a bright blue back that Cherokee legend says was given to them by a Dream Spirit who told the drab-looking birds to bathe in a magic blue lake. Europeans, and Canadians and Americans today, consider bluebirds a symbol of love, hope, and happiness.

Lorne started going farther afield than his parents' farmyard, putting boxes up on fence posts along roads. He had his first pair of nesting bluebirds in 1965. Not long after, he was an operator of the longest continuous bluebird trail in Canada. It stretched east-west from MacGregor, Manitoba (120 kilometres west of Winnipeg), to Indian Head (70 kilometres east of Regina) and north-south from North Battleford to Indian Head. It took over 800 kilometres to go and check Lorne's boxes. As he said, "I kinda got carried away, I guess." But the bluebirds really took to the boxes.

There have been plenty of dedicated bluebirders in Canada and the United States. The first was Thomas E. Musselman from Adams County, Illinois, who started attaching nesting boxes to fence posts in 1934. He actually coined the term "bluebird trail." In Canada, Dr. John Lane from Brandon, Manitoba, started his Junior Birders on a trail task in the early 1960s. Lorne started placing boxes in the direction of Brandon, and by 1968 his trail met Lane's trail. During these years, Lorne became famous in bluebird circles.

Since meeting him, I have learned a lot about bluebird boxes and have even started to notice them along fence posts on the prairies. Lorne considers the establishment of the trail as one of the most successful grassroots initiatives in hands-on conservation in Saskatchewan. In 1969, he received the Saskatchewan Natural History Society's Annual Conservation Award for his work with bluebirds.

Beyond that work in the 1960s, Lorne also got into the art and science of bird banding. It is a skill and passion that he has enjoyed ever since. He met Saskatchewan's most prominent bird bander, Dr. Stuart Houston, in 1964. Originally from North Dakota, he grew up near Yorkton, where he fell in love with birds. Also a physician and an author, Stuart was an ideal mentor for a burgeoning naturalist. Both Lorne and Stuart were avid readers of the *Western Producer*, especially of the "Prairie Wildlife" column written by Doug Gilroy. In the March 19, 1964, issue, Gilroy wrote about great horned owls and requested that if readers "locate a horned-owl on her nest please drop a line to Dr. Houston" and provided his address. Stuart was running a contest for schoolchildren and any youngsters with knowledge of owl nests. The prizes were copies of field guides and subscriptions to *Blue Jay*, a naturalist journal. Lorne was already sixteen and not interested in a contest, but the column did invite any reader to contact Houston and mentioned that it was a "chance to meet a bird bander and help increase our knowledge about the movement of our Saskatchewan owls." So Lorne wrote "rather skeptically" to Stuart, who lived over 300 kilometres away in Saskatoon, saying that "I had found three great horned owl nests and would be glad to take him to them if he wanted to come to band the seven young [ones]." Houston responded immediately and then drove to the Scott farm. It was the beginning of a lifelong friendship.

I went to speak to Stuart in the summer of 2018. His apartment, shared with his wife and outstanding bird bander, Mary, was cluttered with books and papers. The books were on a wide variety of topics but mostly on birds and Tommy Douglas since Stuart had written extensively about both topics. Copies of wildlife magazines and the *Blue Jay* journal lay on chairs and the sofa. It was clear that this bird-banding couple was engaged in the community. In fact, Stuart had just completed a co-edited 800-page book—the definitive book on birds in Saskatchewan. It was published a few months before Mary died (July 2019) and two years before Stuart died (July 2021).

Both Stuart and Mary spoke about Lorne with smiles on their faces. Stuart remembered the day that he drove to the farm near Indian Head to pick up Lorne and find the great horned owls. He drove into the farmyard and honked. Lorne jumped into the car, and they were off. Lorne's dad, Reginald, was beside himself. No people had come into the farmyard before without introducing themselves. Stuart was forgiven for this transgression, but he never forgot it.

For three years, Lorne helped Stuart to band owls, and through his encouragement, in 1968, Lorne obtained a Federal Bird Banding Permit from the Canadian Wildlife Service. Since that time, he has banded over 40,000 birds (including 10,000 mountain bluebirds). To undertake bird banding, you have to apply for a licence from the Canadian Wildlife Service, which sends the tiny metal bands out. You keep track of each bird that you band (what kind and the date). This is done electronically, but Lorne does his reporting by hand and says that "Ottawa still puts up with me." The list of ID numbers matched to birds banded (species, sex, and location) is then sent to the Canadian Wildlife Service, which shares that list with the U.S. Fish and Wildlife Service. When hunters or others find a bird—dead or alive—with a band, they are to record the ID number and report it and/or mail the band to the Canadian Wildlife Service in Canada or the Fish and Wildlife Service in the United States. The information is then provided to the bander. So Lorne knows where his birds are being found.

Throughout his time banding birds, mostly in the 1960s and early 1970s, some birds did return to his boxes. Looking back over his daily journals, Lorne reported that, for mountain bluebirds and tree swallows, about 25 percent of the females were recaptured in following years. He also recalled that one mountain bluebird was captured six years later nesting in the same box. Similarly, he also captured a six-year-old tree swallow. But usually fewer than 1 percent of the young birds that he banded returned to nest in boxes in later years. This might seem to be unfulfilling, but Lorne pointed out that it is generally accepted that half of small birds perish in the first year of life.

🐦 🐦 🐦

FOR LORNE, the 1960s were a time of serious awakening to the larger world around him. And this world was filled mostly with birds. He learned of the group Nature Saskatchewan from Doug Gilroy's column in the *Western Producer* and joined the group in 1965. But Lorne really got his professional start with Ducks Unlimited in 1966 when he was nineteen. He went to a naturalists' meeting in Regina, and the director of Ducks Unlimited was in attendance. Lorne, very shy, worked up the nerve to introduce himself. He chatted with the director and got a job offer to survey birds for two weeks. That was his first job in the nature and conservation world. And it was a great place to start since Ducks Unlimited was the major conservation group in the province at the time.

During the 1960s, Lorne also started work in his first job off the farm. In 1967, he was hired at the Museum of Natural History in Regina, now known as the Royal Saskatchewan Museum. It dates back to 1906 when the provincial Department of Agriculture set aside $557 for the acquisition of "natural history specimens." Minister W.R. Motherwell and Chief Game Guardian T.M. Willing advocated strongly for the development of a museum in which to store and showcase natural history. It was the first museum in Saskatchewan and had a mission to "secure and preserve natural history specimens and objects of historical and ethnological interest." In 1913, the museum hired H.H. Mitchell, its first full-time employee, to oversee the growing collection. The Department of Agriculture was responsible for the museum, and the chief game guardian of the province at that time, Fred Bradshaw, became the museum's first full-time director in 1928.

The museum was known for moving about—getting shuffled from building to building in Regina. But it received a Golden Jubilee project award in 1953, and construction of its permanent building began immediately. The Saskatchewan Museum of Natural History opened in 1955 with exhibits spanning geology, paleontology, zoology, and archaeology. That year 183,000 people visited the galleries. And, most importantly, professional staff were hired, including curators and naturalists. The director from 1947 to 1970, Fred Bard, oversaw the transition and growth of the museum. He was a dynamic and energetic leader with a vision for both the museum and the natural world—past and present. Bard was known for many conservation efforts, notably his work with whooping cranes and, more locally, creation of the Wascana Waterfowl Park and Canada goose breeding and reintroduction. He also hired twenty-year-old Lorne Scott. Like Lorne, Bard was a self-taught naturalist. The job interview consisted mainly of answering questions about birds, familiar territory for Lorne and something that the shy farm kid was comfortable talking about at length.

Lorne moved to Regina and acquired room and board but never spent a weekend in the city. He always returned to his dad's farm, where he lent a helping hand and felt at home. His city job paid a dollar an hour for eight hours a day. As Lorne told me, "I had more money in those days than I do now." But he wasn't there for the money. He loved his job. Bard became a mentor, and Lorne met artist and naturalist Fred Lahrman, a "lifelong friend." Lahrman had many jobs at the museum given his creative talents. They included display painting, taxidermy, bird banding, photography, sound recording, and writing and illustrating for the museum's publications.

Lorne remembers two things about his work at the museum. First, he helped to set up the first nature trails in provincial parks. He spent a lot of time working on different park exhibits. And people who visited provincial parks in the 1970s would come across his work in the form of interpretive signage posted on trails and at visitor centres. Second, Lorne worked with Bard to steward geese. If you can imagine, there was a time when the Canada goose (*Branta canadensis*) was declining and in need of conservation.

Although native to North America, overhunting and loss of habitat in the nineteenth century led to a significant decline of the goose in the early twentieth century. A self-taught naturalist from Abernethy, Ralph Stueck, captured a few crippled geese in the 1940s and raised them at his small sanctuary called Sleepy Hollow. In 1952, he gave a pair of geese to Bard, who started the Wascana Canada goose flock in Regina with the help of eggs collected from wild goose nests in the Cypress Hills. A year later Bard received a few more geese from a private sanctuary at Last Mountain Lake. The birds thrived in captivity.

The Wascana Lake Migratory Bird Sanctuary was officially created in Wascana Centre in Regina in 1956. Bard released thirty to forty birds in the newly created sanctuary, where they were free to roam. The birds stayed during the winter, and the Regina Power Plant kept the water ice free for the geese. Bard and Lahrman fed the birds daily with grain. The flock survived their first cold winter at Wascana Lake, and with careful attention from their caretakers at the museum the geese multiplied. Anyone who has ever visited Wascana Lake is well aware of how successful this program became. Geese now outnumber walkers and other recreationalists by a wide margin.

By the late 1960s, over 100 pairs of geese nested on protected islands in Wascana Lake. In the following years, some of the geese were collected and released in rural Saskatchewan as part of a "restocking effort." It was so successful that Canada geese from the Wascana flock were used to restock populations in Quebec, British Columbia, Florida, and New Mexico in the 1960s and 1970s. Lorne remembers his time at the museum fondly. He would help to collect eggs for safe hatching, and he would help Bard and Lahrman to feed the geese through the winter months.

Everyone who visits Wascana Park sees the geese. They are nearly impossible to miss as they lie in wait to honk at walkers and runners and sometimes give chase to rowers out on the lake. Many visitors have funny Canada goose stories to tell. But more than that, we now see geese all over Canada and across the United States. They have become commonplace. The Canada goose is a success story for wildlife management. And young Lorne had a role to play in it.

🐦 🐦 🐦

THE 1970S WERE A VERY EXCITING TIME in the environmental realm. A lot of the awareness and early action in the 1960s bore fruit in the 1970s as Canada and the United States started passing policies to protect wildlife and water while preventing pollution. In Canada, Pierre Elliott Trudeau and the Liberal Party were at the helm in Ottawa. The governor general gave a rousing speech from the throne in 1969 that laid out an aspirational environmental agenda that Trudeau's government was never able to fully deliver to the nation. But the country was inspired, and the environment was a national issue for most of the decade.

The first Earth Day occurred on April 22, 1970. It technically occurred in 2,000 colleges across the United States. More than 20 million Americans, mainly students, protested to raise awareness of environmental conditions and call for reform and legislation. The big event was in New York City, where between 20,000 to 50,000 people shut down Fifth Avenue, and every major news broadcaster in the city covered the event. Needless to say, this activism did not go unnoticed in Canada, even though no formal gathering was held in the country.

In 1972, the United Nations hosted the Conference on the Human Environment in Stockholm, Sweden. Along with 114 other countries, Canada agreed to the Stockholm Declaration, which included twenty-six principles related to the environment and poverty. Among these principles were that "natural resources must be safeguarded" and that "wildlife must be safeguarded." But there was also recognition that "environment policy must not hamper development." Eventually, these somewhat conflicting ideas would merge into the principle of "sustainable development." But in the 1970s there was simply increasing global attention to the need to balance development with conservation.

The Canadian environmental movement was not as large as the American movement. Federalism might have had something to do with that since in Canada the provinces have the lion's share of responsibility for environmental matters. Thus, protesting at the federal level is never as effective as protesting at a more local level. That said, in 1971 the Canadian Nature Federation (now Nature Canada) formed, bringing together naturalists across the country. Ontario passed the country's first endangered species act, and in 1978 the federal government created the Committee on the Status of Endangered Wildlife in Canada to create and maintain a list of species at risk across the country.

However, in Saskatchewan, the 1970s were less radical and more resource intensive than we might expect considering the environmental revolution happening in other parts of the continent. The decade began with the formation of the Saskatchewan Environmental Society, an exciting new advocacy group focused mainly on energy and pollution. And in 1972 the government created the Ministry of Environment separate from the Ministry of Natural Resources or Agriculture. Thus, the 1970s had all the makings of a great environmental decade, but the government of Allan Blakeney had some other plans. To adequately understand Lorne's motivations for entering politics in the 1980s, we need to better understand the political landscape of the 1970s.

🐦 🐦 🐦

ALLAN BLAKENEY grew up in Nova Scotia and attended Oxford
University as a Rhodes Scholar. When he returned to Canada, he
took a job in the Saskatchewan civil service—simply because there
was a job available there. He entered politics in 1960 and held a seat
in the Saskatchewan Legislative Assembly from 1960 to 1988. (This
means that Blakeney came into office when Lorne was twelve and
remained a political fixture in the province until Lorne was forty-one
and nearly ready to enter politics himself—at forty-three). In 1969,
Blakeney became leader of the provincial New Democratic Party
and premier in 1971 when the party won 55 percent of the popular
vote and forty-five of the sixty seats in the assembly.

Blakeney's government had no qualms about intervening in
the market, and it focused primarily on the non-renewable natural
resource sector. Crown corporations were the order of the day—
the government created the Saskatchewan Oil & Gas Corporation
(SaskOil) in 1973, Saskatchewan Mining Development Corporation
in 1974, and Potash Corporation of Saskatchewan (PotashCorp) in
1975. Although economic diversification was considered necessary
for provincial prosperity, there was still interest in agriculture, especially in getting young families out on farms in Saskatchewan. The
"land bank" became part of the NDP agenda and Blakeney's campaign
in 1970. The idea was that retiring farmers could sell their land to the
government, which would then lease it to young farm families. It was
initially proposed as an alternative to private property by those on
the political left, but Blakeney made it clear that he was not interested in the government owning a lot of land. He suggested that after
five years the leaseholder could purchase the land from the government. In this manner, it would be like a system of land transfer from
one generation to the next—with some help from the government
along the way.

The idea of "government help" was really at the heart of the Blakeney years. He wanted the province to develop its resources as a way
to help the people. And he was dedicated to growing all resource
sectors under Crown corporations. He gave little thought to the
environment. In fact, in his political memoirs, Blakeney said that "I

have not dealt with the important environmental questions facing Canada and the world. I have not done so because they are the subject of lively public discussion to which I can add little." Presumably, he meant that he had little to say in the conclusion of his book about the topic. In reality, the Blakeney government had a complicated relationship with the environment. It was very pro-development but also tried to balance some of that development with new institutions as well as new policies and regulations.

Indeed, Blakeney did do one radical thing that turned out to be an environmental blessing for the province. His government created an Environmental Assessment Policy and an Environmental Assessment Branch of the Department of Environment in 1976. If a Crown corporation was going to extract resources, from oil to potash to uranium, then it would do so by means of an open process that allowed for (at least some) public input. According to University of Saskatchewan law professor Marie-Ann Bowden, between 1976 and 1980 there were 152 projects that went through the process. Fifty-two required a full assessment, but only four were found to be environmentally unacceptable.

One example is the Wintego Dam on the Churchill River. When SaskPower wanted to build a dam on the river for hydroelectricity generation in 1972, Blakeney's government called for an environmental and social impact assessment *prior* to project approval. This was not something that politicians did in the 1970s. In fact, this was probably Canada's first ever impact assessment—two years before the now infamous Berger Inquiry of the Mackenzie Valley Pipeline in the north. The Churchill River Board of Inquiry presented its final report to the government in 1978 with a resounding no to the project. And that was that. The reasons that the board refused a dam on Churchill River were not economic but environmental. This was one of those rare instances when the government chose the biotic community over economic profit. (My grandfather Augustus Hector MacDonald was chairman of the Board of Inquiry and the one who eventually told Blakeney's government not to proceed. I learned this while researching Lorne's life at the Saskatchewan Archives.)

During the 1970s, the environmental assessment process applied only to Crown corporation activity. But in 1980 the government passed *The Saskatchewan Environmental Assessment Act*. It was legally enforceable and applied to private proponents. Although other provinces had similar legislation or policy, Saskatchewan's law was comprehensive and progressive for the time. It was not intended to prevent development, nor did it require public inquiry on different projects. That was left to the discretion of the government. The law was intended to examine the workability of a project and increase its credibility.

Uranium is a natural resource that put environmental assessments in Saskatchewan to the political and environmental test. And it was an issue that would resurface for Lorne while he was the minister of environment in the 1990s. Uranium was discovered in the 1930s in the Northwest Territories, but the story of uranium really dates to the Second World War, when exploration for deposits took place at a rapid pace. In 1944, during the war, Canada put a ban on private prospecting, but that ban was lifted in 1947, after the war. Uranium was then discovered by private prospecting companies in Ontario and Saskatchewan.

Uranium mining often occurs through what is known as "open-pit mining." The deposits are close to the surface, and a crew can go in with heavy machinery and remove layers and layers of earth to get at the uranium. However, some deposits are too deep and must be mined underground. It is similar to mining coal or hardrock mining of gold and silver, where deposits are found deep under the Earth's surface. Shafts and tunnels are dug down, and an excavation area, or "workshop," is created where humans and/or machines can access the uranium. Since radon exposure is very high, and very harmful to humans, mining uranium is done by machines now.

During the 1970s, uranium caused a stir as people became concerned about public health, public safety, nuclear weapons, and environmental impacts. If the 1960s taught people about pollution, the 1970s saw those teachings put into practice. The Saskatchewan Environmental Society, the Saskatchewan Federation of Labour, the

Human Rights Association, as well as the National Farmers Union demanded a public inquiry into uranium in the north. In fact, there was growing tension within the New Democratic Party itself over the future of uranium. Fearful of a call at the 1976 NDP convention for a moratorium on uranium extraction, Blakeney's cabinet decided that an environmental assessment should include a public inquiry to increase the legitimacy of their pro-uranium platform.

The Cluff Lake Board of Inquiry was commissioned on February 1, 1977. This inquiry, dubbed the Bayda Inquiry, after its commissioner, Edward Dmytro Bayda, lasted fifteen months and included formal and community hearings, written submissions, debates, the gathering of scientific data, and cost-benefit analysis. In the end, it recommended that the government go ahead with uranium mining in the north and provided recommendations (e.g., minimizing disturbances to the environment, reclaiming land, and hiring local people for construction) for making such development less risky and more profitable to Indigenous communities in the north.

The uranium debate on development in northern Saskatchewan versus development on the prairies is complicated and rife with racial undertones. Uranium deposits are dictated by geography, and there is no getting around the fact that the largest and richest deposits are in the north. This makes uranium a case study of environmental injustice, because the environmental and public health costs are placed on northern residents, primarily Indigenous Peoples, whereas most of the economic benefits flow south into the government coffers. That is what is known as "distributional injustice." But it is also procedural injustice, because those deciding which mines are approved and how much mining will occur all report to work at the legislative building in Regina and live in the southern part of the province. The people whose lives are most affected by uranium mining have the least say in the process of approving the mines. It is deeply problematic.

To make this point clearer, we can compare the NDP stance on uranium in the north and south. Toward the end of Blakeney's term, in 1979, Eldorado Nuclear proposed the construction of a uranium refinery right outside Saskatoon. The refinery would take uranium from the north and transform it into hexafluoride to be used in nuclear reactors. Opposition was immediate. It was led primarily by members of churches, who opposed nuclear weapons on moral grounds. They were joined by members of environmental groups such as the Saskatchewan Environmental Society as well as many vocal residents of Saskatoon and southern Saskatchewan. The refinery project was cancelled in 1980. Uranium mining in the north was okay, but uranium processing in the south was not.

🐦 🐦 🐦

WHILE OTHER YOUNG PEOPLE during the 1970s in Canada were joining the newly formed Greenpeace group from Vancouver, Lorne was sticking close to home. He left the Museum of Natural History to become the park naturalist for Wascana Centre Authority in Regina in 1975, and that year he also started to farm his own land. Leaving the museum after almost nine years of employment and friendship was difficult, but being a park naturalist appealed to Lorne because it "allows for more out-of-door activities and greater involvement with the public." Indeed, he became a bit of an elementary school celebrity. In the spring and fall, school groups would come to the park, and Lorne would give a short lecture on natural history and show children the trails and the birds, especially the thriving goose population. During the winter months, he would often visit schools. Lorne had a narrated slide show and went on tour in southern Saskatchewan. He says that for nearly a decade afterward people came up to him and said "you came to my school and talked about birds." This is one of the things that makes him most proud—that he influenced a generation of young people in the province and taught them about nature. That is an accomplishment that echoes through time.

In the fall of 1974, Lorne and a cousin purchased sixty-five hectares of land from his uncle near Indian Head. They also rented another half section and began farming in 1975. He commuted to his job in Regina from the farm and worked long days and long evenings.

This dual career continued until Lorne was elected to political office in 1991, when he left his job at the Wascana Centre Authority but continued to farm on his own. Like education, farming is another accomplishment that can echo across generations. Lorne has always been a farmer first. It is the core of his identity, and the farm is where he is most at home in the world.

During the 1970s, Lorne also continued to band birds. As he became more serious about it, he learned the risks associated with his hobby. In 1969, banding owls with his own permit, he had a run-in with a mama owl that left him with a small scar and a good reminder to bring a football helmet and goggles while banding. Banding also requires some serious backcountry driving skills. Sure, Saskatchewan has some nice grid roads, but birds (and other wildlife) do not always stick to the nice roads. Lorne is rather infamous for his old vans and his detours along the way to anywhere. When his 1966 Fargo panel truck finally drove its last kilometre, Lorne wrote its eulogy for the *Purple Martin Capital News*:

> I would like to pay a final tribute to the panel truck which served me so well. It provided transportation for setting out my last 800 bluebird and tree swallow houses. All my bird banding, which amounts to some 7,000 birds, was done with the use of the panel. Perhaps the most useful service the panel provided was the many field trips it made with groups of young people including: scouts, guides, 4 H clubs, and school classes. The field trips ranged from before sunrise visits to the dancing groups of the sharp-tailed grouse, to evening banding trips and weekend camp-outs.

When Lorne crashed the $1500 van in 1972, the odometer read only 108,000 miles (174,000 kilometres), but he restored it. When he officially retired it in 1988, it had 420,000 miles (675,000 kilometres) racked up. This was in part because of spectacular years like 1974 when twenty-six-year-old Lorne drove across the province to band

900 mountain bluebirds and 1,700 tree swallows—with 1,000 of them banded during two long June days. Lorne would drive from bird box to bird box along highways and grid roads. He has a knack for quickly snatching baby birds and slipping bands over their tiny legs. He banded another four species of birds that summer, including American avocets, great horned owls, purple martins, and yellow-headed blackbirds.

Sharing his passion for birds and wildlife extends beyond his family to younger generations across the province. In 1973, the Saskatchewan Natural History Society held its annual meeting in Hudson Bay, close to the first wilderness area established in the province, the Wildcat Hill Wilderness Area. Lorne attended the meeting and took ten high school students from Indian Head with him for a weekend camping trip. Their first stop along the way was at a bluebird house where Lorne banded six young mountain bluebirds. He took the students to Duck Mountain Provincial Park, where he was lucky enough to show them not just white-tailed deer but also a black bear. The forest grounds by the campsite featured red-neck grebes, warblers, thrushes, and of course ravens, not to mention the rather rare ram's-head lady's slippers.

One of Lorne's most memorable banding trips occurred in June 1971 with his friend Gary Seib. The two men took a few farm boys in search of hawk nests in the area. They spent an entire day banding twelve red-tailed hawks and looking for other birds. They dropped the boys off around 10 p.m. and decided to camp at a small campsite about sixty-five kilometres from Indian Head. Their plan was to get up early and take some wildlife photographs if nature cooperated. But at 5 a.m. they were awoken by the Royal Canadian Mounted Police knocking on their van door. Scampering quickly out of the van, nearly speechless, Lorne and Seib showed their banding materials and cameras to the officers and tried to explain the delicate art of bird banding. The police, convinced by their story as much as by the looks on their faces, said that someone had reported them as "suspected cattle rustlers," so an all-points bulletin had been put out in southeastern Saskatchewan for a blue-green van with Lorne's plate number on it. Laughing off the mistake, Lorne and Seib packed up and tried to keep their minds on banding hawks. When Lorne returned to the farm later that afternoon, one of his sisters charged out of the house to meet him. The police had been calling all night, and an RCMP officer had shown up at 2 a.m. looking for Lorne but refused to inform the family why. Fearing the worst, his family was happy to see the bird bandit return safely.

THE 1970S WERE FORMATIVE YEARS for Lorne. But not radical years. Despite the drastic politics happening around him, he rooted himself in his community. He did participate in conservation groups such as Nature Saskatchewan and Ducks Unlimited. And he did take his first job in the environmental realm but as a park naturalist and not as a leftist waffle maker from the youth movement of the radical wing of the 1960–70s NDP. He started to farm and began a family. But he was not involved in any politics and certainly was not thinking of a career in that field.

It might seem to be unlikely, or maybe even disappointing, that Lorne could live through the 1960s and 1970s and not become radical or invested in the political and social problems of his day. There were significant debates in the province over energy, land, uranium, and other resources. It appears as though Lorne either did not notice or simply buried his head in the sand by deciding to spend his time watching and banding birds. That is not accurate, though. Instead, Lorne was learning—becoming an expert naturalist—and observing. As a young man, he was figuring out his values, which included birds, community, family, and farming. He would go on to spend the rest of his life fighting to protect those values.

CHAPTER 3
THE 1980s: A DAM AND DEVINE DECADE

If we decide to continue the destruction, that will not be because
we have no other choice. This destruction is not necessary. It is not
inevitable, except that by our submissiveness we make it so.

—WENDELL BERRY

The 1980s and early 1990s are sometimes referred to as "third-wave environmentalism" because this era represents a time in American and Canadian politics when there was direct, intense, and passionate attention to the issues of acid rain, the ozone layer, wildlife, climate change, and sustainable development. In Canada, Brian Mulroney, prime minister from 1983 to 1994, was arguably the "greenest" prime minister in Canadian history. He signed the Air Quality Agreement with the United States on acid rain and passed the *Canadian Environmental Protection Act*. In some ways, he was acting on the vision that Trudeau set out the decade before. However, Mulroney was also implementing neo-liberal policies and is credited (as well as blamed) for the North American Free Trade Agreement.

No story better exemplifies the 1980s in Saskatchewan than that of Lorne Scott and Grant Devine—first teaming up to protect habitat and then going head to head over a dam in southeastern Saskatchewan. It was the tug-of-war of "grow" versus "conserve" so common on the prairies. And it is suggestive of the larger notion that "resources" are not a fixed or agreed upon concept. What is a resource

to some is nature to others. Really, the 1980s were a decade of contradictions. It is fitting that it all culminated in the construction of a
dam and the creation of Canada's *Environmental Assessment Act.*

Devine's government swept into office in the spring of 1982. The
Progressive Conservative Party won a shocking fifty-five of sixty-four
seats and reduced the New Democratic Party to just nine seats. His
background was in agriculture. Devine grew up on a farm and went
on to earn a PhD in agriculture from Ohio State University in 1975.
He was a professor of agriculture at the University of Saskatchewan
when he entered politics.

When I contacted Devine regarding this book, he immediately
invited me out to his farm near Moose Jaw. I was eager to go—in
part to meet Devine in person and in part to see the area. My grand-
mother grew up on the farm next to the Devine family farm, and I
had never been out that way before. So, on a windy day, I met Devine
at a gas station on Highway 1 and followed him out to his property.
It was very quiet. Felt empty. I learned that he had just sold all his
horses and was in the process of selling the house and land in order
to move to Saskatoon. He seemed to be sad to be leaving the area,
and it was obvious why. His home, part Eaton's catalogue order and
part Ikea, backed onto an artificial lake. It was serene. I have never
seen a farm like it.

We immediately connected over our pursuits of PhDs in the
United States. I had gone to Indiana, and he had gone to Ohio. But
unlike me he had come home to Saskatchewan after obtaining his
PhD. He told me that returning from Ohio was "a bit like returning
to the old country." The recommendations of the day were "summer
fallow really well and grow wheat." This ran counter to what he had
learned through extensive research in the United States. There was
so much more that he wanted to do for agriculture in the province.
I could relate—what I had learned about conservation policy ran
counter to what Saskatchewan was doing, and there was so much
that I wanted to do for wildlife in the province.

Devine's main focus was always agriculture. In 1986, Devine
appointed himself, as premier, the minister of agriculture in

Saskatchewan. He told the *Western Producer* that "it's a high priority here and because I have a good working relationship with the prime minister. I thought, why not me?" Without regret, he told me that "our administration pumped a lot of money into agriculture." And Devine is very proud of Saskatchewan's farming and ranching industry. Sipping a Coca-Cola facing me across his kitchen table, he stated matter-of-factly that "we are among the best dryland farmers in the world. Bar none." I knew this but still wanted to roll my eyes. Being polite, I asked him whether he saw any problems with the *way* that we farm in Saskatchewan.

No. He did not consider mechanization or chemical use exceptional or problematic. He admitted that "there are environmental concerns about drainage. Because of fertilizer. That is something that will continue to need to be addressed." He referred to the prairie wheat fields as "solid gold." And he said that, "if you are going to change that, you have to change it in a way that allows people to make a living. And make a good living." Devine was suggesting that any change to how we farm in Saskatchewan cannot undercut a corporation's bottom line.

Outside agriculture, Devine focused on oil and natural gas privatization and development. He believed in privatization. Full stop. Saskatchewan Mining Development Corporation merged with Eldorado Nuclear to form Cameco, then one of the largest uranium firms in the world. In 1989, Devine privatized PotashCorp. His government built the first two oil upgraders in Canada and a fertilizer plant. "When I came back from the U.S., we imported all our nitrogen fertilizer from other jurisdictions. Hello!?" He laughed as he told me the story. "As a farm boy and economist, I would think 'we have all this gas. We got to save it.' So anyway we did a project. It made nothing but money. And it helped keep the price of fertilizer lower here because we had a local source." To his credit, Devine was trying in his own way to answer the economic paradox of the west by producing and manufacturing goods at home in Saskatchewan. We might destroy our natural resources, but at least we would do so for ourselves and not for Ontario or foreign (U.S.) manufacturers that would take the lion's share of the profits.

Needless to say, Devine's government is remembered for many things, but conservation policy is not one of them. His government, like those of Douglas and Blakeney, was focused on resources: oil, potash, uranium, and agriculture. But *privatization* was the word of the decade. Devine didn't believe—and still doesn't—that the government needed to have a direct hand in farming, ranching, mining, forestry, or any other resource sector. The private individual, and by extension the private corporation, can do it better and more profitably. This was unlike Blakeney's government even if the result of resource extraction was the same.

🐦 🐦 🐦

DESPITE HIS INVOLVEMENT in conservation and his work with various non-governmental organizations, Lorne is not a particularly political person. Growing up, he wasn't a member of any political party. In 1978, Allan Blakeney appointed George Reginald Anderson Bowerman as the minister of environment. Ted Bowerman, as he was known, had been elected first in 1967, and he held his seat until the 1982 election. As the minister of environment, he created an Advisory Committee on the Environment composed of non-elected environmental experts. Lorne served on this committee from 1978 to 1980.

He had actually forgotten about this committee. When I interviewed Pat Atkinson, a long-time MLA from Saskatoon, for the book, she brought it up. It is where she first met Lorne and where they first worked together on issues that mattered to both of them. Once reminded of the committee, Lorne remembered that "it was a useful committee in that we discussed things like Grasslands Park, forestry, and other broad issues." But he didn't remember it as being particularly political.

However, in the early 1980s, Lorne joined the Progressive Conservative Party, not an uncommon affiliation for people in the Indian Head area. The first political issue that grabbed his attention was not birds per se but habitat. Or really what one might call "land." As

Lorne recalled it, in 1971 Blakeney declared that "our crown jewels are not for sale"—meaning that Crown, or public, lands would not be sold. And his government stuck to that promise for a long time. From 1971 to 1981, the provincial government did not sell any Crown land. But in 1981 the New Democratic Party, losing some rural support, decided to start selling Crown lands. The party thought that farmers and other rural people would be happy to see the government reducing its control of rural lands. Plus the government needed revenue, so selling natural resources, including land, was always part of that strategy.

This government decision created a flurry of activity among conservationists in the province. Lorne was president of the Saskatchewan Natural History Society at the time, and he worked relentlessly with his friends Dale Hjertaas and Dennis Sherratt to stop the sale of Crown lands. At the time, Sherratt was working within the government as a research biologist with the Wildlife Branch. According to Lorne, conservation advocacy was "letters, briefs, meetings with politicians, political memberships, conventions, and resolutions." He recalled that a group of farmers and conservationists met with the NDP caucus in 1981 to try to convince them to retain Crown lands in the grasslands. According to Lorne, they said "no, we are not changing our minds."

So he went to Graham Taylor, the MLA in the Indian Head area. Taylor told Lorne to buy a membership in the Progressive Conservative Party and go to the party convention in 1982 to get the issue on the government agenda. Lorne did exactly that—he put in a resolution saying that Crown lands with important habitat should not be sold. At the convention, the resolution passed by over an 80 percent majority. And it was really the beginning of *The Wildlife Habitat Protection Act* (WHPA), passed by the Devine government in 1984. As Lorne said, it was a "persistent lobby by the conservation community" and the help of Sherratt working inside the government that led to 1,375,931 hectares of native habitat protected by the Act in 1985. Although grazing and haying could continue on the lands, they could not be cleared, broken, drained, or—most importantly—sold.

The role played by Lorne here cannot be overstated. He visited many Wildlife Federation branches and encouraged them to write to the government and identify local lands that should be protected. He also made many phone calls. He created that "persistent lobby" effort. Importantly, a lot of the pressure came from rural areas, from the people whom Devine needed to get re-elected.

This was a huge accomplishment for Lorne and the conservation world. It was one of the key conservation laws in the province and remains so today even though it has been severely undermined by the Saskatchewan Party governments. Indeed, *The Wildlife Habitat Protection Act* helps to preserve the integrity, stability, and beauty of the prairie biotic community. It was unquestionably the right thing for the province to do, and alongside Fish and Wildlife Development Fund lands, Grasslands National Park, provincial parks, and protected areas, the Act is one of the most important wildlife and habitat policies in Saskatchewan. Interestingly, it is an Act that Devine doesn't recall. I asked him about it in the summer of 2018. Lorne spoke about the Act with such passion and clarity that I assumed Devine would have equally powerful memories of the historic Act. But he didn't. He wasn't sure what WHPA lands are. Later, when I mentioned this to Lorne, it made him roar with laughter and exclaim that "next time I see Devine I will have to tell him the best thing he ever did was WHPA."

DEVINE DOES REMEMBER VIVIDLY, however, the Rafferty-Alameda controversy. What started as a little water project on a muddy creek in southeastern Saskatchewan turned into a political circus involving the United States, Canada, Saskatchewan, Manitoba, North Dakota, dozens of lawyers, multitudes of environmentalists, and hundreds of bureaucrats. It is a story about unlikely beginnings and unclear endings.

The Souris River starts southeast of Regina and flows past Estevan and into North Dakota, where it loops back to the northeast, near

Minot, and then crosses the international border again between Manitoba and North Dakota until it makes its way through southwestern Manitoba and joins the Assiniboine River near Brandon. This is not unusual for rivers in North America since many of them flow over the international border, a straight line that divides the two countries and ignores nature's boundaries. In Saskatchewan, the two main tributaries (or creeks) that branch from the Souris River are Long Creek and Moose Mountain Creek. They move through southeastern Saskatchewan without crossing any political border.

Drought and flooding are the historical norms in the region. Many Canadians know that in 1857 an Irishman by the name of John Palliser reported back to England that much of Saskatchewan—known today as the Palliser Triangle—is too dry to support farming. But lesser known is that in 1872 another Irishman (and Canadian naturalist) named John Macoun visited the same area as Palliser and called it "fertile" because of the seasonal rainfall. The difference between the two observations is that Palliser visited the area during a drought. And the area has seen many droughts, the most famous of which was the dust bowl, a series of extreme dust storms that persisted for much of the 1930s.

In the case of floods in the creeks or the Souris River, the source can be snowmelt in the spring or thunderstorms in the summer. In fact, since the Souris is dependent on precipitation (as opposed to other rivers in Saskatchewan fed by water from the Rocky Mountains), snow and rain are always to blame for flooding. And significant floods of the Souris have occurred in the past 150 years. The average is a flood two of every ten years. This tendency to swing between extremes led Devine to refer to the Souris as "either mud or flood."

In terms of ecology, the Souris River is surrounded by mixed-grass prairie and some aspen groves. There were wetlands along the river and creeks. However, prior to the 1980s, this part of Saskatchewan was transformed into agricultural lands and already under intense cultivation and some livestock production. The native prairie in the Souris area was important in part because so little of it is left in the province. And the watershed was home to over 200 bird species (including the threatened Baird's sparrow and burrowing owl). The area was so important to wildlife that it was part of the land protected under *The Wildlife Habitat Protection Act.*

The Souris River and its creeks already had dams and reservoirs in Saskatchewan, which provided municipal as well as industrial and agricultural water supplies. For example, the Boundary Dam on Long Creek supplies cooling water for the thermal power station and municipal water for Estevan. Similarly, the Nickle Lake Reservoir supplies water to Weyburn. Indeed, it is important to keep in mind that farming and ranching in Saskatchewan are as much about water management as soil management. The province has been constructing dams and controlling water since Europeans settled the area. And the Souris was one such river already controlled by humans. By the early 1980s, there were forty dams, with ten in Saskatchewan, on the river system.

🐦 🐦 🐦

ON FEBRUARY 12, 1986, Grant Devine announced the Rafferty-Alameda dam projects to a hand-picked audience of 150 people in Estevan. He declared that, subject to environmental approval and U.S. (financial) support, Saskatchewan would construct the Rafferty and Alameda dams as well as the Shand Power Station. While on a roll, Devine also announced the creation of the Souris Basin Development Authority (SBDA), a special-purpose Crown corporation, to coordinate the project.

As fate would have it, February 12, 1986, was also the day that Lorne Scott was declared the president of the Saskatchewan Wildlife Federation (SWF) in Lloydminster. This was really just a coincidence because at the time there was no way for Devine to know that the federation would be opposed to the project. Indeed, its members were a large part of Devine's base—rural and conservative. And, until that time, Lorne had been a card-carrying member of the Progressive Conservative Party. If Devine heard the news that Lorne was the SWF president, then it likely pleased him. So how did the tables turn so quickly?

In the beginning, Devine wanted to build a dam, and Lorne wanted to make sure that wildlife habitat would be protected. Perhaps there was a way to do both, but compromise was off the table almost from the start. When I asked Devine why his government built the Rafferty-Alameda dams, he told me that

> it happened in good part because in Estevan, the riding I represented, people had been talking about damming up that piece of water for years and years and years. They would do some studies on it and talk about it and talk about it. So, when I became leader and premier, they said it is time you really take this seriously. Because when it rains you are going to see no end of water. It floods farms, it floods communities, and it floods all the way into North Dakota.

That is why Devine pursued the project. From his perspective, it was a water project geared to flood prevention. He recalled that there were "lots of people, including the media, and wildlife folks, who said this is not a good project. You can't do this." And he vividly recalled people, especially those in the opposition party, saying that the dam reservoir (Rafferty) would never fill up. He told me that his "good opposition buddy Dwain Lingenfelter said 'I will be able to walk across that body of water any day in the future.' So, one day in the legislature, when the speaker wasn't looking, I sent over a snorkel mask and some fins across the aisle over to Dwain. And we all had a good laugh." And here Devine does get the last laugh, because Rafferty did fill up and today is a huge lake with plenty of recreational uses.

Lorne opposed the project because the Souris River Valley was a narrow ribbon of habitat. Wildlife from many kilometres around flocked there in the winter. The valley was also a migration corridor for species coming up from the United States. To him, it was a very important piece of native habitat, and the dams "would destroy some of the best and only remaining riparian habitat in southeast

Saskatchewan." Plus, as the SWF president, he had ranchers and some farmers contacting him saying "we don't want to lose our land." A dam would create a reservoir that would flood otherwise productive farmland.

When I asked Lorne "how did a guy from Indian Head get so involved in a project about a dam in Estevan?" he said that it was Jerry McKinny's fault. Jerry was from Manitoba and involved with the controversial Red River transfer of water between Manitoba and North Dakota. When Jerry caught wind of the Rafferty project, he got in touch with Don Wilkinson, a rancher from the Weyburn area who also ran a federal pasture. He also contacted Joe Dolecki, a professor of economics at Brandon University. Together they discussed the implications of the Rafferty dam and decided to contact Lorne and a lawyer friend, Rod MacDonald, from Radville.

This "rag-tag team," as Lorne called it, of a rancher, small-town lawyer, professor, and farmer was officially forged. Unfortunately, his health failing, Jerry had to back away from the project, but the other members became close and expanded their group. As Bill Redekop points out in his book about the Rafferty-Alameda dams, these men weren't typical tree huggers and probably "wouldn't be caught dead being seen with so-called environmentalists before the dams were planned." They were just a bunch of guys who loved the land. They called themselves SCRAP: Stop the Construction of the Rafferty-Alameda Project.

SCRAP was up against two Georges in charge of Devine's lofty dam ambitions. First, George Hill became the president of the Souris Basin Development Authority, the new Crown corporation to oversee the project. Hill was an Estevan lawyer and then vice-chair and chair of the Board of Directors at SaskPower until being called by the federal government to the Court of Queen's Bench in 1984. With his background in law and experience working at SaskPower, he was the ideal person to head the SBDA. Second, George Hood was then hired as the director of planning and operations at the SBDA. He went on to become the vice-president. Hood was originally from Milton, Ontario, and remarked in his own book about the Rafferty-Alameda project that, when he saw small-town Saskatchewan, "I remember thinking, I have moved to a place that was, at best, thirty years behind the times and, at worst, somewhere near the end of the earth." After his work with the SBDA on the dams, Hood returned to Ontario and took a job in administration at Queen's University.

When I interviewed Lorne in 2018, I innocently asked "who is George Hood?" Lorne, laughing, said "oh, my friend George Hood. He was sorta the hitman of SBDA and basically the bureaucrat Devine had appointed to make this project go." A few years ago, the Rafferty Dam was officially renamed the Rafferty–Grant Devine Project. And in 2018 Devine told me that he wanted the Alameda dam to be renamed "The Georges Dam" after Hood and Hill. That is how important the SBDA and the two Georges were to the project.

The Souris Basin Development Authority was given authority over and responsibility for designing and building the main components of the project, along with SaskWater and the Ministry of Environment. The SBDA was required to meet all the conditions of *The Saskatchewan Environmental Assessment Act*, created in 1980 by Allan Blakeney's government. The purpose of the Act as you might recall from the uranium debates of the 1970s, is not to prevent development but to ensure that environmental aspects of a project are considered in each phase. Moreover, on rare occasions, the Act can determine that a project's environmental costs outweigh its economic benefits. In these cases, a project is either redesigned or cancelled.

Hill went to work quickly, and by the summer of 1987 the environmental impact statement was complete, weighing in at eighteen volumes and 1,700 pages! It included three main components: pre-project conditions, a prediction of the project's impacts on the physical and human environments, and the project's plan to mitigate the environmental effects. Those were all fine, but one of the major problems with the process was that the same minister, Eric Berntson, was simultaneously responsible for SaskPower and SaskWater— essentially a conflict of interest. To be clear, the entity requesting the project, SaskPower, needed approval from SaskWater, but both had the same minister at the helm. The Ministry of Environment, of course, also had to approve the project. But by the time the assessment was complete, Herb Swan was the minister of both SaskWater and the Ministry of Environment. In reality, the project developer, the Saskatchewan government, was also the project regulator. That was absurd. And it was why a Board of Inquiry was appointed in 1987.

The Brennan Inquiry, chaired by John Brennan, dean of the College of Commerce at the University of Saskatchewan, was charged with assessing the environmental impact statement. It sought to push the changes through quickly, decisively, and without any real public input. To be sure, it ordered meetings in local communities for public consultation. But it gave the public only about three weeks of notice, during harvest season at that. Making things even more ludicrous, to properly understand the issues, one had to read an eighteen-volume legal treatise.

Farmers love it when the government does that—holds important meetings about issues that will directly affect farming communities during harvest. It is even better when you ask them to read a government study immediately prior to a public meeting. Soon troubles started to erupt. Don Wilkinson, that rancher from Weyburn who was part of SCRAP, quite reasonably asked the Brennan Inquiry to extend the public review for an additional sixty days. His request was denied. So he went to court—he filed suit against the minister of environment, the Board of Inquiry, and the government of Saskatchewan. His lawyer argued that, since Wilkinson could be affected directly by the project, he should have adequate time for input. However, the judge dismissed the case because the Board of Inquiry's recommendations would not be legally binding on the government, so public opinion (even that provided by affected landowners) would not change the outcome of the project.

After a few months, in January 1988, the Board of Inquiry responded to the environmental impact statement and approved the project subject to thirty-four conditions. The Minister of Environment also approved the project subject to twenty-one conditions. These conditions were on top of the already existing mitigation strategies that Hill had laid out in the environmental assessment. For example, the SBDA would replace habitat loss hectare for hectare, which meant purchasing sixty-one quarter sections of land adjacent to the reservoirs to plant native prairie and trees. The goal was no net loss of habitat to wildlife.

These mitigations were not enough. The members of SCRAP were concerned about land and nature. At the least, they wanted to ensure that all conditions and all mitigation strategies would be legally binding. But really they still wanted to prevent the dams from being built. They could not, however, sue the government on behalf of nature. Valleys do not have rights in Saskatchewan. SCRAP members needed to take the government to court for failing to conduct a proper environmental assessment—one that included all interests, such as those of Manitoba and the United States. Thus, their eyes were really on the federal government, which they thought should be involved in approving the project.

In the 1980s, the federal government was not in the habit of regulating provincial projects or private projects occurring on federal lands. The federal government had only Environmental Assessment and Review Process (EARP) guidelines, created in 1973 by Pierre Trudeau's federal cabinet. It was adjusted by cabinet in 1977, and then, importantly, it was strengthened in 1984 when an order-in-council was issued under the *Government Organization Act*. To be clear, the EARP was not passed in Parliament—it became a guideline by way of Trudeau's cabinet. Thus, its status as "law" was a bit questionable at the time. The Federal Environmental Assessment Review Office was in charge of the EARP and tended to focus on projects in places of sole federal jurisdiction, such as national parks. But, technically, the EARP scope included more than that.

Even if the Environmental Assessment and Review Process could apply in Saskatchewan, the question still remained whether SCRAP could really prove that a proper environmental assessment had not been done in the province. SaskWater had applied to the federal Department of Environment for an *International River Improvements Act* licence. Since the Rafferty-Alameda project involved international waters, it required a licence from the Canadian government under the *International River Improvements Act* (IRIA). Environment Canada could have required an environmental assessment under the EARP but decided against it, thinking that the provincial one was good enough.

Members of SCRAP disagreed, and they were ready to go to court. But taking the government, provincial or federal, to court wasn't easy because SCRAP didn't have any "standing" before the court. SCRAP was not directly affected, and courts focus on private interests. Sure, some of its members, such as Wilkinson, landowners in the area, would be directly affected. But only they as individuals could go to court, and then their arguments against the dams would be limited to their specific interests and impacts. Thus, the first challenge for SCRAP was to illustrate that its case was about more than just local interest. Lorne did this in a brilliant and clever way—he had the SWF Board of Directors formally pass a resolution to support the lawsuit's objective. He got Nature Saskatchewan's Board of Directors to do the same. Thus, 52,000 people, the members of those two groups, became direct participants in the lawsuit.

On May 12, 1989, SCRAP had its day in court. It argued a statement of claim against the federal minister of environment and the SBDA. The government argued that SCRAP had no status to sue, but Justice Eugene Scheibel disagreed. He noted that SCRAP included landowners directly affected and that, since dams are so serious an issue, non-landowners have genuine interests, so there was "status to bring this action." This was major. It was a turning point.

However, it was not a total victory. The judge also ruled that the federal government was not required to describe what an environmental assessment must contain. The government was not required to include Manitoba or other interests. That was not the way in which the provincial law worked. Thus, if SCRAP was to continue its claim, then it would have to take the federal government to court, because only the federal government was (maybe) required to conduct an assessment with broader interests considered.

Time was of the essence. Construction at Rafferty was happening almost around the clock. If SCRAP didn't hurry, then it would be too late. It needed the court to halt construction. So, a week after the provincial case, SCRAP filed an injunction to halt Rafferty, but the judge immediately dismissed the case. The group needed a new strategy.

If the EARP applied to cases in which a project affected federal responsibility, then SCRAP needed to prove that Rafferty-Alameda was in that scope. The project did not have federal funding, so that course of action couldn't be used. The dams did involve an international waterway, the Souris River, but the federal government had already granted the project an IRIA licence, the equivalent of discharging responsibility to Saskatchewan for that river. So that wasn't going to work either.

What SCRAP discovered was that Rafferty-Alameda would flood federal lands because there were Prairie Farm Rehabilitation Administration (PFRA) lands in the area. Wilkinson knew this because he managed some of them. And SCRAP, through the *Freedom of Information Act*, had access to SBDA documents, which included a letter from Hood to the federal government referencing federal lands. It was just a passing reference. But it was enough to catch the attention of SCRAP members, who decided to do a property title search on the future flooded lands. They quickly learned that some of the pasture lands had never been officially signed over to the Saskatchewan government and were, in fact, federal responsibility.

SCRAP had its hook: federal pasture lands. But what it needed to move up to the next level, and into the federal arena, was a larger public profile and more funding. Rod MacDonald, SCRAP's lawyer, had been working for free. But he needed help. He needed resources. And Lorne Scott could provide them since he was linked to a high-profile and wealthier group, the Canadian Wildlife Federation (CWF).

Using his connections through the Saskatchewan Wildlife Federation, Lorne discussed the dams with Stephen Hazell, the CWF policy director and legal counsel. Hazell really supported legal action. I spoke to him in the summer of 2018, and he recalled the case in great detail (in part because he wrote a book about it and in part because it was such a groundbreaking case in Canadian environmental history). Hazell said that "ultimately we, Lorne and I, decided that we would try and bring something forward to the CWF to get them to take action." Lorne brought forward a motion to a CWF Board of Directors meeting authorizing staff to proceed with an application for judicial review. His argument was based upon three important points: first, the environmental impact statement in Saskatchewan was flawed because it did not consider effects in North Dakota or Manitoba; second, there were legal grounds for believing that the federal EARP applied to the project; and, third, a CWF victory would serve as an important precedent.

These arguments were salient, but perhaps more important was the fact that people respected Lorne. As Redekop details in his book, Joe Dolecki, another member of SCRAP, thought that "Lorne was a legend in the wildlife community," so people would listen to him. And the fact that "Lorne was at the time a card-carrying Progressive Conservative nullified any hint of political motivation." The CWF Board of Directors agreed. Hazell recalled that board meetings were rarely occasions for oratory, but Lorne was fired up that day. "When he concluded, the resounding applause made it clear that the resolution would pass." And it did, without a single no vote.

With approval from the CWF board, Hazell pursued the issue. The federation hired a litigation lawyer, Brian Crane, based in Ottawa, and went to court. But during the process in Ottawa, Lorne was still involved in the group. According to Hazell, Lorne was "really the key guy in Saskatchewan—he was our guy on the ground. And it is always hardest for the local folks who have to deal with neighbours and local politicians who really want the project and who don't understand why we should care about a little riparian vegetation. And that was Lorne." Although the SWF board had approved opposition to the Rafferty-Alameda project, not all branches agreed, nor did all members. For example, Estevan had a strong SWF branch, but "because of local pressure" it ended up supporting the Rafferty-Alameda project. Lorne recalls getting all kinds of harassing phone calls and even a death threat once while at work in Regina.

The case was heard on March 30, 1989, before Justice Bud Cullen. Crane, the CWF legal counsel, argued that the EARP guidelines were legally binding, that the federal government did not follow them, and thus that the government's decision to grant an IRIA licence was not valid. Judge Cullen concurred. The Environmental Assessment and Review Process was not just policy but also law, and, more importantly, the law had to be applied because the Rafferty-Alameda project clearly would affect an area of federal responsibility (PFRA lands). He ordered that the licence for Rafferty-Alameda be cancelled and construction halted. Redekop refers to this as "an extraordinary moment in Canada's environmental history."

The moment passed quickly, though, for the federal environmental assessment was completed within a month, and federal Minister of Environment Lucien Bouchard reinstated the licence for construction on August 31, 1989. Hood and Hill put people to work immediately—construction occurred twenty-four hours a day seven days a week. Bouchard did not appoint a panel to review the project—he just attached twenty-two conditions to the licence, many of which dealt with mitigation and reclamation of habitat.

It wasn't long before the Canadian Wildlife Federation announced that it was going back to court. If the project was ever about the environment, it wasn't any longer. Construction on the Rafferty dam was past the point of return, so the environmental damage was already done. From that point forward, it was all about process. The Canadian Wildlife Federation wanted to ensure that the EARP guidelines were environmental law in Canada. Before a Federal Court judge in Winnipeg on November 29, 1989, Crane argued that the minister had failed to appoint an independent inquiry by a panel of experts, as spelled out by the EARP, at Rafferty. This case was heard in conjunction with that of the Tetzlaff brothers, local landowners whose property would be flooded, who filed suit in the Court of Queen's Bench against Bouchard for violating their *Charter of Rights and Freedoms* protections. The judge took a month to consider the case, and he determined that the federal minister of environment should have been compelled to hold a full environmental assessment. Another victory for the Canadian Wildlife Federation. However, the judge—who put full blame on Minister Bouchard—allowed Saskatchewan to continue construction for the time being and set the date of January 30, 1990, by which time Bouchard and the province had to agree on an independent panel, or the licence would be revoked.

Hood and Hill were angry with the federal government's mishandling of the project and, according to Hazell, threatened to embarrass Bouchard if he stalled on appointing a panel. At this point, things started to go the way that the Souris Basin Development Authority wanted. Bouchard agreed to pay Saskatchewan for any delay in construction caused by the federal government. And he appointed a five-member panel to review the project. The trucks kept rolling in Saskatchewan, and then Bouchard resigned from the federal cabinet (over the Meech Lake Accord, not over Rafferty). He was replaced by Robert de Cotret. Within a few weeks of being on the job, Cotret flew to Saskatchewan to tour the dams, first with Hill and then with Devine and the North Dakota governor by air the next day. There are different versions of the agreement struck between Devine and Cotret on that trip, but whatever happened—and no one seems to know for sure—Saskatchewan continued construction. The five-member panel charged with assessing Rafferty-Alameda resigned. And construction continued.

In an interesting turn of events, the federal government then took Saskatchewan to court. Yes, this is a true story. The federal government had been dragging its feet for years on applying the EARP, and now it was prepared to take Saskatchewan to court over its right to apply it. Cotret was adamant that he had never approved anything—that he had not okayed construction. He signed an affidavit stating as much. Devine said that Cotret did approve it. And, as ridiculous as this sounds, SaskWater and the SBDA wanted to take Environment Canada to court. Federal Court Justice Donald MacPherson ruled that construction be allowed to continue.

In a last gasp, the Tetzlaffs, whose land near Alameda had been expropriated by this point, attempted to get a court injunction to stop construction. The brothers appealed the first decision issued by Federal Court Justice Francis Muldoon and argued that the IRIA licence should have been revoked immediately after the first CWF court case.

The judge in the appeal case, Chief Justice Frank Iacobucci, ruled that, though the federal government was required to apply the EARP and conduct an environmental assessment, it was not required to do so *before* issuing the IRIA licence. This was because the law didn't state as much. It was a literal interpretation. And perhaps a bizarre one. But it was the last say on the matter.

SCRAP AND THE CANADIAN WILDLIFE FEDERATION lost the battle. Rafferty, completed in 1993, is six kilometres northwest of Estevan. When the dam stops the water and the Rafferty Reservoir fills, it stretches fifty-seven kilometres and stores 444,000 cubic decametres of water. Alameda, completed in 1995 and now called the Grant Devine Dam, is on Moose Mountain Creek near Oxbow and the North Dakota border, and it creates a twenty-five-kilometre reservoir when full. The Rafferty Reservoir has a pipeline that supplies cooling water to the Shand coal-fired power station outside Estevan. This was a main objective of the dam. It also has a diversion channel that connects the reservoir to the nearby Boundary Reservoir so as to allow the movement of water in either direction. As for the rare southern prairie valley and wildlife habitat, they were flooded.

Mitigation and reclamation were required by the government. But reclamation of an area is never that simple, and environmentalists argued that valley plant life cannot be reproduced outside the valley. Eight hundred hectares of critical wildlife habitat were cleared for the Rafferty Reservoir; the valley bottom woodlands were eliminated; habitat was lost for white-tailed deer, sharp-tailed grouse, and pheasant; fourteen rare plant species were lost; and breeding habitat for waterfowl was lost. The project destroyed a valley and replaced it with grass and trees. Adding insult to injury, the SBDA went on to plant non-native species such as Scotch pine and Colorado blue spruce trees. It is not the same. And it will never be the same again.

This was difficult for Lorne to accept. In his book, Hood points out that Lorne's reaction to the Federal Court of Appeal ruling on

December 21, 1991, as told to CKTV News, was that "what we did get was the Federal Court of Appeal upholding the previous court decision that a federal environmental review has to be done on the project. This is what we've said for the last several years and the courts have always come down on our side. So, I guess we're right but we've lost, if you can make sense out of that." Lorne lost. The members of SCRAP were right—they were the ones preserving the integrity, stability, and beauty of the prairies. But SCRAP still lost, and the dams were built.

However, Lorne, SCRAP, and the Canadian Wildlife Federation also got the process started on revamping the EARP into a new federal law, the *Canadian Environmental Assessment Act*. During the Rafferty-Alameda contest, the Supreme Court decided another case. In *Friends of Oldman River Society v Canada* (1991), the court determined that the federal government does have the right to conduct an environmental assessment. The EARP might have been called "guidelines," but the court decided that Pierre Trudeau's cabinet, when creating them, really created a regulatory policy intended to be law. Thus, after this decision and what happened in Saskatchewan with Rafferty, the federal government got to work on creating a new law.

The *Canadian Environmental Assessment Act* (CEAA) was passed by Parliament in 1992 under Brian Mulroney's government. Although the law was rewritten by Stephen Harper's government and Justin Trudeau's government, it remains a cornerstone of sustainable development across the country. The Act forces consideration of the environment in economic projects, with the goal being to negate, reduce, or mitigate the impacts of human development on the natural environment. The idea behind the CEAA is not to stop development but to ensure that it occurs sustainably. As Hazell said, "environmental assessment is potentially the most powerful tool in the hands of government, citizens, and the private sector to protect the environment." And we can't forget that this law came out of Alberta and Saskatchewan because of little rivers and passionate conservationists. Hood might have thought that Saskatchewan was "near the end of the earth," but Lorne and the Canadian Wildlife Federation demonstrated that grasslands are at the heart of this world.

It is nearly impossible to find follow-up stories on the Rafferty-Alameda project. For the most part, people have moved on. No one talks about it anymore. Hood suggests, and I would agree, that "Rafferty-Alameda is like a political inkblot test" because "everyone who looks at it will come away with a different image." I asked Devine and Lorne to look back and reflect on this controversy of almost thirty years ago.

Sitting at his kitchen table at the farm near Moose Jaw, Devine told me that the reservoir "has filled many and many times. I think it is about forty miles long and about forty feet deep. And probably some of the best walleye fishing in western Canada. People come from the United States, and they can't believe it. There is a golf course around it. And it's . . . it's popular." He went on to say, with no hesitation, that, "when you look back at it, it was obviously the thing to do. Despite the difficulties we faced politically, we did it."

Devine pointed out, correctly, that after his government lost in 1991 the New Democratic Party completed the project. He recalled that, "when we were defeated, a former NDP cabinet minister, and I would consider a friend of mine, Jack Messer, became the president of SaskPower. And Jack did a really good job of completing the project after 1991. There were some things he had to tidy up. He took a hold of it. It ended up a popular project." It strikes me that the NDP really had no choice—the dams pretty much had been built, and the whole affair had been dragged through the courts so many times that there wasn't any reason to think that any other outcome was possible. But it is correct to say that, technically, the NDP did complete the Rafferty-Alameda dam project.

What resonated with me while talking to Devine was how he told me repeatedly that on this issue "there is no common ground." I thought that he meant between environmentalists and right-wing politicians. But he really meant between Ottawa and Saskatchewan. Devine is not against protection of the environment per se. But for him, I think, it is about western alienation. This dates back to the settlement of the west, when the federal government treated it like a colony of the east by trying to extract wealth and resources from the west with little concern for the people living there. As DeVoto said of the western United States, it was a fiefdom.

For Devine, it is about grain and railways, oil and pipelines, and everything else that the west has produced and tried to market. While the west tries to prosper, Ottawa tries to restrain it and control it. He believes, and this is common in Saskatchewan, I think, that there is no help from the federal government—just bureaucracy and regulation. This is why he favoured privatization and why he wanted to manufacture goods, such as fertilizer, right in Saskatchewan—so that the east couldn't take a share of the profit. This resentment has spilled over into the realm of environmental regulation, and Devine, and many people on the political right, see environmental assessments, species at risk acts, and carbon taxes as nothing more than a way to regulate and control land, people, and profit.

"It is deep seeded" is how he explained it. He added that, "whether you like it or not, it is huge. The resentment is huge. *The Environmental Assessment Act* flies in the face of pipelines. I see no common ground. Everyone wants to make a living. A higher standard of living. We have resources, and we are land locked." This is why Devine thinks that he was right on Rafferty-Alameda. It was a local project that the federal government should have stayed out of. For him, it was never about the environment—it was only about the east controlling the west. It was the western paradox of wanting a long-term and stable local economy. However, Devine was too willing to allow the destruction of the west in an attempt to save the west. He bought in to the paradox hook, line, and sinker.

On the other side, Lorne was trying to protect the west from itself. He still believes that the environmental degradation caused by the dams far exceeded any benefit. The dams do not preserve the integrity, stability, and beauty of the prairie biotic community. It was the wrong call. And he thinks that history has proven that the dams were not necessary. He pointed to the flood of Minot in 2011. Why didn't the dams stop it? More importantly, he wonders why North Dakota didn't just build its own dam if flooding there was such a problem. Lorne sees the two dams as "monuments to Devine."

🐦 🐦 🐦

THE 1980S ARE A METAPHOR for conservation on the prairies. It was a decade of give and take with zero ideological consistency among political parties or politicians. *The Wildlife Habitat Protection Act* is one of the most important regulations for wildlife ever enacted on the prairies. But what the right gave with one hand it tried to take away with the other. Devine's government quickly took land out of the Act to build a dam and flood a riparian ecoregion. Devine wanted to protect land but only when it was politically convenient to do so. And there was little to stop him as he spent money on projects across the prairie region. To his credit, he wanted to create projects that would keep Saskatchewan resources (and jobs) in the province. But he gave little thought to the environmental consequences of unrestrained resource development.

For Lorne, the 1980s were a confusing and frustrating time. He found himself having to switch teams depending on which way the wind was blowing. He had to be pragmatic and willing to work with whoever wanted to protect land and wildlife. Thus, he quickly found himself leading a battle against the very government that he had just worked with to protect land. In 1986, it was not impossible to think that the Rafferty project could be halted. It was not even ten years earlier that the Churchill River project was cancelled on account of environmental reasons. However, Devine was a different premier, and the federal government was an inconsistent and unreliable ally for SCRAP. In the end, this experience prepared Lorne for a new career that he thought was now inevitable if he wanted to conserve the grasslands from further policy failures.

In 2009, Lorne was awarded the Saskatchewan Order of Merit, intended to "recognize individual excellence and outstanding contributions to the social, cultural, and economic well-being of the province and its residents." Notice that the categories do not include environmental contributions. Lorne's entry in the program points to his work securing "3.4 million acres of Crown land under *The Wildlife Habitat Protection Act*, ensuring it would continue to be leased for grazing, and not be developed or sold." Perhaps this is considered a social or cultural contribution in the province.

Devine was awarded the Order of Merit at the same time—literally at the same award ceremony. His entry in the program speaks mainly to his work in agriculture and politics. It also states that under his leadership Saskatchewan "built Canada's first two heavy oil upgraders, Saskatchewan's first paper mill, and a Japanese-Saskatchewan electric turbine manufacturing facility. He also led the implementation of a province-wide natural gas distribution system and power and *water projects like the Rafferty and Alameda dams*" (emphasis added). There is no doubt that Saskatchewan considers these to be economic contributions to the well-being of the province.

No matter how you interpret it, you have to admit that it is a bit ironic that Lorne and Devine received their awards on the same night. It is as though the province itself can't make up its mind about Rafferty and Alameda or conservation in general. How can you award two people for doing opposite work? One compromised nature for development projects, and the other fought tooth and nail to prevent those projects for the protection of nature.

CHAPTER 4

THE EARLY 1990s: FROM POLITICS TO POLITICIAN

We may love a place and still be dangerous to it.

—WALLACE STEGNER

T he early 1990s were still part of the third wave of environmentalism in Canada and the United States. In 1992, the United Nations hosted the Conference on Environment and Development, known informally as the "Earth Summit." The main achievements were agreements on climate change and biological diversity. The world was coming together for the first time to tackle two of the most pressing problems facing it. Canada, under the leadership of Brian Mulroney, signed both agreements.

In fact, 154 countries signed the UN Framework Convention on Climate Change. The goal is to stabilize the amount of greenhouse gas in the atmosphere at a level that will prevent dangerous and human-made changes to the climate and the Earth's ecosystems. However, the key caveat is that this stabilization has to occur in a way that does not infringe human safety or sustainable economic development in each country. Every year since 1992, all the countries that signed the convention (there were 196 signatories in 2022) have attended a two-week meeting to discuss progress and strategies moving forward.

Mulroney stepped down as leader of the Progressive Conservative Party in 1993 with high disapproval ratings. His minister of defence, Kim Campbell, became leader and prime minister for a four-month period. In the November election, the Liberal Party won a majority, and Jean Chrétien became prime minister. His first and ongoing concern was debt reduction, which included some cuts to environmental programs as well as many other areas of the government. By 1998, Chrétien introduced the first balanced budget in Canada since 1969.

Most of the mid-1990s were focused on Quebec and the sovereignty movement. This was a huge and pressing issue. The referendum in 1995 seemed to stoke the flames, and the federal government, as well as most of the country, continued to attend to the nationalist fire burning across the country. However, amid this domestic crisis, Chrétien did sign the Kyoto Protocol in 1997. This was an extension of the 1992 agreement on climate change.

In Saskatchewan, the 1990s were action-packed on environmental issues. Grant Devine's government came crashing down in 1991 as the debt rose to $15 billion and the North American Free Trade Agreement, unpopular in rural areas, was supported by Devine in 1989. Scandals among top government officials were also deeply problematic. Among the fifty-five Conservative MLAs, sixteen were charged with account fraud, and some of them served jail time. They included Eric Berntson, one of the key MLAs who supported the Rafferty-Alameda project. He represented Souris-Cannington, and the Alameda dam was built in his riding. At the time he was charged, Berntson was a federal senator and had to resign in order to serve a short jail term. Devine was not implicated in any criminal wrongdoing, but the scandals left a black mark on his reputation.

His downfall was a chance for the New Democratic Party to regain some of its lost ground in the province. Roy Romanow emerged as the premier. He was first elected to the Legislative Assembly in 1967. And he served in Premier Allan Blakeney's cabinet from 1971 to 1982. He lost his seat in the 1982 election but regained it in 1986 and became leader of the party in 1987.

Romanow was a very different leader from Blakeney and NDP (or CCF) leaders of the past. He was what is often considered part of the "third way," more a traditional Liberal than a social democrat. His third way was less about equality of outcomes and government allocation of benefits and more about creating opportunities through the private sector. Essentially, he was a step away from the "government-based" solutions that Blakeney was so fond of in the 1970s. Romanow's government would look to the market and private forces to bolster the economy.

However, his government got off to a rough start. It inherited the spending mishaps of the Devine years and had to overcome a $15 billion debt. By 1993, the province was faced with the possibility of declaring bankruptcy. It was later revealed, by Roy Romanow and Janice MacKinnon, his minister of finance, that the federal government and Prime Minister Brian Mulroney provided emergency financial assistance to Saskatchewan. In a 1997 *Globe and Mail* article, Romanow recalled how MacKinnon made a secret trip to Ottawa to discuss the province's precarious situation with Donald Mazankowski, the federal minister of finance. As Romanow said in the article, "I must pay a little tribute to Mr. Mulroney here, because he was able, through his minister of finance, to grease some payment from the federal government to the Province of Saskatchewan."

While Saskatchewan held it together and kept the government running on a low-cost budget, there was little time or money for new environmental initiatives. This is partly why Romanow is not known for any environmental leadership. If anything, history books recall how he opposed the Kyoto Protocol and Canada's chance to join the world in combatting climate change in the 1990s. More locally, people in Saskatchewan likely recall that Romanow was pro-uranium and opened up the province's largest mines during his tenure. He also lowered royalty rates for oil and industry in the hope of attracting more business to the province. Of course, in the conservation world, he did announce the creation of the Representative Areas Network at the Saskatoon Prairie Conservation and Endangered Species Conference. But largely, with the exception of the work done by Lorne Scott, his minister of environment, in the late 1990s, Romanow's government is likely not remembered for its conservation policy.

I WONDERED WHY Lorne didn't run for the Liberals or the Conservatives in 1991. He wasn't committed ideologically to the New Democratic Party at the time. Sure, he made friends there during the Rafferty days, but he had not joined the party, and it wasn't immediately obvious that his allegiance would fall there. I also knew that Lynda Haverstock asked him to run for the Liberals. She told me as much when I met her for coffee at a bookstore in Saskatoon during the summer of 2018. Still a fireball of wit and energy, Haverstock recalled how she immediately took to Lorne because he was a pragmatist. She thought that this made him a natural Liberal, like her.

When I asked Lorne about the Conservatives and Liberals, he shrugged, smiled, and said "I guess Romanow asked me first." This made me laugh out loud. Lorne is—and was even during his ten-year career as an MLA—non-partisan and non-ideological. Haverstock was right about that. But I knew that it wasn't that simple. Politics rarely is. Pushing him further, I asked "who really talked you into running?" Without hesitation, he recalled that it was "Bob Lyons and Lorne Calvert." He explained that they asked if he would go to an NDP executive meeting and give a talk about the Rafferty-Alameda project. He had an expired Conservative Party membership at the time and was a member of no other party. The meeting was in Moose Jaw, and Lorne gave his talk. After a rousing applause, he asked if anyone had questions. Apparently, Fred Clipsham, a party member and future Regina city councillor, stood up and said "we want you to run for us." And Lorne replied "any serious questions?" That day Lyons, Calvert, and Romanow all asked Lorne to run for the New Democratic Party.

Calvert remembers this time well. On the same trip when I met with Haverstock, I also met with Calvert in Saskatoon. He has a kindness about him that relaxes a person, and conversation flows easily. In fact, I had to switch to decaf coffee as the conversation wandered from topic to topic. He spoke fondly of Lorne and, like Haverstock, remembers instantly connecting with him.

Calvert was elected to the Saskatchewan Legislative Assembly in 1986 and met Lorne through the Rafferty-Alameda controversy because "that was one of the hottest issues." Calvert shared an office with Lyons, "passionate about this topic." They travelled to North Dakota to see what could be done about it. Calvert was impressed with Lorne's zealous approach and perseverance. When Lorne spoke in Moose Jaw at the NDP executive meeting, Calvert knew that he would make a good political candidate for the party. "I was still a novice to the political world" is how Calvert described himself. "And I think we [he and Lorne] rather connected. I had come from a rather non-traditional background and not a particularly partisan world. And Lorne was coming from a non-partisan point of view. A passionate view. A gentle passion. It was very attractive." Calvert was not in the practice of recruiting candidates, but "it struck me that this man was a contributor, to the party and to the broader public sphere."

Lorne won the NDP nomination in 1991 and became the candidate for the Indian Head–Wolseley riding. He ran against Dwight Dunn of the Progressive Conservatives and Jack Hosler of the Liberals. When I asked Lorne what it was like to campaign for the New Democratic Party in his area, he said that it was a very good experience. He vividly remembers Hosler and thought that they were allies against Dunn. "It was quite comical," he explained, giving the example of going to fall suppers when he and Hosler would sit together and watch Dunn go around bumping into people and upsetting their meals. Lorne and Hosler would wait until the supper was over, and then "we'd walk around talking with people. In the end, Hosler and I agreed to vote for each other." Lorne kept true to his word and suspects that Hosler did the same.

Lorne enjoyed getting out and meeting people. He said that "people by and large were really polite. The odd one raised a Rafferty card. And others would slam the door." His real strength in the area was with hunters and wildlife folks. Lorne was already well known and well liked and extremely respected in those circles. So, once he declared that he was running, he started signing those people up for NDP memberships. Although not normally the stronghold of the party, these people wanted to vote for him. "I think people voted for the individual—not the premier"—is how Lorne explained it. On election night, he won 2,725 votes or 39.82 percent. Hosler and Dunn almost tied with a difference of only three votes: 2,069 to 2,066 votes.

Lorne officially became the member of the Legislative Assembly for the Indian Head–Wolseley riding. Geographically, the riding was rather large—obviously including the towns of Indian Head and Wolseley but extending to the Qu'Appelle Valley. The First Nations in the district included Carry the Kettle, Sakimay and Ochapowace bands. Outside those reserves, the district was largely agricultural.

Although it might seem to be uncommon for a farmer to run for the New Democratic Party and win, it is important to remember that the CCF and NDP grew out of rural Saskatchewan, and farmers were their bases. Moreover, in 1991, the New Democratic Party won pretty much everywhere, both urban and rural. It claimed more than half of the popular vote and fifty-five seats of sixty-six in the Legislative Assembly. The Progressive Conservative Party held on to ten seats but lost the popular vote to the Liberal Party in many ridings.

During the 1991–95 term, Lorne learned the political ropes. He was not part of cabinet and not privy to many of the decisions made during that time. But he was chair of the Environment and Resource Caucus Committee. He worked behind the scenes on getting more land into *The Wildlife Habitat Protection Act*. Haverstock remembers Lorne as being "completely relatable. I think because he is so kind, so approachable, non-dogmatic in his field." Indeed, that was a big element of their friendship. Haverstock and Lorne are what you would call the classic non-partisans. As she explained, "we are associated with political parties, but there is a complete understanding that we are not purists in terms of ideology. We don't believe that any one political party has purview of good public policy." Haverstock and Lorne were first brought together through the assembly's seating arrangement. There were so many NDP candidates elected in 1991 that they "spilled over into the opposition benches." And for Haverstock, in a place where "every day of my life was miserable," there "was a thing of great solace. His name was Lorne Scott."

♠ ♠ ♠

I MET ROY ROMANOW in his office at the University of Saskatchewan on a beautiful August morning. He was busily writing his memoirs and in a self-reflective mood. I asked him about his government's
environmental legacy. He talked about two things: uranium and
climate change. That was interesting because, in all the hours that I
had spent talking with Lorne about his life's work, these two topics
never came up. This was in part because they are bread-and-butter
"environmental" issues as opposed to "conservation" issues. And, in
part, because he does not like talking about them. The Romanow
government was pro-uranium and anti–climate change policy. These
were not radical positions at the time and perhaps stances that Lorne
might have supported had he stayed in the Progressive Conservative
Party. But I am sure that Lorne, having been the environment minister who opened uranium mines and did nothing to address climate
change, would prefer that I not even mention these issues.

One of the most important uranium deposits in Saskatchewan
was discovered in 1981 at Cigar Lake. This deposit was the richest
(18 percent uranium oxide) undeveloped deposit in the world. It was
also one of the largest. But then, in 1988, the McArthur River deposit
was discovered—also one of the largest high-grade uranium deposits in the world. The problem for Romanow was that his party was
really split on the issue of uranium development. In fact, in 1982, after
a stunning election loss that nearly ruined the party, delegates to the
NDP annual convention passed a resolution calling for the phasing
out of uranium mining in the province.

Following this, a joint statement by church leaders in Saskatchewan called for a moratorium on uranium mining until more was
known about the potential consequences and because of the use of
uranium in nuclear weapons. Thirteen church leaders from Angli-
can, Lutheran, United, Roman Catholic, and Mennonite denomi-
nations signed the statement. But Devine's government nonetheless
proceeded with uranium development. And with privatization of
the industry. In 1988, Eldorado Nuclear and Saskatchewan Mining

Development Corporation merged to form Cameco Corporation, Canada's largest uranium producer (and Canada was the world's largest producer until 2009, when Kazakhstan overtook it). The company began privatizing in 1991 by selling public shares and was fully privatized by 2002. While in opposition during the Devine years, NDP MLAS opposed expansion of the uranium sector and wanted a complete phasing out of all existing mines.

Thus, the question for the Romanow government was whether or not it would pursue uranium development despite opposition from the public and within the New Democratic Party. This wasn't an easy decision. There was a deep divide within the party over the issue. In 1992, a year after the party was returned to power, it reversed its position on uranium. Officially, this happened "after a close vote at an acrimonious convention." However, it was not an approval of all uranium mining carte blanche.

Romanow's government decided to approve new mines only if they were acceptable after an environmental review. In August 1991, the provincial government and the federal government appointed a federal-provincial environmental assessment panel to review several proposed uranium mines in northern Saskatchewan. The first review panel considered three proposed mines: the Dominique-Janine extension (at Cluff Lake), the Midwest Joint Venture, and the McClean Lake Project. It released a report in 1993 approving the first, rejecting the second because of unacceptable mining methods, and delaying the third by five years. The governments then went on to review two other projects: Cigar Lake and McArthur River. Those reports were completed in 1997 while Lorne was the minister of environment. Both projects were approved.

Uranium extraction is a dirty, toxic business. It is profitable, creates jobs, and grows the economy. But it produces immense pollution at every stage of mining and processing. It is then used for nuclear energy, which causes low greenhouse gas emissions but creates much toxic waste. Or, worse yet, it is used in nuclear weapons that pose catastrophic human and environmental risks. These are the issues that must be weighed in any cost-benefit analysis. And we cannot lose sight of the fact that costs and benefits are distributed unequally given the geography and population demographics of Saskatchewan. Most of the costs occur in the north, whereas most of the benefits occur in the south. Uranium, as it turns out, is both messy and political.

Romanow's government supported the panel's decision regarding conditional approval of Cluff Lake but rejected the call for a delay at McClean Lake. Apparently, it was not worried as much about toxic waste storage as everyone else in the north and everyone else on the environmental review panel. Berny Wiens, the minister of environment and resource management at the time of the first report, was satisfied "that any adverse environmental impacts will be successfully minimized without the need for a five-year delay."

This is exactly the western paradox: wanting a stable and steady economy while destroying the resource (the environment) on which that economy depends. In hindsight, the paradox seems to be clear. Well-intentioned governments want to "develop" so-called resources to benefit people and create prosperity. And in doing so they destroy certain resources, people, and avenues for prosperity. The Saskatchewan government mined uranium to create jobs and clean energy. It believed—perhaps rightly so—that with regulation it could minimize resource depletion through efficiency and technological advancement.

I asked Lorne what it felt like to be minister and approve the mines. He looked around the small diner in which we were eating lunch and joked "I think I am going to go and sit somewhere else." But then he explained that "we took the line that uranium is here in Saskatchewan, and there is a demand for it, and if we don't provide it some other place will. But if we provide it, we will be using the best environmental safeguards and technology available. We will develop it to the best of our ability. Knowing that years down the road there might be new information."

That is how the government justified uranium mining. And Lorne was careful to align himself with the Romanow government when discussing this with me. He never used the phrase "I thought" or "I did" or "I wanted"; he only spoke in terms of "we" on this issue. And he meant "we" as "the government." Lorne really had no choice, for the government decided to approve the mines, and as the minister of environment he was chosen to be the mouthpiece of the government on this issue.

Prior to going into politics, Lorne never gave much thought to uranium extraction. He was aware of it but not involved in it and had no real opinion on it. My own thoughts on uranium and nuclear energy are muddy at best, but I had to ask him again "do you really think uranium can be developed in an environmentally sustainable way?" Lorne was quiet for a few seconds. "The storage. You can reduce accidents. You can reduce human error." He explained further: "I went on a tour. Yellow cake, I guess they call it. And there were open barrels. I was standing right beside it. But it is not harmful until it is produced [into uranium]." Like many politicians both before and after him, Lorne didn't really answer the question.

He also felt some assurance in the fact that the New Democratic Party had arranged for funds to be set aside for cleanup and management over the long term. His hope was that new technology will help to make the extraction, transportation, and production of uranium safer. I asked him if this is something that he follows or has kept track of over the years. But he admitted that it is not an issue on his radar.

I am a bit surprised, and perhaps a little disappointed, that after all the hullabaloo that uranium production caused in Saskatchewan, and that nuclear energy has caused across the world, the minister responsible for okaying the world's largest uranium mine didn't have more to say on the matter. How could he be so blasé? The nature of democracy is that you get elected on a party's platform, and you support its implementation. You get to have influence and make progress on the issues that matter most to you. Lorne did. His issues were always wildlife, habitat, and protected areas. Uranium was not his driving issue, but knowing him I expect that he would have resigned as minister had he been fundamentally opposed to its development in the north.

Joe Phelps, the minister of natural resources in the early 1940s under Tommy Douglas, thought like Lorne on the issue of uranium.

As Kathleen Carlisle points out in her book *Fiery Joe: The Maverick Who Lit Up the West*, Phelps thought of uranium as being "a little bit apart from the people," and he considered himself "a prairie person." That is, Phelps was more familiar with prairie issues, and his constituency was in Saltcoats, near Yorkton, not in the north. He also said that "the forest, the fish, and the game were all in trouble. This impressed me more." Lorne felt the same way as Phelps. He too is a "prairie person" whose constituency was in the southern part of the province, and he is interested primarily in prairie wildlife and habitat. And, like Phelps, and every political party to form the government, Lorne, as minister, was also willing to turn a rather blind eye to the Indigenous Peoples living with the environmental consequences of resource extraction in the north.

The decisions on uranium mining were made by forces larger than Lorne. The Romanow government, and the NDP executive, had already decided that the path forward was uranium mining. That was how the government would generate much-needed revenue for the province. Most of these decisions were made before Lorne became minister, and he was not at that decision-making table. To be clear, he never voted against or spoke against uranium development in the north. He diligently supported his government's policy, and today, looking back, he acknowledges that the government needed revenue and that the north needed economic development. He is convinced that the federal and provincial environmental assessments were procedurally just and that measures were put in place to reduce environmental damage.

🐦 🐦 🐦

The 1990s were an exciting and hopeful time for climate change policy. By the mid-1990s, Saskatchewan was leading the country in growing greenhouse gas (GHG) emissions. The province wasn't first in absolute terms, but its growth rate in emissions was higher than that of any other province. Emissions grew in Saskatchewan by 25.6 percent from 1990 to 1995, putting the province well ahead of second-place Alberta (18.8 percent) and third-place British Columbia (14.8 percent).

However, rising GHG emissions were not a cause of concern in Alberta or Saskatchewan at the time. In fact, Premier of Alberta Ralph Klein's concern was the potentially "catastrophic" effect that GHG *limits* could have on the oil and gas sector. Klein warned that reducing emissions to 1990 levels could cost billions, perhaps trillions, of dollars to the Alberta economy. In Saskatchewan, Premier Romanow was more tempered but still thought that Canada's record on GHG emissions was "not that bad." Both Klein and Romanow were committed to protecting the oil industry and the economy.

What Saskatchewan and Alberta opposed was the idea of replacing the system of voluntary regulation with binding regulation. The federal New Democratic Party wanted Canada to cut GHG emissions by 20 percent within thirteen years. The Saskatchewan New Democratic Party did not support such a drastic cut. Lorne was quoted by the Saskatoon *StarPhoenix* as saying that "this is not realistic." He further claimed that "certainly a twenty per cent reduction would be wonderful. As governments in power, we have to look at the reality of it." Minister of energy and mines, Eldon Lautermilch supported Lorne and thought that voluntary measures had illustrated some "success" and should be the pathway forward.

The Kyoto Protocol occurred at the sixth meeting of the United Nations Framework on Climate Change Convention in 1997. Prime Minister Jean Chrétien signed the protocol, but his cabinet was hesitant to ratify it because of the commitments required of individual provinces. The final and internationally agreed upon target was 6 percent below 1990 levels by 2012. To be clear, Chrétien committed Canada to reducing its carbon dioxide emissions to 6 percent below what it was currently emitting. That was challenging because as time passed the population of the country grew, as did the economy. Thus, reducing emissions below a level emitted by fewer people and a smaller economy requires significant effort by the government, industry, and citizens.

Prior to the December meeting in Kyoto, there was a November meeting of the joint ministers of environment and energy in Canada. The provincial representatives agreed that Canada could lower its emissions below 1990 levels by 2010. However, there was no agreement that it could be 6 percent lower. Thus, provinces felt betrayed by the federal government's commitment on the international stage.

To address some of the frustration, the federal government hosted a dinner in December 1997 with the first ministers in Ottawa. There was agreement for cooperation—provinces and territories would take an honest look at what would be required for success in implementing and monitoring the Kyoto Protocol. Romanow did not send Lorne to Ottawa with all the other provincial environment ministers. When asked by the media, staff said that Lorne had "other commitments."

But the truth is that he was not the lead minister on this file. That job went to Minister Lautermilch, who defended voluntary mechanisms with every breath. And he had the support not just of Romanow but also of the province's Ralph Goodale, the federal minister of natural resources. Yes, Goodale stood not with Chrétien and his federal party but with Saskatchewan on the climate file. In the 1990s in Saskatchewan, climate change denial was predominant, and there was an even larger reluctance to confront the policy implications of a changing climate. As economists and world leaders started to discuss emissions trading and carbon pricing, Goodale decided to stand with the province. He was against a price on carbon.

And so was Lorne. In 1997, he thought that "any tax would penalize Saskatchewan, a province with a dispersed rural population that contains twenty per cent of the nation's road system." He went on to say that "global warming is very serious and it's not a figment of anyone's imagination, but a tax on gas or any energy project would very unfairly impact Saskatchewan people." Although climate change was real, the solution put forward by the federal government was unfair. This argument should sound familiar to readers today.

The topic of climate change is notably absent from the Saskatchewan legislative record in 1996–97 and 1997–98. No one in the government raised the issue of climate change, global warming, Kyoto, or a carbon tax. There was zero discussion about implementing any type of emissions reduction policy in the province. Although these issues were debated in cabinet, they were not discussed in the assembly. The fact that no member of the opposition Liberal Party raised questions indicates that there was broad cross-party agreement that climate change was not a pressing government issue in the 1990s.

As history played out, Canada went on to ratify the Kyoto Protocol in 2002, and then in 2011 it became the first country to formally withdraw from the international agreement. In 2015 at the Paris meeting of the United Nations, Justin Trudeau agreed that Canada would reduce its emissions to 17 percent below 2005 levels by 2030. This was a target already promised by the government of Stephen Harper in 2014. Wasting little time in fulfilling a campaign promise, Trudeau met with the premiers of the provinces and territories to discuss a Canadian climate strategy.

In 2016, the Pan-Canadian Framework on Clean Growth and Climate Change was agreed to by all provinces except Saskatchewan, which refused to implement a cornerstone piece of that agreement—a price on carbon. In 2018, Doug Ford was elected to office as the premier of Ontario, and he immediately ended the province's cap-and-trade policy (trading with Quebec and California). Ontario has joined Saskatchewan, along with Manitoba and New Brunswick, in challenging the federal government on its demand for a national price on carbon. In 2019, the NDP government in Alberta lost to the United Conservatives, and the new premier, Jason Kenney, opposed a carbon tax.

🐦 🐦 🐦

LORNE'S VIEWS ON CLIMATE CHANGE POLICY have not changed in the past twenty years. "Obviously, we need to reduce our carbon emissions, or we are in serious trouble." He said this as he looked over his shoulder at the Dairy Mart in Indian Head. That is how controversial this topic is in a town in rural Saskatchewan. You don't even want to be caught talking about it in public. But a carbon tax, in his understanding, means that you buy gas and pay a tax on it—only for that money to come back to the government or the people. "Take it with one hand and give it with the other hand. It doesn't achieve anything." This is a common refrain in the province. And it is incorrect. The economic and policy implications of a carbon tax are more complicated because pricing carbon creates behavioral incentives that lead people and corporations to use less carbon over time. They are also some of the best tools that economists and policy makers have devised for reducing carbon emissions.

Lorne is the first to admit that in 1997 he didn't have "the answer." He still doesn't today. He lives in a place where a 4x4 truck is a status symbol and he and his neighbours have to drive thirty kilometres round trip for a carton of milk. Unlike his views on wildlife and public lands, which are unwavering and crystal clear, climate change leaves him fumbling a bit. It is clear that he doesn't want to talk about it. And he said as much by proclaiming nervously that "I haven't discussed this with anybody."

I am not surprised that someone on the prairies is conflicted over climate change policies. As a writer-in-residence at the Wallace Stegner House in Eastend, Saskatchewan, I felt a million kilometres away from the impacts of climate change—those that stare me in the face in Toronto as I take the overcrowded subway in sweltering heat or as I sit in traffic on the *twelve-lane* 401 Highway. In the Cypress Hills, climate change and biodiversity loss are not apparent threats. Spring just arrived on time with the bluebirds. And when I went for walks, as I often did in the mid-morning and early evening, I saw life all around me: coyotes, gophers, deer, sometimes moose, budding trees, and all kinds of plant forms ready to be transformed by the warmth of spring. This didn't feel like a crisis. Indeed, it felt like peace, beauty, and safety.

It is the political winds of climate change that put the issue in the air. In Alberta, Rachel Notley tried to convince people that a carbon tax can work and is right. Her government collapsed under its own weight in the spring of 2019. In Manitoba, there is confusion—first the province accepted the idea of a price on carbon, but then it quickly joined Saskatchewan in its proposed challenge to Trudeau and the federal plan. My guess is that, for a lot of people in the west, fighting a price on carbon is more about fighting Trudeau than about fighting the responsibility to act on one of the largest threats facing humanity. As one resident said to me, "farmers believe in climate change, they just don't believe in the solutions." I think that Lorne is a good example of that kind of farmer.

CHAPTER 5

THE LATE 1990s: HIGH TIDE OF CONSERVATION

The direction is clear, and the first step is to throw your weight around
on matters of right and wrong in land use. Cease being intimidated by
the argument that a right action is impossible because it does not yield
maximum profits, or that a wrong action is to be condoned because it pays.

—ALDO LEOPOLD

The late 1990s were a high tide of wildlife and land conservation in Saskatchewan. This was largely because Lorne Scott was the minister of environment and resource management. In the election in 1995, the New Democratic Party held on to its majority government but was reduced from fifty-five seats to forty-two seats in the Legislative Assembly. Lorne's electoral district was merged with part of the Bengough–Milestone district to create the Indian Head–Milestone district. Lorne won 3,440 votes or 43.45 percent of the vote. He beat Liberal candidate Steve Helfrick by a few hundred votes. The Liberal Party, under Lynda Haverstock's leadership, was having a renaissance in the province. Indeed, it captured one-third of the popular vote and eleven seats in the assembly, becoming the official opposition.

With forty-two MLAs in the government, Roy Romanow went about choosing his cabinet. He once wrote that choosing a cabinet in Saskatchewan is different from doing so in other places because the individuals must have "a feeling for what it means to be a prairie person." He went on to write that "some of my best ministers were those people who were the sons and daughters of people who had

worked or were still working our prairie soil." Lorne was thus a natural choice. Pat Atkinson, also chosen as a cabinet minister numerous
times throughout her twenty-five-year career, told me that "Lorne
was perfect for us. He was a farmer. He was rural." But more than
that, she said, he came to us "as an expert." Everyone knew Lorne the
conservationist and naturalist.

Lorne Calvert also spoke of Lorne's expertise but noted that it
was mixed with an unusual passion. He recalled that Lorne came
into the legislature one day, and Calvert thought that some tragedy
had befallen him. But no, Lorne had accidentally killed a crow that
morning that he had meant only to scare. "It was like he had lost a
child" is how Calvert explained it. "He is just genuine. He is authen-
tic." There have been no other environment ministers in the history
of Saskatchewan who could match Lorne's expertise and passion for
the province's landscape and wildlife.

Lorne had already been the chair of the Environment and
Resource Caucus Committee and thought that he was ready to be
the minister of environment and resource management. But it wasn't
easy to be in the environment branch of the government in the 1990s.
Looking to reduce the public debt, Romanow made cuts everywhere
that he could—including in the civil service. In the wildlife branch,
there was a good depth of expertise. Wayne Pepper, a thirty-one-year
civil servant with that branch, explained to me that the cut essentially
gutted it. Pepper took a retirement package, but at age fifty-five he
thought that he was just at "the peak" of his career. He was trained as
a biologist and an ecologist and worked in wildlife for the province
for over thirty years. His expertise was unmatched save for that of a
few others in the branch who had come into public service with him.

Unlike in other sectors of the government, such as health or
education, there wasn't much movement out of the wildlife branch.
Experts came into it and stayed their whole careers. So, when Romanow offered a cohort of senior civil servants in the branch retirement,
it contributed to a loss of knowledge and proficiency. This was the
situation that Lorne walked into as minister. The whole Department
of Environment and Resource Management had its budget cut, and

the branches beneath it, wildlife and fisheries, were significantly trimmed. This was a difficult time for wildlife folks in the government.

When I asked Lorne in 2018 about his undertakings as minister, he spoke first of provincial parks. Admittedly, I knew little about this topic since I have not visited many parks in the province. I quickly learned that Saskatchewan has twenty-nine provincial parks and ten historical parks spread across the landscape.

Parks have been part of his life since Lorne worked for the Museum of Natural History in Regina in the 1970s. Part of his job there was to create the information displayed in parks across the province. The signs included mainly pictures and descriptions of wildlife and plant life in the particular park. From this experience, he gained knowledge about the conservation value of the parks. This is something that he has never forgotten.

Lorne remembers parks as being the first big issue that he worked on as minister. He recalled that, "right after I became minister, I was told we had to close six provincial parks—including Blackstrap, Echo, Katepwa, and Buffalo Pound." In July 1996, it was made public that the government could no longer afford to run twenty-nine provincial parks. At the time, some of the buildings in the parks, especially those built before 1970 (about 60 percent of all buildings), did not meet health and safety regulations or building codes. When making the announcement, Lorne said that closure "is the last thing we want to envision."

Indeed, he was appalled by the prospect and vowed that he would not be the minister to close parks. His team put together numbers on visitations, fees, and long-term costs of park management. They also launched a review and consultation program called Saskatchewan Provincial Parks: Where to Tomorrow? that brought together the government, environmental groups, and the public. The goal was to create a new vision of the park system for the twenty-first century that would address aging infrastructure, changing recreational trends, and limited government funding.

At the same time, Lorne went to his colleagues one by one to seek support for the parks. He first got support from Lorne Calvert. And then Janice MacKinnon, the minister of finance at the time and key to getting some resources for parks. Although some other ministers were surprised that Lorne got MacKinnon's support, he said that "I always got along with her, although some didn't." This was typical since Lorne got along with almost everyone. He wasn't quick to give up on his priorities, but he was not a bully. He would seek people and talk to them about an issue and see where he could connect with them.

Lorne asked cabinet for six months to devise a plan to save the parks. The cabinet members supported him. He looked at all kinds of options—from reducing services in the parks, to cutting staff, to reducing operating hours. The main problem was that just maintaining the park system cost about $12 million annually, whereas park revenue was only about $6 million. At the time, park visitation was strong—2.4 million visits in 1995.

Within six months, it was clear that Lorne was considering every possible solution to keep the parks open, including corporate sponsorship of the park system. It started with allowing Labatt Breweries to spend $10,000 to replace picnic tables. This was not without controversy, for some people feared that this type of sponsorship would promote and encourage drinking in the parks. To the media, Lorne claimed that "we will have very discreet, small signs. There certainly won't be neon, flashing lights saying 'This is sponsored by so-and-so.' It'll be done in a very tasteful manner and at the same time, we certainly appreciate the sponsorships." That is a diplomatic statement.

When I asked Lorne about the corporate sponsorship, he did "vaguely remember something about that." It is a bit ironic that someone who does not drink alcohol was able to secure sponsorship from a beer brewer. He laughed and joked that he'd start drinking beer if the breweries started paying for all the parks in Saskatchewan. Although in the long term the government came up with the necessary funds, Lorne's creative thinking and his support from colleagues were the stopgap measure necessary to save the six parks from the cutting block. In fact, all twenty-nine parks remained open, and the province has never had to close a park since that time.

♪ ♪ ♪

A NEW FORESTRY ACT was the first thing that Lorne introduced in the Legislative Assembly. It was a significant piece of legislation for the Romanow government because it would open up forestry development, mainly in the north, and create some much-needed revenue for the province. However, it was not a throwback to the days of Tommy Douglas and Joe Phelps, when the government planned to use natural resource revenue to subsidize other public projects. Instead, it was a continuation of Grant Devine's neo-liberal approach to public resources. This meant privatization. In 1995, the government merged Sask Forest Products (a Crown corporation created by Phelps and Douglas) with MacMillan Bloedel, a private company. By 1999, privatization was complete. Weyerhaeuser bought out Bloedel, and the province transferred forest management licences. Forestry in the province is private, not public.

For Lorne, forestry was about more than revenue. It was also about forests. At the second reading of the bill in the assembly, he introduced the bill with reference to the intrinsic value of forests before moving on to their economic value. He said that "our forests are much more than trees. They are complex communities of plants and animals nourished by the soil, air, and water. The quality of our physical environment, the air we breathe, the water we drink, and all living things around us depend on the health of our forests." Lorne was proud to stand in the Legislative Assembly and speak about the intrinsic value of "resources." In fact, his statement sounds like something that Aldo Leopold would have said about forests and a biotic community. Saskatchewan's section of the boreal forest is an impressive and interconnected system that sustains all life in the north.

But that was not how other people in the government, or the province, saw forests. Lorne recalled that, "up until then, forestry in the province was just cutting trees." He wanted to be part of a transition to the sustainable development of forests. From his perspective, the Act would replace a thirty-year-old piece of legislation that ignored environmental considerations and Indigenous input. He was interested in the health of the forests and how that connected to the health of the local Indigenous communities.

However, the pragmatist in Lorne also spoke about the 8,000 jobs that depend on the industry and the billion dollars of revenue that it provides to the provincial economy. The Act was intended to create a system by which forest companies must negotiate a twenty-year plan with the province. And the Act increased fees for the industry while making restoration of forests (replanting trees) mandatory and financed by the industry. The Regina *Leader-Post* summarized the new legislation by stating that "forestry companies will pay more, the public will gain a louder voice and treaty rights will be reaffirmed." At the time, Lorne summarized it as legislation "designed to balance our economic needs with environmental and social demands." It was an excellent example of how Saskatchewan could start to answer the western paradox. Lorne wanted to protect the forests and ensure the restoration of harvested forests so that the industry could provide long-term and steady revenue for the province, including jobs and royalties.

Sustainable forestry management dates back hundreds, if not thousands, of years. But in a professional setting, it was brought into the North American governance of forests with Gifford Pinchot, the first director of the U.S. Forest Service, and Aldo Leopold, the first graduate of Yale University's School of Forestry and a champion of environmental conservation. Canada was slower to adopt sustainable forestry practices, in part because it was slower to develop its forestry industry. But in the 1990s, Saskatchewan's forests were in dire need of long-term management plans and environmental assessments. Lorne was pleased to oversee this new era of forestry in the province.

With the passage of *The Forest Resources Management Act*, timber fees were to increase substantially, to almost double what they had been in the province. But there was no outcry from the industry because Lorne had met with representatives prior to the announcement of the Act. The government had secured advanced support. In nearly every other province, the fees were higher. Saskatchewan had the lowest timber fees in Canada at the time and perhaps among the lowest in the world. But it is important to note that fees did not double in Saskatchewan. Initially, the goal was to double fees and to include fees for insect and fire control. However, Lorne and his fellow ministers were unable to negotiate successfully on these matters. Timber fees increased, but not as much as first proposed, and insect and fire control were left out of the Act.

It also required a "State of the Forest Report" every ten years to increase public transparency and accountability. More importantly, an integrated forest land use plan had to be prepared for every forest management unit in the province. This helped to move forest management from just "harvest" to "sustainable harvest." Overall, Lorne's first substantial piece of legislation was a success but fell short of his lofty goals. The industry was not quite as prepared as Lorne to solve the economic and sustainable development problems of the province.

ONE OF LORNE'S CROWNING ACHIEVEMENTS from a conservation perspective was *The Conservation Easement Act*. More so than forestry, conservation easements were near and dear to his heart. The basic concept of an easement is to place restrictions on development and use of land for the purpose of conserving it. This is often done through a third party, a land trust, by which a landowner surrenders the rights to develop and sometimes use the land for a set number of years or in perpetuity. For example, if a farmer has a wetland on her property and wants to ensure that even after she sells the land the wetland can never be destroyed or plowed, then she can put a conservation easement in place on that section of land. An organization such as Ducks Unlimited or the Saskatchewan Wildlife Federation can arrange and hold that easement. It is a voluntary but legal agreement, and the landowner cannot decide to back out if she needs money down the road and suddenly wants to sell that patch of land or plow it up for agriculture.

This was not a new idea in the 1990s. In fact, it was a commonly used conservation tool in the United States. The National Park Service had purchased easements (for scenic vistas) in the 1940s and 1950s to protect land in Virginia, North Carolina, and other southern states. The first state to enact conservation easement legislation was California in 1959, followed by New York in 1960. Within a decade, forty U.S. states had some sort of legislation in place to allow for conservation easements. In Canada, conservation easements were slower to develop. It was not until 1995 that Ontario, British Columbia, and Alberta introduced such legislation.

In the Legislative Assembly, Lorne argued that *The Conservation Easement Act* "will allow governments, private conservation agencies, and landowners to use conservation easements to conserve a full range of space[s] we in Saskatchewan value for their natural, historic, heritage, culture, and scenic qualities." Although Liberal Party MLAs had a few questions during the debate, they pertained mainly to the process and the overall intent of easements. Were they really for conservation of land and wildlife? It seemed that people in Saskatchewan could not understand the concept of conservation. They were looking for some sort of economic or regulatory hook. Was this just an attempt to regulate private property? Or was this just a way for environmental groups to make money? People just couldn't understand the "real" purpose of conservation easements.

Lorne was adamant in the Legislative Assembly and in media appearances that the purpose of the Act was to protect existing habitat. It really was that simple. Many of the organizations that he had joined or worked closely with prior to his time in politics favoured the bill. He had support from agricultural groups as well as conservation groups. This was huge. And for Lorne it was the crowning achievement of his time in office. Wildlife habitat will be protected— legally protected—forever in Saskatchewan because of this law. For a home-grown conservationist, there is no greater legacy.

In the first ten years of enacting that legislation, sixty-four parcels of land, in total 190 hectares, were donated, mainly to Ducks Unlimited for the protection of wetlands. This far surpassed Alberta (61 hectares) and British Columbia (96 hectares) in that ten-year period. Today thousands of hectares of land are in conservation easements in Saskatchewan. And Lorne made it possible. This was not something that the New Democratic Party had campaigned on and not something that its membership base was demanding. When Romanow and I discussed environmental legislation, he acknowledged that Lorne thought that conservation easements were vital. Cabinet supported the initiative, but it was completely driven by Lorne.

🐦 🐦 🐦

THE 1990S WERE AN IMPORTANT DECADE for Métis people's rights on the prairies. And for a brief period, hunting was at the centre of a battle over identity, land, resources, and sovereignty. It is difficult not to interpret the public outcry over this issue as veiled (sometimes loosely veiled) racism in Saskatchewan. And in many ways, the story is like a continuation of the demise of the bison on the prairies over 140 years ago. At the end of the nineteenth century, it was government policy to destroy the Métis and First Nations ways of life by making hunting increasingly difficult. With no bison to hunt, Indigenous people were forced to give up that way of life. But they have continued to hunt—for sport and subsistence—in Saskatchewan.

In 1995, John Grumbo was charged under the Saskatchewan *Wildlife Act* as a "non-Indian" who received a deer from an "Indian" (the term used in the Constitution). This was illegal. Non-Indians cannot harvest or receive a deer out of hunting season. Grumbo argued that Métis are Indians under the Natural Resources Transfer Agreement of 1930. This is a bit complicated, but when Saskatchewan became a province in 1905 the federal government retained ownership of lands and resources (also true for Manitoba and Alberta). It was not until 1930 that Ottawa relinquished lands and resources to the prairie provinces. When the lands were in federal possession, Indians had the right to hunt and fish on them for subsistence. The question then became, when the lands were transferred to the provinces, did

Indians lose their right to hunt and fish on them? And exactly who is an Indian (not defined by the Constitution)?

The Supreme Court had ruled that treaty Indian hunting and fishing are subject only to federal regulations, not provincial regulations. For example, a wildlife act cannot override the constitutional right of an Indian to hunt or fish, whereas the federal *Migratory Birds Convention Act* can. But the court had not determined whether or not a Métis person is an Indian for the purposes of hunting and fishing in the prairie provinces. That was the very thing that John Grumbo was challenging.

In provincial court, Grumbo lost and was convicted of a crime under *The Wildlife Act*. But that decision was overruled a year later in the Court of Queen's Bench. The decision was crucial. The overruling meant that any person who could prove to be Métis could hunt without a licence in Saskatchewan. At the time, a journalist for the *StarPhoenix*, Randy Burton, argued that the court ruling made Saskatchewan a "hunting playground for Métis." This was in part because, as Burton pointed out, courts in Manitoba had ruled that Métis people did not have the right to hunt without a licence, and in Alberta only Métis people who lived on the land could hunt unlicensed. This meant that Métis from Alberta and Manitoba denied hunting rights could hunt unregulated in Saskatchewan. Adding to the discrepancies in wildlife regulations, Manitoba and Alberta had bans on night hunting in place, whereas Saskatchewan did not. The implication was not only that Métis from other provinces could come and hunt unlicensed all day in Saskatchewan but also that they could hunt all night.

This topic received a lot of media attention and public outcry at the time. According to a 1997 *StarPhoenix* article, the Duck Mountain Provincial Park manager said that "people are getting antsy along the border because there is a major influx of aboriginal hunters coming from Manitoba." The manager went on to describe the challenges in the region and confirmed an increase in the number of unregulated hunters. From his perspective, it made "game management very tough" and was "a safety concern." Another article in the *StarPhoenix* referenced "petitions and widespread outrage in rural Saskatchewan" over Métis hunting. The archival record supports this: there was no other topic on which Lorne received more letters from the public during his time as minister.

This issue also arose at the same time as moose numbers started to drop in the province, and residents were quick to see causation where only correlation existed. A farmer from Blaine Lake, Saskatchewan, wrote an op-ed for the *StarPhoenix* in 1997 that put the issue rather bluntly and had an accusatory tone regarding Lorne's handling of the situation:

> Environment and Resource Management Minister Lorne Scott would like us to believe moose numbers in this region are down for a variety of reasons. The plain truth is that they are down because of the Métis slaughter. Why did Scott not exercise some control over this Métis issue? A multitude of people (myself included) wrote to inform him of the carnage taking place. Rather than take control of the situation, he stuck his head in the sand. A Métis card can be had by almost anybody for a $50 fee, with the Métis Nation of Saskatchewan policing it, and it's amazing how many people have come out of the woodwork. Now, the license-buying, bill-paying sport-hunter will have to pay again through hunting-privilege cutbacks. Scott's conservation initiatives, habitat charges and depredation grabs are ringing pretty hollow. It is time he did something, before we have no big-game animals left. It is time to speak out and not sit idly by. I'm posting my land "no hunting" this fall and I urge all concerned citizens and sports hunters to do the same. It's time to bring this neglect and abuse to light.

"Depredation grabs" was a key statement in this op-ed. A special depredation fee was introduced while Lorne was minister to provide funds to address wildlife depredation of crops. It was unpopular and repealed after a year. It probably contributed to the tone of this piece.

Members of the public were not the only ones to attack Lorne. The topic also arose in the Legislative Assembly in December 1997. Dan D'Autremont, a Progressive Conservative MLA from the southeast riding of Cannington (bordering Manitoba), accused the government of allowing night hunting to escalate in the absence of legislation. Indeed, he specifically accused Lorne of appearing before the media with a "deer-in-the-headlights look" while "slinking about in the dark" on the issue of night hunting.

Lorne was quick to defend the government by pointing out two major oversights: first, section 41 of *The Wildlife Act* and, second, a Supreme Court case from 1964. Section 41 reads that "no person shall, at any time, use a searchlight, spotlight, flashlight, jacklight, night light, headlight or any other light or cast a ray of light for the purpose of hunting any wildlife." That pretty much makes night hunting illegal. However, the government did not make it outright illegal because of the Supreme Court decision ruling that Indigenous people can hunt day or night by any means.

Burton, again reporting for the *StarPhoenix*, highlighted Lorne's insistence on working with the Métis Nation-Saskatchewan (MN-S) and Federation of Saskatchewan Indian Nations (FSIN) to come to an agreement. At the time, the MN-S constitution opposed night hunting but didn't enforce it. And Lawrence Joseph, the FSIN vice-Chief, noted that Chiefs and Elders recognized night hunting as a dangerous activity that should be eliminated. In fact, "Elders call it taboo because it is spiritually wrong" to hunt an animal with the use of spotlights at night.

Lorne said that, instead of taking a "heavy-handed approach," he wanted to work directly with the FSIN and MN-S to address safe and sustainable night hunting. That was the only way that it would work long term. The government could pass regulations, but there was a good chance that enforcement would be impossible. So the FSIN had to agree from the outset for lasting change to take place. There was not a lot of trust on either side, First Nations or the government.

Lorne recalled that "I worked with Lawrence Joseph. Our message was safety. Together we did greatly reduce the night hunting."

To appease the public, in 1998 the government, under Lorne's direction, regulated the use of spotlights for night hunting. The government also made it illegal to discharge a firearm at night from a road, shoulder of a road, or ditch. However, night hunting itself—such as that done by moonlight—was still legal in the province because First Nations and Métis have rights to hunt at any time on reserve land and unoccupied Crown land.

However, Lorne's and the government's actions did not quell public outcry. Many Saskatchewan residents thought that the new regulations did not go far enough. Lorne received a lot of criticism from farmers and members of the Saskatchewan Wildlife Federation over the issue. There were calls for a moratorium on Métis hunting altogether. But Lorne held his ground until the Court of Appeal ruled that all applicable provincial hunting and fishing laws applied to Métis and non-Métis alike. That pretty much settled the public's complaints about unregulated Métis hunting in the 1990s. However, recognizing that northern Métis are subsistence hunters, Lorne wanted to make an exception. In May 1998, his office implemented a policy giving Métis living in the Northern Saskatchewan Administrative District the equivalent of an Aboriginal right to hunt.

Since that time, Métis people have had their rights affected by two Supreme Court cases. The first, *R v Powley*, affirmed that Métis have an Indigenous right to hunt for food as recognized under section 35 of the *Constitution Act, 1982*. This decision was made in 2003 as a result of a Métis community in and around Sault Ste. Marie and, as such, applied directly to that community. However, it did establish a legal test to determine the Indigenous rights of other Métis groups. In the second case, *Daniels v Canada* in 2016, Métis were determined to be "Indians" under the *Indian Act*. This gave them the right to hunt and fish as Indians. In Saskatchewan, this meant that all Métis people could hunt and fish on federal and provincial lands (similar to First Nations people in Saskatchewan). But in 2018 the province limited that right to include hunting only during the recognized dates listed in the annually published *Hunters and Trappers Guide*.

Métis-government relations are ongoing. On July 20, 2018, the Métis Nation—Saskatchewan signed an agreement to develop a nation-to-nation relationship with the federal government. The issue of hunting is still central. And it will remain so for the Indigenous people of the prairies.

🐦 🐦 🐦

FROM MY PERSPECTIVE, one of the biggest failures and successes of Lorne's years as minister was *The Wildlife Act*. I have studied this topic in great detail and written about it in another book. It is also how I came to meet Lorne.

In 1992, Canada signed the UN Convention on Biological Diversity at the Earth Summit, the same summit at which it signed the UN Framework Convention on Climate Change. The agreement on biodiversity committed Canada to protecting biodiversity across the country and in its water and ocean territories. Four years after the convention, the provinces and territories met with the federal government and agreed on a set of criteria for species-at-risk legislation at the subnational level. This was known as the Accord for the Protection of Species at Risk. Roy Romanow assured me that he signed the accord in good faith, as did the premiers of the other provinces, and that "there was a lot of enthusiasm" at the time for this type of legislation. However, following the accord, the governments struggled to pass the legislation.

Saskatchewan had already passed *The Wildlife Act* under Allan Blakeney's NDP government, but it was not a conservation law per se. It simply established rules and fees for licences and gave conservation officers the authority to enforce the rules. It did prohibit entry into a series of wildlife refuges in the province but offered no special protection for or recovery of endangered wildlife and provided no habitat for wildlife. And there was no mention of species that were declining or at risk of overexploitation. The purpose of *The Wildlife*

Act had always been to provide the means to sustainably hunt the province's game species as opposed to a means of protecting or conserving wild species.

Signing the Accord for Protection of Species at Risk in 1996 meant that Saskatchewan would have to do better. It would need to create a law that could protect species at risk from further decline across the province. In 1997, Lorne introduced amendments to *The Wildlife Act*. He did not try to introduce a separate piece of legislation, such as an *Endangered Species Act* or *Species at Risk Act*. Other provinces were introducing such legislation—except for the three western provinces. In British Columbia, Alberta, and Saskatchewan, any attempt to fulfill accord promises came by way of amendments to existing wildlife regulations.

Lorne prefaced the amendments to *The Wildlife Act* by pointing out that "Saskatchewan contains one of the most diverse and unique ecosystems in the world. Our lush prairie grasslands, productive wetlands, diverse aspen parklands, and the wilderness forests and lakes in the North are renowned for their beauty and abundance of wildlife." He went on to discuss the new species-at-risk provisions of *The Wildlife Act*: Saskatchewan would add a definition of wild species, use government science to assess species, and add species under threat of extinction to a list contained in *The Wildlife Act*. And that was all.

To be clear, the amendments to the Act, as proposed by Lorne, allow for the categorization of species (extirpated, endangered, threatened, and vulnerable) and give the minister of environment the legislative discretion to determine how a species is to be classified and whether or not a species is to be added to the official list. This means that the government, not scientists, can decide which species are threatened or endangered with extinction. To make decisions, the minister relies on data provided by the Saskatchewan Conservation Data Centre, an organization formed in 1992 through a partnership with the Ministry of Environment, the Nature Conservancy (U.S.), and the Nature Conservancy of Canada.

In the Legislative Assembly, Lorne claimed that "Saskatchewan is committed to the principles of the accord," but this never turned out to be true. Perhaps he believed that he could give the province the *Species at Risk Act* that the New Democratic Party had promised. The accord, agreed to by the provinces, set out fifteen different criteria that a provincial *Species at Risk Act* should contain, such as the development and implementation of recovery plans. The amendments to *The Wildlife Act* met only three of the fifteen promised criteria. Recovery plans were not one of them.

There was little debate in the legislature over the protection of species at risk. Instead, the main debate was over the increased cost of hunting licences in the province through new "big-game damage provisions" in *The Wildlife Act*. Those were the other amendments that Lorne introduced at the same time. The Act passed in June 1997, but already the following year there was an amendment about new penalty provisions: raising the maximum fine to $100,000 for damage to wildlife habitat. The amendment passed without much opposition, and the new *Wildlife Act* received royal assent on June 11, 1998. Today this legislation remains the province's only law to protect species at risk.

On the next page in Table 1 is a list of "at-risk" species added to *The Wildlife Act* in 1998. Extirpated species are recognized to be native to Saskatchewan but no longer found in the wild. Endangered species are native wild species threatened with extirpation or extinction, and threatened species are native wild species likely to become endangered. For species on the list, the Act makes it illegal to "kill, injure, possess, disturb, take, capture, harvest, genetically manipulate or interfere with or attempt to do any of those things to any designated species." But the Act does not create any regulation or mechanism to identify and protect critical habitat for listed species. Instead, Saskatchewan's approach to habitat protection has been through *The Wildlife Habitat Protection Act*, not geared specifically to species at risk.

TABLE I

Species Protected by the Saskatchewan *Wildlife Act*

Common Name	Latin Name	Status in the Act
black-footed ferret	*Mustela nigripes*	extirpated
grizzly bear	*Ursus arctos horribilus*	extirpated
greater prairie chicken	*Tympanuchus cupido*	extirpated
Eskimo curlew	*Numenius borealis*	extirpated
white lady's slipper	*Cypripedium canadium*	extirpated
burrowing owl	*Speotyto cunicularia*	endangered species
piping plover	*Charadrius melodus*	endangered species
greater sage-grouse	*Centrocercus urophasianus*	endangered species
whooping crane	*Grus americana*	endangered species
swift fox	*Vulpes velox*	endangered species
sand verbena	*Abronia micrantha*	endangered species
western spiderwort	*Tradescanthia occidentalis*	endangered species
tiny cryptantha	*Cryptantha minima*	endangered species
hairy prairie-clover	*Dalea villosa*	endangered species
slender mouse-ear-cress	*Halimolobos virgate*	threatened species

As of 2022, the list of species had not changed since the original list was created in 1998. Not a single species has been added or removed from the list. However, in Canada there is a federal institution that tracks flora and fauna and assesses their status in the wild. The Committee on the Status of Endangered Wildlife in Canada was already assessing wildlife with ranges in Saskatchewan and able to say with scientific authority which species were secure and which were declining. As of 2022, the committee had classified thirty-three threatened, twenty-one endangered, and two extirpated species in the province. Yet its *Wildlife Act* remains unchanged. Independent scientists indicate that there are fifty-six species at risk with ranges in the province. Saskatchewan's government says that there are fifteen. That is a huge gap. The first number was determined by scientists and the second by politicians.

Four provinces and two territories in Canada lack stand-alone legislation for species at risk: British Columbia, Alberta, Yukon, Nunavut, Prince Edward Island, and Saskatchewan. The other seven have an *Endangered Species Act* or *Species at Risk Act*. And looking at all thirteen jurisdictions, it is clear that Saskatchewan has among the weakest provisions for species at risk. The province is part of the global temperate grassland biome, among the most altered and least protected biomes on the planet. Through consistent government inaction, the grassland ecosystem continues to decline.

The provincial government signed the accord in 1996 and had the opportunity to really do something to address biodiversity loss. Lorne has explained to me, on more than one occasion, that the support was never there. The agricultural community had zero interest in species-at-risk protections because it meant habitat, or land, restrictions. There was a culture of fear based upon misunderstanding of how the American *Endangered Species Act* works. American media perpetuated the myth that the Act appropriates land for wildlife protection. Farmers and ranchers in Saskatchewan came to believe that an endangered species meant that the government would come out to the farm or ranch and either take over the land or regulate it out of production. And without support from agriculturalists, the most numerous and important land managers in the province, there was no point in forcing a *Species at Risk Act*.

So Lorne did what he could do. He added a list of species at risk to *The Wildlife Act* in the hope of raising awareness of their existence and decline. The species-at-risk provisions in the Act were not even intended to be enforced. Lorne admitted that "it was there in name only." He said this with deep sorrow. He has spent the better part of his life working with landowners to conserve habitat and protect species at risk. He knows that good stewardship of land in Saskatchewan is possible, but he was unable to get regulated or legally enforceable stewardship. And, since his time as minister, there has been little political will to do anything about species at risk in Saskatchewan.

🐦 🐦 🐦

IN 1992, the Brundtland Commission on the environment determined that a minimum of 12 percent of an ecoregion is required to ensure species survival and diversity. By 1991, when the New Democratic Party formed the government in Saskatchewan, only 5 percent of the natural landscape had some sort of protection. Lorne couldn't get a *Species at Risk Act* that enabled the identification and protection of critical habitat for species. Instead, he had to work to keep lands in *The Wildlife Habitat Protection Act* and add other lands when possible. Conservation easements also added habitat to Saskatchewan's protected ecoregions. And, of course, there were the provincial parks and federal lands, such as PFRA lands, national parks, and bird sanctuaries.

The Ministry of Environment, under Lorne's leadership, decided to create a Representative Areas Network (RAN) as a list of all the "ecologically important land and water areas across the province" meant to protect habitat for wildlife while providing recreational spaces for the public. The goal was to create the list and challenge the government and Saskatchewan residents to add lands to increase the total to 12 percent. As Lorne explained to me, "RAN is basically an inventory of all areas that have some form of protection." It is a way of "taking stock." That includes provincial parks, provincial lands (pastures too), federal (PRFA) lands, Ducks Unlimited lands, and other NGO lands. It is just an inventory and does not "afford any protection." Although there are no legal provisions under RAN specifically to protect the lands listed, theoretically they are already protected by another entity (government or private). For example, close to forty designated areas in the Representative Areas Network are also designated under the *Representative Area Ecological Reserve Regulations*. Lorne, in his typical humble fashion, undervalues his accomplishment as the minister who started the program. Indeed, the RAN process increased protected areas in the province by over 1 million hectares. That's significant by any measure.

Moreover, there were efforts to get landowners outside the Ministry of Environment's direct control to agree to manage their lands to support RAN principles. Lorne had to verify with each parcel holder whether the land could be included as protected and listed in the Representative Areas Network. Substantial new protected areas were added over the years, primarily using *The Ecological Reserves Act*. These areas were mostly in the north and often developed through the land use planning exercises mandated by *The Forest Resources Management Act*. They required study to achieve the representation goals based upon enduring features and extensive consultations, especially with First Nations and Métis, and the regulations for the areas often accommodated traditional use. (Section 5(1) specifies that trapping, hunting, angling, mushroom picking, berry picking, and so on are allowed in all Representative Area Ecological Reserves unless prohibited for a specific reserve.) Some of the significant areas were the Wapawekka Hills Representative Area, Seager Wheeler Lake Representative Area, Amisk Lake Representative Area, Sturgeon-Weir River Representative Area, Jan Lake Representative Area, Halldorsen Bay Representative Area, Perry Lake Representative Area, Mari Lake Representative Area, and Selenite Point Representative Area. Most were not brought into place during Lorne's term as minister, but Lorne did start the processes, and 29 additional Representative Areas were added between 2002 and 2021.

According to him, one of the most significant agreements was signed by the Prairie Farm Rehabilitation Administration committing all of its community pastures in the province to the RAN program, totalling about 650,000 hectares. This was crucial; as Lorne pointed out, "in many areas of the province, these pastures are the only remaining grasslands of any size." The provincial Department of Agriculture followed the PFRA lead and committed about 320,000 hectares of community pastureland to the Representative Areas Network. Partnerships were also signed with the Canadian Wildlife Service, Department of National Defense, and Ducks Unlimited, and the Saskatchewan Wetland Conservation Corporation added its land. Thus, the 5 percent that had been put into protection between 1905 and 1991 quickly jumped to 10 percent in the years that Lorne was minister.

Unfortunately, the amount of land designated as protected land varies a great deal from region to region. The "representative" in the Representative Areas Network meant that the province was naturally broken into different ecoregions, such as mixed-grass prairie or boreal forest, and that 12 percent of the land in each region should be protected. However, that goal remains elusive. The aspen parkland had only about 6 percent of land designated for protection in 1999, and that number is likely less now with the advancement of agriculture and intensive livestock operations in the region. The Cypress Hills area has the highest percentage of protected area—as much as 20 percent in 1999—because of parks and conservation easements by large landowners. Lorne admitted that "the goal was 12 percent, but we didn't get there." And without serious intervention, we never will. The province isn't working on it. Lorne acknowledged that, since he left office, the Representative Areas Network has been "put on a shelf and collecting dust." That is somewhat true—many areas were designated, especially in the north, and this continued after his term as minister ended. Work continued under subsequent governments, including the Saskatchewan Party governments, but the momentum started under his leadership waned after he left office.

🐦 🐦 🐦

ONE PROTECTED AREA of the province where the federal *Species at Risk Act* does apply, giving protections far beyond the Saskatchewan *Wildlife Act*, is Grasslands National Park. Initially proposed by Dr. George Ledingham in 1957, the idea had support from the Saskatchewan Natural History Society and the Canadian Nature Federation as well as many other organizations. However, since the proposed land for the park included mainly provincial Crown land already being leased to ranchers for grazing, there was little enthusiasm among ranchers for a national park that would see the lands transferred to the federal government.

In 1973, federal minister of environment and Parks Canada Jean Chrétien spoke at the twenty-fifth anniversary meeting of the

Saskatchewan Natural History Society and was fully in support of a park in the Val Marie area. A memorandum of intent was signed in 1975, and an agreement to create the park was signed in 1981. Parks Canada started purchasing land at that time. However, the final federal-provincial agreement to create the park was not signed until 1988. That delay could raise an eyebrow. Lorne told me that "the province was using the Grasslands Park as a bargaining chip to obtain a federal licence for the Rafferty-Alameda dam projects." This was a story that Elizabeth May broke to the media during the Rafferty-Alameda days.

Long before she was the leader of the Green Party of Canada, or the executive director of the national Sierra Club, May was a senior policy adviser to Thomas McMillan, the federal minister of environment in the late 1980s. In a newspaper article featured in the *Winnipeg Free Press*, May acknowledged that she had resigned her position over the Rafferty-Alameda project. Specifically, it was a deal between the Deputy Prime Minister's Office and the Province of Saskatchewan to exchange a permit for the Rafferty-Alameda dams for Grasslands National Park. If the province would hand over the land necessary for a federal park, then the federal government would green-light the dam projects. May has always stood by this story even though the federal government has denied it.

If Grant Devine did trade Rafferty-Alameda for Grasslands, he doesn't remember it now. Or he didn't want to tell me about it. Sitting at his kitchen table in his farmhouse, I asked him about parks. "We did some things," he said and clarified that "I can't remember. There wasn't a big debate about parks." When I specifically mentioned Grasslands National Park, he asked "when was that?" I told him 1988, since that was the year of the federal-provincial agreement. All he said was "well, really? 1988? It was a little tough in that area but supported." And he moved on to a discussion about his love of ranching and being on horseback, like the people out in that area of the province.

Should we believe Elizabeth May or Grant Devine? Is it possible, or even likely, that Devine's government would have traded a licence for Rafferty-Alameda for the provincial lands necessary for a federal park? It doesn't really matter. The record already demonstrates that his government was desperate to get Rafferty-Alameda built and that the federal government was accustomed to making all kinds of mistakes in matters related to those dams. Exactly how Saskatchewan and the federal government came to agree on the matter is unclear, but there was a formal agreement in 1988.

Things moved forward, albeit slowly. Land acquisition proceeded on a "willing seller, willing buyer" approach. Ranchers began to sell their lands to the federal government. But the transfer of provincial Crown lands to the federal government took decades to complete. The provincial government wanted to conduct an exploration for coal, oil, and gas mineral rights that might be transferred in the process.

So, in the end, it was Devine who agreed to a park, but Lorne was the one who handed over the lands that made the park possible. On August 14, 1997, as minister, Lorne announced the provincial transfer of 31,181 hectares of land to the federal government. That gave the government 50 percent of the land within the proposed park boundaries—enough to initiate legislation to create the park. In 2000, after Lorne was out of provincial politics, the federal government amended the *Canada National Parks Act* and proclaimed Grasslands National Park. If you have never been to the park, you should go. There is nowhere else in Canada where you can watch black-tailed prairie dogs chatter and play across a field in which bison stand and burrowing owls hide. The vastness of the landscape and the horizon will shake you. It is as beautiful as it is memorable.

♪ ♪ ♪

GRASSLANDS NATIONAL PARK was a huge accomplishment for Saskatchewan and Canada. It received national press. And it certainly put Lorne in the limelight when he officiated the ceremony in the park. But while in office, he also took the time to support much smaller projects. Heather Wiebe, at the time the director of the Burrowing Owl Interpretive Centre in Moose Jaw, said that she called the minister's office and invited the minister or someone from his

office to the official opening of the centre in 1997. She hoped that
someone would at least return her call and was absolutely shocked
when she listened to her messages one morning and heard Lorne's
voice. Lorne said that he would be there. Wiebe saved the message
and played it for her mom later that night; she could not believe that
the minister himself had called back.

Sharon Butala, a Saskatchewan author and friend of Lorne's,
explained that even as minister Lorne was "friendly and warm with
absolutely no ego." She remembered that he would travel out to
rural areas to meet with ranchers and farmers on their own lands or
in their own communities. But he always "spoke the same to everyone" and never gave the impression that "he knew more than they
did." When Butala and her husband, Peter, donated their ranch to
the Nature Conservancy of Canada and created the Old Man on
His Back Prairie and Heritage Conservation Area, she worked with
Lorne. He was a "man of the highest integrity" and "the salt of the
earth." He was the kind of minister who, driving to a ceremony in
a provincial park, asked the driver to pull over so that he could
step out and help the park staff with a small project. He was "never
afraid to roll up sleeves and get to work in the dirt" is how Wiebe
explained it.

And it seems as though Lorne was always working behind the
scenes to find compromises on important issues. For example, he
worked to have conservation officers in the province carry sidearms.
Not everyone in cabinet agreed about this, and Lorne believed (erro-
neously) that Pat Atkinson was still upset about this issue. That is
how hotly debated it was inside the government. But he met with
conservation officers, and he talked to his colleagues. He even went
on night patrol with officers to witness first hand what it was like to
charge people found hunting illegally. He recalled the whole political ordeal as a "really interesting exercise." He had Lorne Calvert talk
to some officers in his riding, and Calvert agreed that they "are usually alone and in the middle of nowhere. They are sometimes chased
by poachers. Guys have had rifles stuck in their chest." Thus, it was
obvious to Calvert that the officers needed guns.

Lorne figured out a way to ensure that conservation officers would have more training with guns than city police. This seemed to ease some concerns. After getting support from cabinet, he worked with the government in Manitoba so that the two provinces could announce on the same day that officers would be getting sidearms. After the controversy in cabinet, Lorne was expecting a big public backlash, so in the days after the announcement, he said, his office was determined to keep track of all calls about the issue, but it got only three calls from the public. And I found only one letter in the Provincial Archives that spoke disapprovingly of the issue. Lorne's ability to work out common-sense solutions with stakeholders demonstrates not only great patience but also wisdom.

The last time that Lorne Scott appears in the legislative record is on the matter of WHPA lands. This seems to be fitting. However, it was not for the purpose of expanding the Act or even of adding land. Indeed, on April 29, 1999, Lorne introduced amendments to the Act that actually would remove 2,115 hectares of land from it. This was to "accommodate the interests of farmers and ranchers" who wanted to buy that land for agricultural purposes.

But all was not lost. Lorne was able to secure the addition of two large blocks of land totalling 1,084 hectares. One area, 583 hectares, was next to a provincial forest, and the other area, 500 hectares, was in what is known as the Fur Lakes area, east of Shell Lake. So, though it was a net loss to WHPA lands, arguably it was an overall gain for habitat protection. Lorne swapped disparate parcels of land for large tracts of land. There was no opposition to this exchange. The third reading of the bill took place on May 3, 1999, and that was the last time that Lorne stood on policy in the Legislative Assembly.

🐦 🐦 🐦

THE 1990S WERE BIG. From a wildlife and land perspective, despite limitations, it was Saskatchewan's conservation decade. However, looming large in the background were fights over uranium and climate change. Saskatchewan is one of the world's largest producers of uranium today. And, leaving aside the production and use of nuclear energy (or weapons), there is no sugar-coating the environmental externalities associated with uranium mining. Since mining occurs in the north, it does not have a direct impact on the prairie ecosystem. But the issue is still emblematic of the government's stance on resources and environmental policy. The New Democratic Party did an about-face on the issue and then pushed through environmental assessments in the supposed economic interests of the province. Despite clear opposition from the Saskatchewan Environmental Society, as well as other environmental groups, Indigenous Peoples, churches, and some residents, the government turned Saskatchewan into a uranium powerhouse. The yellow-cake mining is a black stain on the province's environmental policy and Indigenous rights.

Regarding the Kyoto Protocol and climate change, the New Democratic Party was also on the wrong side of history. It said no to a price on carbon and framed the discussion in a way that would echo through the decades. Roy Romanow, his minister of energy (Eldon Lautermilch), and Ralph Goodale, a federal cabinet minister, all agreed that reducing Saskatchewan's GHG emissions would hamper the oil industry and other industrial development in the province. They sought to protect natural resource extraction instead of the grasslands and the larger biotic community. Today Saskatchewan is still fighting carbon pricing, this time under the leadership of the Saskatchewan Party. There is consistency on this issue from both the left and the right. The consequences for Saskatchewan's prairies could be dire. Climate change will have devastating effects on grassland ecosystems, putting pressure on the hydrologic cycle and pushing species already at risk to further extremes.

I find that it is hard to judge Lorne fairly as minister of environment. He was caught between the grow versus conserve battle faced by every government since 1905. Romanow faced the western paradox head on and ultimately decided that immediate resource development was more important than sustainable development. As minister, Lorne was able to pass into law *The Conservation Easement Act* and *The Wildlife Act* as well as oversee the creation of the

Representative Areas Network and Grasslands National Park. Each of these initiatives, and especially when combined, do preserve the integrity, stability, and beauty of the biotic community. These policies were right, and as such they also provide a partial answer to the western paradox. Saskatchewan can conserve both the lands and the resources on which it depends for long-term prosperity.

Lorne was one of the longest-serving ministers of environment in Saskatchewan. In fact, since the Ministry of Environment was created in 1971, only one minister, the first one, Neil Erland Byers, has served longer than Lorne (for six years, from 1972 to 1978). As mentioned, Lorne lost his seat in the 1999 election. But for more than four years, he was able to shape the Saskatchewan landscape. He was not always able to enact the kind of stringent legislation necessary to protect the land and its wildlife from forces beyond his control. However, he did put habitat conservation and biodiversity loss on the political map and raised awareness of the issues that matter most to him. And those are issues that should matter a lot more to people in Saskatchewan.

CHAPTER 6

THE EARLY 2000s: FROM POLITICIAN TO LOCAL ACTIVIST

My heart is moved by all I cannot save.

—ADRIENNE RICH

The first decade of the twenty-first century is not associated with any environmental movement or really even any environmental event. The world watched Al Gore win and then lose the presidential election in the United States. Gore was a huge spokesperson for the climate change movement and made it central to his campaign. For a brief period, Americans—and by extension Canadians, exposed to U.S. media—regularly discussed climate change.

There is no question that the terrorist attack of September 11, 2001, changed the course of world history. The United States shifted its focus, and budgetary spending, to homeland security. Other issues, from education to health care to the environment, were put on the back burner. The devastation caused by Hurricane Katrina in 2005 did force some attention back to climate change and, to a lesser extent, the importance of wetlands. However, attention quickly shifted back to security issues and oil politics. President George W. Bush was focused on security and the U.S. economy, even at the expense of the environment. He stopped listing species on the *Endangered Species Act* because wildlife regulations slowed, and sometimes prevented, oil and gas extraction. He made exemptions to environmental laws so that hydraulic fracturing could boom, and it immediately did across Texas and Pennsylvania.

In Canada, the Liberal Party struggled to keep power federally. Prime Minister Jean Chrétien, who had signed Canada on to the Kyoto Protocol, designed to reduce greenhouse gas emissions, was unable to convince the provinces that climate change mitigation was necessary. When he stepped down in 2003, Paul Martin came to the helm as prime minister, but his government was reduced to a minority position in 2004 and then lost in 2006. During the first six years of the decade, the Liberal government did not focus on the environment.

Stephen Harper was prime minister of Canada from 2006 to 2015. During that time, he significantly cut funding to the environment and repealed or weakened many federal environmental policies, including the *Canadian Environmental Assessment Act*. He was famous for his climate change denial rhetoric and for his animosity toward science. He cut funding for research, and Canada stopped tracking data on certain environmental indicators. This period was a dark time in Canadian environmental history.

Saskatchewan environmental policy also entered a similar dark period in the later part of the first decade. The New Democratic Party was reduced to a minority government and eventually a coalition government with the Liberals. Lorne Scott lost his seat in the 1999 election. Don McMorris, a Saskatchewan Party candidate, won the Indian Head–Milestone riding with 3,877 votes compared with Lorne's 2,305 votes. The New Democratic Party hasn't won in Lorne's riding since.

Lorne did not lose on account of his record as the minister of environment. He believes that it had to do mainly with the closing of hospitals, very unpopular in his riding. Even his good friends admitted that they just couldn't vote for the New Democratic Party again. His loss was part of a much larger trend away from the party in rural Saskatchewan. Indeed, there was a major shift in Saskatchewan politics in the late 1990s with the emergence of the Saskatchewan

Party, a somewhat united right-wing party. In 1997, the Saskatchewan Party was created from the union of four Progressive Conservative and four Liberal Party MLAs who created a caucus in the Legislative Assembly.

Roy Romanow retired in 2001, and Lorne Calvert became the NDP leader and premier of the province. NDP support was waning, and in the 2003 election the party won 45 percent of the popular vote and only thirty seats, whereas the Saskatchewan Party won 39 percent of the vote and twenty-eight seats. The Liberal Party won 14 percent of the vote and no seat in the Legislative Assembly. From that point onward, the province has functioned basically as a two-party system, with the Liberal Party unable to gain any seat in the assembly.

Calvert, premier from 2003 to 2007, perhaps did value the environment more than prior provincial leaders. This was difficult given the realities of the slim NDP victory and a two-member majority in the assembly. Although again land and wildlife were not focal points for the government, sustainable agriculture, renewable energy, and climate change were priorities. Calvert chose David Forbes and then John Nilson as the minister of environment and Peter Prebble as the legislative secretary for renewable energy and energy conservation (2006–07). In June 2007, the government released the Saskatchewan Energy and Climate Change Plan, which called for a 32 percent reduction in greenhouse gas emissions by 2020 and as much as 80 percent by 2050. The route to success would be via voluntary conservation measures by industry, carbon capture and storage, increased renewable energy, methane release reduction in the oil and gas sector, and attention to increasing carbon sinks (forests and grasslands) across the province. The government established a wind farm and put alternative energy rhetoric into practice. It also imposed regulations requiring that automotive gasoline contain 7.5 percent ethanol.

At the same time, the government continued to promote uranium and invested in carbon capture and storage (known as "clean coal" at the time). In many ways, the Calvert government followed the Romanow government's lead by enriching several targeted tax incentives, further reducing royalties for oil and gas, decreasing small business taxes, and bringing in broad tax cuts for large corporations in the 2006–07 budget. Thus, in some sense, the government had trouble prioritizing when it came to the environment. Calvert wanted to grow the economy, as past premiers had, but he also wanted to conserve the resources on which economic development depended. There was tension in those goals. His government thought, perhaps hoped, that environmental policy could feed into the economy. Wind and solar energy might create jobs and revenue. Calvert was willing to try.

In 2007, Brad Wall and the Saskatchewan Party came to power. In an attempt to capitalize on the oil boom, the government streamlined environmental policy to "reduce red tape." Attention turned from renewable energy to oil and coal. The carbon capture and storage project was touted as the answer to climate change problems—Saskatchewan would just bury its emissions and not worry about them. And the government would foster the hydraulic fracturing boom in the province. There is no place in North America, or perhaps the world, with fewer regulations for hydraulic fracturing of oil. Jobs increased, the oil sector grew, and the economy continued to improve. But the province entered a period of soaring CO_2 and methane emissions. There was no thought given to a balance between growth and conservation.

🐦 🐦 🐦

IN THE EARLY 2000S, Lorne found himself out of a regular day job. He still farmed, as he had continuously since 1975. But he had never done so full time. It was not surprising, then, that within a year, in February 2000, he was busy as the executive director of the Saskatchewan Wildlife Federation. This position allowed Lorne to pick up where he had left off on a few important conservation issues, such as the gun registry and game farming. These issues grabbed his attention professionally while he continued to volunteer with conservation groups and community organizations in Indian Head.

Handguns have been registered in Canada since 1934. All guns were subject to registration during the Second World War, but following it only handguns required registration. All other guns and their ownership were highly regulated, but registration was not required. On December 6, 1989, Marc Lepine shot twenty-eight people, killing fourteen women, with a Mini-14 semi-automatic rifle at École polytechnique in Quebec. It was, and remains, Canada's largest mass shooting.

On the heels of that event, in 1990, Kim Campbell, the justice minister at the time, introduced significant gun regulation in Parliament. The bill died when Parliament was prorogued a year later. In 1991, she introduced a new bill, but it was strongly opposed by the gun lobby. A weakened version of her bill passed in the House and the Senate, but guns were not prohibited and registration of rifles was not required.

Chrétien's government picked up this legislative issue and passed the *Firearms Act* in 1993, with royal assent given in 1995. This Act, parts of which are still enforced today, required the licensing of all gun owners and the registration of all firearms. Yes, *all firearms* across the country were supposed to be registered with the government. A federal institution, the Canadian Firearms Centre, was created to oversee this process. Gun owners were given a generous deadline— January 1, 2003—to register their non-restricted firearms. To register a gun, you needed a licence, and the timeline for that was 2000.

Rural opposition to the gun registry was enormous. Anyone living in Canada during the late 1990s remembers the debate over this registry. In fact, Canadians continued to hear about it until April 5, 2012, when Stephen Harper's government repealed the clause related to the registration of non-restricted firearms. That move, which Harper's government had campaigned on in the western provinces, was immensely popular.

On this issue, Lorne, and most of rural Saskatchewan, sided with the Conservative Party. The Saskatchewan Wildlife Federation was relentlessly anti-long-gun registry. In some ways, its stance was consistent with small *c* conservativism still prevalent in Saskatchewan.

Rural people don't think that it is in the government's authority to regulate their right to hunt and protect themselves. But opposition to the registry is also more nuanced.

Guns are a fascinating political topic. Unlike Americans, most Canadians are opposed to handguns and fully accept regulations for their registration, ownership, and use. That said, gun ownership is on the rise. The report in 2017 from the RCMP's commissioner of firearms showed 839,295 restricted and prohibited guns—many of them handguns—across the country, almost double the 480,000 in 2005. The mass shooting in Toronto in July 2018 had some Canadians questioning the *Criminal Code* and wanting increased regulation of handguns.

But when it comes to other firearms, such as farmhouse rifles or long guns (hunting rifles), Canadians can be rather blasé on the topic. There is a major difference of opinion on urban gun regulation and rural gun regulation. In rural areas, guns are for protection and/or hunting. They can also be about status and culture. For example, in April 2019, I was at the Ducks Unlimited annual banquet in Maple Creek. Lorne's nephew was contemplating bidding on one of the long guns being auctioned. He joked that, if he won the bid, he'd need to bid on a gun cabinet because his would be too full for another gun. "Oh, are you a big hunter?" I asked. His response was a straight-faced "nope." His wife elaborated that "everyone just has guns here." I didn't need to act surprised because I wasn't surprised.

But instead of making it about culture and identity, the Saskatchewan Wildlife Federation focused on hunting. To the federation, gun control was "the biggest barrier to the recruitment of new hunters in Saskatchewan." That is what Lorne said when pressed by the media. And it was an issue of utmost concern since SWF membership was declining. The problem was clear: if people can't (easily) own guns, then people can't hunt. And people who do not hunt are not going to join hunting organizations. Hunting organizations are key to wildlife habitat protection in the west.

Lorne thought that the long-gun registry illustrated clearly that federal politicians do not understand hunting. He also acknowledged that some gun owners believed that the gun registry was just a stepping stone to gun confiscation. A bit conspiracy theory perhaps, but some SWF members told Lorne that their worry was that ultimately, once the government knew who had guns, it would come to take away the guns. And this meant that some people would rather get rid of their guns than register them with the federal government. To that end, Lorne continued the SWF Guns for Habitat Program in which gun owners could donate their guns instead of registering them.

Lorne told delegates at the SWF annual convention that "the best strategy to fight the Act is to delay complying for as long as possible." I have a hard time imagining Lorne actually saying that—or believing it or doing it. My impression is that he is a rather eager law-abiding citizen. So this suggests how much some people opposed the legality of having to register long guns. The penalty for not registering them was pretty steep: up to five years in prison and seizure of all guns.

By February 2002, Lorne and the Saskatchewan Wildlife Federation were considering "peaceful disobedience" in opposing the gun control law. However, that resolution failed. Lorne went on record saying that the federation "has not and will not encourage people to break the law." To be clear, the federation always supported gun control in the form of regulations regarding safe storage and use, but it adamantly rejected the "costly, complicated, and basically ineffective legislation from Ottawa." By December 2002, Lorne wrote a final plea to the federal government to shut down the registry for long guns. It was published in the *Prince Albert Herald*, but the plea fell on deaf ears. January 1, 2003, came and went. Lorne never registered his guns. Nor did many farmers and rural dwellers in Saskatchewan. The Saskatchewan Wildlife Federation continued to oppose the long-gun registry but never encouraged anyone to break the law. It took almost another decade before Harper was able to repeal the registry law.

Although gun registration might seem like a trivial issue for Lorne to focus on after his departure from government service, it was a continuation of the work that he did as minister on easements, *The Wildlife Act*, and the Representative Areas Network. More importantly, as a salaried SWF executive director, he had to either show leadership on an issue of great importance to his board and membership or get out of the way. Gun control can affect other conservation issues, but it was the issue of most importance to the people who paid his salary and thus could not be taken as a trivial issue, regardless of his personal beliefs. Hunters in Saskatchewan are part of the conservation base membership. They value wildlife and habitat protection. By trying to help hunters and make it easier for the Saskatchewan Wildlife Federation to recruit new hunters, Lorne was working directly on wildlife and land conservation. In his own way, he was still trying to preserve the integrity, stability, and beauty of the biotic community—a community that includes hunters as well as deer and their habitat.

🖋 🖋 🖋

OF ALL THE ISSUES that I spoke to Lorne about regarding his lifetime of work in conservation, it was game farming, and by extension trophy hunting on those farms, that animated him the most. In fact, it was the only time that I heard him speak in ideological terms. It turns out that this non-partisan is willing to tolerate the "right-wing free market" only up to the point where keeping wild animals enclosed for the purpose of trophy hunting is concerned. Lorne draws the line there.

Game farming, or game ranching as it is sometimes called, is a multi-faceted issue. It basically refers to keeping game species— such as bison, elk, boar, or deer—contained within a fenced area. Why would someone want to do that? Same reason that people keep cows—for the money. But sometimes these farms are for the purpose of hunting. People can pay to come and hunt elk or bison or white-tailed deer. They are basically guaranteed to kill an animal since there is nowhere for it to flee.

Game farms are not new. In the northern district, the concept of conservation farms for fur-bearing animals such as mink dates back to the Tommy Douglas government in the 1940s. On the prairies, the *Game Farming and Game Products Merchandising Regulations* were passed under the Grant Devine government in 1989. Saskatchewan was not the first province to allow game-meat farms or game-trophy farms. In 1982, Manitoba opened its door to elk farms for meat and scientific research. But by 1985 Agriculture Canada destroyed thirty-two elk imported from the United States that had tested positive for blue tongue, an unknown disease in Canada until that time. Yet by 1987 there were over 250 game ranches in Manitoba, Saskatchewan, and Alberta. By 2019, Saskatchewan alone had 279 game farms.

It should seem unreasonable that Saskatchewan would allow game farms after the clear risks posed in Manitoba—it took less than three years for disease to take hold of animal stocks there. Disease can easily put wild stocks at risk as well as the public if anyone eats tainted meat. So why did Saskatchewan go ahead with game farms? I talked to Lorne about the relationship among hunting, game farming, and chronic wasting disease a number of times over the summer of 2018. These interrelated topics often came up in our discussions about Saskatchewan's conservation story. For Lorne, chronic wasting disease as a result of permissible and legal game farming is an ugly stain on the provincial record.

He explained that "agriculture diversification" was the justification that Devine's government used in the 1980s for game farming. The government was not going to stand in the way of people making money. He also mentioned that the regulations were rushed through, with MLA Graham Taylor as the champion. It was not lost on Lorne that one of the first game farms—out near Wolseley and Indian Head—was opened by Taylor's son. As Lorne explained, "Graham Taylor's son brought in some red deer, which was illegal until it was made legal." As SWF president, Lorne met with minister of environment Herb Swan, who assured him that there would be no change to government policy, but then two days later the government enacted game farming—making it legal in Saskatchewan. Lorne observed that "people were going to get rich raising elk." They brought them in from South Dakota. The two big farms—one by Saskatchewan Landing park and one by Lloydminster—are where chronic wasting disease started in the province.

From an agricultural perspective, the idea was that producers could sell meat and antlers and allow people to "fly in from *New York City* and shoot an elk in a pen and then go back to the airport," Lorne explained (with emphasis on New York City to express his total disgust). A brilliant idea on paper, game farming with trophy hunting turned out to be a problem for wildlife and recreational hunting in many parts of the province.

From the SWF perspective, shared by many wildlife biologists, game farms, even those for the purpose of meat, are dangerous to wildlife (animals not in captivity). Animals bred and kept in close quarters have a higher chance of contracting and spreading disease. Lorne was worried about blue tongue and chronic wasting disease. A game farm animal would contract a disease, and then the animals at the farm would have to be destroyed. That alone is a sad and disturbing problem, but the real conservation problem is that disease could spread to wild populations. Animals could break free from captivity and mix with wild animals. Game farming was a threat to the wild gene pool. And that, of course, is what happened. As Lorne explained, "basically everything we said would happen did. It was all true. They [game farms] will bring disease, and there will be poaching and trafficking. And escaped animals." It was a known risk, one that the government willingly took.

While in office, Lorne did have to deal with game farms. And new regulations were passed in 1999. He recalled that "game farmers hated me. They met with the premier and asked him to fire me." The first case of chronic wasting disease was discovered in 2000, and this issue occupied Lorne as SWF executive director in the early 2000s and has continued to occupy him since then.

Chronic wasting disease is a nervous system disease that can infect the deer family, including elk, moose, and caribou. The disease is so aggressive that once contracted it is 100 percent fatal. And it plays out as the name suggests. An animal loses weight over time despite eating. And symptoms of nervousness and/or lethargy set in as the animal withdraws from normal herd behaviour. The disease does not affect human beings—although the Canadian Food

Inspection Agency cautions that more medical evidence is necessary to understand transmission of the disease.

The first discovery of the disease dates to 1967 in a captive mule deer herd in Colorado. It was then discovered in wild herds of elk and deer in 1981 in Colorado and Wyoming. And so it began. Making its way to a farm in South Dakota. And into the wild in Saskatchewan and Alberta. For the 2021–22 hunting season, the government of Saskatchewan reports on its website that it received more than 3,300 submissions to its hunter surveillance program. The result was "644 positive cases: 459 mule deer, 167 white-tailed deer, 16 elk and two moose." These animals were in the wild. Across the province, the disease appeared in forty-five of eighty-three wildlife management zones in 2018 and as many as fifty-nine zones by 2021. The government reports that "the disease is considered endemic across southern Saskatchewan, south of the boreal forest."

Any time that we discussed this issue, Lorne quickly became excited. His frustration and anger surprised me, for normally he is such a gentle soul. One of his main political complaints concerning the issue is something that I did not know about: game farming is subsidized as part of agriculture. Worse yet, taxpayers are the ones paying to have animal heads tested to see if the animals had the disease. If the result is positive, then taxpayers pay the owner market price for the animals destroyed. This is likely expensive, though no data on the cost in Saskatchewan are publicly available. The risk is borne entirely by the public since private game farmers bring animals into the province and then insist that the public subsidize them if the animals have or get the disease. Lorne blurted out his frustration to me one afternoon: "They [game farmers] are big free-enterprise right-wing cowboys, but they just love taking the taxpayer money." This is the most politically charged that Lorne gets on an issue. He is angry.

Why hasn't the conservation movement in Saskatchewan been able to stop game farming? To me, this seems to be something that more people should be concerned about even if they aren't interested in hunting or conservation. I have friends mad that taxpayers subsidize health care and other friends mad that the government subsidizes big oil in Saskatchewan. Surely the same friends would be furious to know that they are paying private game farmers to destroy their animals.

Lorne suggested that "the unfortunate myth is that government can't stop somebody from making money." This is what the government says anytime someone implies that game farms should be illegal. They are about agriculture and the economy, not conservation values. Lorne also noted "wild boar farms. We have been saying to the province buy them out at fair market value, there are about eighteen farms left, and then just get rid of them. But oh, no, we can't do that. That would interfere with diversifying in agriculture. Well, now we have wild boar in over a hundred RMS in the province." Wild boars also rile him up. They are an invasive species in Saskatchewan today. I know that they are in the Rural Municipality of Keys because I see them from my ATV when out riding. Wild boars do not belong on the Saskatchewan landscape. They destroy crops and everything else in their path. They eat everything from bird eggs to frogs to cow feed. They can also spread disease.

But Lorne's opposition to game farming isn't really about the economics of it. Sure, "right-wing free enterprisers " are looking to make a profit, but that isn't at the heart of the issue. Instead, Lorne opposes game farming because of its relationship to hunting. First, it decreases the number of hunters in the province. In areas where chronic wasting disease is rampant, few people will hunt in them. In many regions, people just quit hunting. It is too risky—what if the animal you shoot is infected? It takes about three months to get the animal tested. Although it is true that chronic wasting disease has not spread to humans, many people feel uneasy about eating a diseased animal.

Second, Lorne opposes game farming because of its ethics. The idea of trophy hunting is simple: go for large ornamented males trapped inside an enclosure with no chance for escape. The hunter removes the antlers or tusks from the dead animal and keeps them as a trophy. Or, as Aldo Leopold says, "a certificate." This type of recreational hunting, when the carcass is then used for meat, is acceptable.

As Leopold explains, "it attests that its owner has been somewhere and done something—that he has exercised skill, persistence, or discrimination in the age-old feat of overcoming, outwitting, or reducing-to-possession. These connotations which attach to the trophy usually far exceed its physical value." However, if the animal is wasted, if the hunter has no interest in the meat, then trophy hunting becomes less tolerable to conservationists. Worse yet, if the hunter pays to kill a *captive* animal for the purpose of gaining a trophy, then all respect is lost. Game farm hunting really bothers Lorne. In fact, as SWF president, he famously said that "real men don't shoot their pets."

From my perspective, Lorne has an uneasy relationship with hunting. As a child, he killed animals with a slingshot for sport. He got a gun when he was about fourteen. But he used it only to hunt ducks with his dad and family. Today he shoots only raccoons and stray cats. He admitted, and probably didn't want anyone else to know, "I have never shot a deer."

How does a guy who has never shot a deer become president and then executive director of the largest hunting group in the province? Lorne has nothing against regulated hunting and Indigenous hunting. And he respects hunters. They tend to share similar conservation principles. Hunters want to conserve animals so that they can continue to hunt them. Lorne wants to conserve animals because he loves them. The rationale is not the same, but the goal of conserving wildlife and habitat is the same.

Sport hunters tend to share a code. They kill animals, but they only kill wild ones with fair chase. And hunters do not let animals suffer. Lorne respects hunters who hunt this way. He too will kill animals, such as stray cats, to reduce suffering. That isn't fun for him. And it isn't always to protect baby bluebirds. In part, it is also out of compassion, as he explained: "Many cats released into the countryside die a slow, agonizing death from starvation and exposure." Sometimes the humane (or human) thing to do is end suffering.

On game farms, animals suffer. Nature suffers. The biotic community suffers. Trophy hunting of this magnitude, in which individuals pay to hunt an already captured animal, devalues nature and disrupts the ecosystem. Leopold argued that hunting is valuable because it highlights humankind's dependence on nature. But game farming and paid trophy hunting are far removed from wilderness preservation. An animal becomes a market commodity bought for an excessive amount of money in the service of private gain.

𓅓 𓅓 𓅓

EVEN AS EXECUTIVE DIRECTOR of the Saskatchewan Wildlife Federation, Lorne kept a toe in politics. In fact, Lorne Calvert talked him into running for the New Democratic Party again in 2003. Lorne quickly won the nomination, but he lost the election. He lost to Don McMorris again: 4,070 votes to 3,258 votes. Closer than the 1999 election but still far from victory. Nevertheless, Calvert said that Lorne had an impact on his government from 2003 to 2007.

During this time, "Lorne was always accessible" to Calvert, who relied on him for advice about conservation policy. One example that Calvert remembered was the deepening of Wascana Lake in 2003–04 before the spring. The earth-moving project, known as "The Big Dig," was necessary because the lake was silting up, causing increased aquatic weed growth and declining water quality for nature and recreation. Engineers devised a plan to save $1 million: instead of trucking all the dirt from the lake out of the city, they wanted to dump the dirt into the Wascana Marsh area, on the lake's east side. This sounded like a great idea to Calvert at the time. But when Lorne heard about this, he immediately called Calvert. "No one had bothered to tell me that there was a colony of endangered turtles, and should we put the dirt on the turtles while hibernating there would be no more turtles," Calvert recalled. So he called the engineers and said no.

Lorne was a friend and someone whom Calvert "just trusted." He still does. During his time as premier, if Lorne spoke to an issue, "I had to listen." "Always a gentleman but not a pushover either. He stands his ground." Of course, Calvert also listened to his ministers of environment as well as his energy adviser. Lorne was not elected and not accountable to the public. But he was respected in conservation circles and someone whom the government could go to for counsel.

Lorne also ensured that the government made the Representative Areas Network a priority. During Calvert's tenure, lands were added to the list. Calvert recalled that "we reached 9 percent provincially." One region with expanded protection was the Great Sand Hills, and Calvert credits not only Prebble and Forbes but also Lorne, who worked behind the scenes. The Sand Hills, for those who don't know, are naturally occurring sand dunes—between 8,000 and 10,000 years old—north of the Trans-Canada Highway near the Alberta-Saskatchewan border. In 2004, the government announced an environmental study of the almost 2,000-square-kilometre area. In 2007, the final report recommended enhanced protection, especially of eighteen ecologically sensitive areas in the sand dunes. The Calvert government went on to implement protections in the area. That was significant because there is also substantial oil and gas interests in that region. By creating the protected area, the government was able to prevent "development" in that region.

Calvert told me that "I have met a lot of people in public life. Lorne is genuine. He is bonafide." And he pointed out, correctly, that "he keeps on giving. He is very active in the little church in Indian Head. He was reeve. And still farming." And his influence on the people whom he meets is probably immeasurable because it is the little things that create ripples and then waves. Calvert now puts up bluebird boxes, and he had a nesting pair in 2019. I wonder how many people, after meeting Lorne, have put out a bird feeder or bird box. I am reminded of the purple martin boxes that I saw at Grant Devine's farm as I drove away from his land. At the time, I wondered if the same birds that visit Lorne also visit Devine. Maybe I should have told Devine that the birds are what we all have in common.

🐦 🐦 🐦

CALVERT WAS RIGHT that Lorne is a natural giver, and while out of office he found more time to devote to his local community and his beloved bird and wildlife community. In fact, the early 2000s were a very fulfilling time for Lorne despite the gun control and game farm noise. With experience and excellent leadership skills, he went on to some high-profile positions in nature groups at local, regional, provincial, and international levels.

I highlight Lorne's volunteer work here, as mentioned at the beginning of this book, to illustrate that Lorne subscribes to a land ethic and places himself inside a "biotic community." That term was coined by Aldo Leopold to describe a group of organisms that live together and interact with each other, including everything from human beings to insects to birds to animals to soil. In a biotic community, in which everything is interdependent, Leopold said, "we see one common denominator: regard for community welfare is the keystone to conservation." Lorne's life is evidence of this.

The Indian Head area is his home. Lorne has lived there his whole life. This might not seem to be extraordinary to some people, but I have had well over twenty different home addresses in my life. And I spent 2018–19 with no real address at all—just living out of a Ford Escape with my husband and our cat as we bounced from place to place along the West Coast from Anchorage to San Diego collecting research for our various projects. That is more normal than Lorne realizes. In fact, Wallace Stegner pointed out that "deeply lived-in places are exceptions rather than the rules in the West. For one thing, all western places are new; for another, many of the people who established them came to pillage, or to work for pillagers, rather than to settle for life." Thus, the fact that Lorne settled for life near Indian Head is remarkable.

He grew up attending the United Church and has maintained his faith and community through adulthood. Lorne has been a fairly active member of the church community in Indian Head and always willing to lend a hand. In April 2010, on Earth Day actually, Miles Russell, president of the Saskatchewan Conference of the United Church of Canada, formally recognized Lorne's work. Russell pointed out that "part of the United Church Creed says that as [a] church we are called to *live with respect in creation.*" He said that

"Lorne has been involved since a youth in this 'Calling' of the Spirit even before these words were placed in our United Church Creed. And so he is an example to all of what it means to live out our faith in practical ways that bring real change to life."

Living his calling has meant some hardship for Lorne. He has always been one to stand by his friends—in good times and bad. In 2003, Fred Lahrman passed away with Lorne at his side. Lahrman and Lorne had been close friends since their days at the museum in the 1960s. They had also been comrades in arms for wildlife in the province. In 2007, Peter Butala lost a short battle with cancer. Close to the end, Lorne travelled to Shaunavon to visit Peter. Sharon, Peter's wife, remembers vividly the comfort that Lorne offered her husband. When Peter started to vomit blood, Lorne didn't call a nurse or back away—he just held the tray close to Peter's mouth and then disposed of it. He wiped Peter's face and continued to talk to Peter. Lorne never wavered in friendship, especially not in difficult times. In 2012, he lost his long-time partner, Leona, to colon and lung cancer. Again, forever at her side, Lorne had to say goodbye too soon.

But living his calling has also brought Lorne immense joy and fulfillment. In 2004, he helped to found Friends of Wascana Marsh. In many ways, this was a direct continuation of the work that he had started back in the 1960s at the Museum of Natural History. Wascana Marsh is 223 hectares of marshland in Wascana Park in Regina. The marsh was originally established in 1913 alongside the Wascana Game Preserve. In 1956, the preserve became a federal migratory bird sanctuary (Wascana Waterfowl Park) because it is a migration site for over 100 species of birds. When Wascana Lake was deepened in 2003–04, Friends of Wascana Marsh developed as a way to raise awareness and funds for the important marshland habitat.

The group is small but does offer "outdoor, nature-based educational and interpretive opportunities and promote environmental sustainability within an urban setting." Close to Lorne's heart, Friends of Wascana Marsh co-host an annual school day that sees Grades 4–6 classrooms come to the park to learn about nature. In the 1960s, Lorne hosted these visits. Also essential to him is the

Junior Naturalist program that Friends of Wascana Marsh helps with financial support.

Ever since Lorne attended the opening of the Burrowing Owl Interpretive Centre in Moose Jaw in 1997, he has remained an avid supporter of it. He has helped to organize and host big fundraising events. He convinced Premier Lorne Calvert to support and attend some of these events. He also convinced Fred Lahrman to create a painting of a burrowing owl for auction. Heather Wiebe, director of the centre at the time, explained to me that "Lorne understood the centre. He always just supported us." Wiebe, who went on to work for the PFRA pasture program and then, after it closed, the BC government, remains friends with Lorne.

At the provincial level, Lorne has been involved with SaskTIP for over a decade. SaskTIP is a charity dedicated to wildlife crime. It is like a Crime Stoppers for wildlife. If you have knowledge of illegal hunting or wildlife abuse, you can call the hotline and report it. Sask-TIP takes the information and works with conservation officers to see the apprehension and prosecution of individuals who "violate resource and environmental laws." I was naive about the extent of illegal hunting and poaching in the province before Lorne told me about it. Who knew that bear gall bladders are extremely valuable on the black market?

Internationally, Lorne has worked mainly with two groups, both focused on birds. He was a founding member of the North American Bluebird Society and has served as its director. Its slogan is "Effective Conservation," and the group, across the United States and western Canada, seeks to "educate, persuade, and enlighten the public in methods that an interested person could use to help bluebirds or other native cavity nesters." Although Lorne no longer maintains his extensive bluebird trail, he still makes boxes and hangs them along rural roads in Saskatchewan. If you look, you will notice them.

At the North American Bluebird Conference in 2016, Lorne was a keynote speaker. In his introduction, it was noted that "no one has done more for bluebirds in Canada than Lorne." The society presented him with an award at that conference for a lifetime of contributions to bluebird conservation. Much to his chagrin, his talk is available on YouTube and is certainly worth listening to if you are interested in bluebirds. It is clear from the reception in the room that Lorne is an excellent public speaker—both funny and passionate—as well as a beloved member of the bird-banding and naturalist community.

He also worked extensively with the Whooping Crane Conservation Association and served as its president a few times. This work with the cranes dates back to the 1970s, and it was through Fred Bard and Fred Lahrman at the Museum of Natural History that Lorne came to the association. The saga of the whooping crane, explored in the next chapter, is a reminder to Lorne that "conservation does work." Over the years, he has helped to educate the public and lobby the Canadian government for better habitat and protection for the cranes.

Finally, and perhaps most importantly, Lorne is also a mentor and an informal recruiter for the conservation movement. There is an entire generation of children who either visited Wascana Park in the 1970s and remember Lorne showing them around or who sat in class and listened to him as he presented his wildlife slides to them. He has also spread his joy of nature to his family and friends. Heather Wiebe said that Lorne is never "selfish with his time or knowledge" and "always open to everyone" because "there is no hierarchy with him." He taught her about bird banding and the fine art of playing the card game Spades.

Jared Clarke, a birder and science teacher, is another mentee of Lorne's. Like Lorne before him, Clarke was the park naturalist at the Wascana Centre (actually the first person to hold that job full-time in 2013 since Lorne left in the 1970s). Clarke remembers that one day he was at the park, and this "tubby farmer in a plaid shirt and old dirty hat" introduced himself as Lorne Scott. The two became fast friends, and Clarke soon found himself spending weekends bird banding with Lorne, Stuart Houston, and other local birders.

However, Lorne often gives Clarke the gears for trying to *reduce* the number of geese in the park. When Lorne started at Wascana, the geese were almost extirpated, and he spent ten years trying to revive the birds. Alongside Bard and Lahrman, Lorne did such a good job that Clarke's primary task was to reduce geese numbers. Clarke was responsible for catching goslings and shipping them up to Cumberland House to be released into the wild. He would also oil eggs to prevent them from hatching. Although this was popular with the public, it did grind Lorne a bit. Nevertheless, the two embarked on a project to start banding geese again, which hadn't been done in over thirty years in the park. In their first summer, the two banded over 1,200 geese.

Looking back at his record, it is clear that Lorne has served his community for decades. In 2010, Lynda Haverstock, then CEO of Tourism Saskatchewan, wrote a letter to Earth Week Celebration in Indian Head in which she acknowledged that "Scott is a champion of our beloved province on so many levels—from his activism on environmental issues to his community involvement to being a generous supporter of worthy causes. Our world is truly a better place because of his integrity, humanity, and countless good deeds." Everyone whom I interviewed for this book spoke of his commitment to family, community, and conservation. Lorne Scott has "given his life to his ideals" is how Sharon Butala explained it. The biotic community has been well served by him.

🐦 🐦 🐦

NOT UNEXPECTED given his volunteer work, Lorne has won many awards and accolades throughout his life. Arguably, the most prestigious include the Saskatchewan Order of Merit and the Order of Canada. Most of his awards hang on the walls in his farmhouse. Others clutter his desk and coffee tables. The plaques and certificates are scattered in with a vast array of wildlife pictures, Lahrman paintings, wooden ducks, antlers, and photographs of special events. Prominent in the living room is a picture of Lorne holding an owl out to Prince Philip.

In 1986, the World Wildlife Fund Canada came to the prairies to launch the Wild West program as part of a larger acknowledgement that the prairies are home to more species at risk than any other ecoregion in the country. From 1986 to 1988, Lorne served on the Wild West Steering Committee. By providing funds for modest projects, wwf-Canada stimulated a significant increase in activity on species at risk and developed the Prairie Conservation Action Plan.

Related to this, in 1987 Canada celebrated its Centennial of Wildlife Conservation in recognition of Last Mountain Lake Migratory Bird Sanctuary (the first and oldest North American bird sanctuary). wwf-Canada invited Prince Philip to the prairies to commemorate the milestone. The main events were the Ramsar International Convention on Wetlands, which Canada was hosting in Regina, and Philip's visit to Last Mountain Lake National Wildlife Refuge. Fortunately, the World Wildlife Fund supported the development of Operation Burrowing Owl, and Philip had some time in his schedule. The director of wwf-Canada, Monte Hummel, was able to arrange Philip's participation in the program launch, making both it and the program major successes. Lorne and about 600 other people gathered at Grant and Sheila Fahlman's farm outside Regina to see fifteen pairs of burrowing owls and, of course, Prince Philip. Unfortunately, since that photo was taken, all the owls have disappeared from the farm. It is a bittersweet memory for Lorne.

In his office, the pictures are more personal—Lorne with Lorne Calvert, photos of his grandchildren, and a cabinet full of slides from thirty years of wildlife photography. Lorne keeps his Order of Canada medal in its original box. He struggles to find it among all the papers and wildlife magazines. He was awarded the medal in 2008. This honour dates to 1967 and is intended to "pay tribute to Canadians who exemplify the highest qualities of citizenship and whose contributions enrich the lives of their contempories." The Latin motto is *desiderantes melioren patriam,* which translates to "desire a better country."

When Lorne received the award at a ceremony held in 2009, his entry in the program read thus:

A committed environmentalist long before "thinking
green" became popular, Lorne Scott has devoted his life
to nature conservation in Saskatchewan and across Canada. Actively involved with organizations such as the Wascana Centre Authority, the Saskatchewan Wildlife Federation, and the Nature Conservancy of Canada, he also
served four years as provincial minister of environment
and resource management. During his tenure, he significantly strengthened Saskatchewan's environmental policy,
and is renowned throughout Western Canada as a staunch
defender of wildlife and natural habitats.

The first sentence is a bit off-putting. Lorne does not consider himself an environmentalist and would reject the slogan "thinking green."
This is perhaps just the governor general office's misunderstanding of conservation on the prairies. But the entry is otherwise an
apt description. It does leave out the Rafferty-Alameda project, but
Ottawa should be careful in giving out any award on that issue. The
entry also highlights wildlife and habitat, the issues nearest to Lorne's
heart and the issues on which Lorne most "desire[s] a better country."

He flew to Ottawa with his partner, Leona, for the ceremony. It
was a fancy affair, and Lorne still has his printed invitation and photographs of himself with Michaëlle Jean, the governor general at the
time. Back home in Saskatchewan, the Saskatoon *StarPhoenix* ran
an article about Lorne's life, pointing to his work on the protection
of WHPA lands, conservation easements, and endangered species.
Dennis Sherratt, who had served as the provincial fish and wildlife
director during Lorne's time in office, was interviewed for the piece.
Sherratt said that Lorne was "always polite, never condescending
and wanted to work with others. He saw politics as a means to get
the job done, not the end." *Conservator*, the Ducks Unlimited magazine, published a piece in 2008 recognizing Lorne's Order of Canada.
Peter Carton, chair of the board, said that "Lorne is, without a doubt,
one of the finest ambassadors for wetland and waterfowl conservation in the country." These accolades ring true.

CHAPTER 7

THE 2010s: MISSING THE TREES AND THE LAND

To sing the praises of the beauty of the earth. To do what we can
to persuade other people to share those feelings. To name the
problems that we see. I think it is all tremendously important.
—CANDACE SAVAGE

I f Canada ever was a leader on environmental issues, former Prime
Minister Stephen Harper significantly marred that reputation. In
2011, Canada became the first country to formally withdraw from
the Kyoto Protocol on climate change. This was a symbolic move
because Canada had done nothing to implement the necessary
emissions reductions and because there were no penalties for
failing to reach targets. His government also shocked the country in
2012 with omnibus Bills C-38 and C-45, which passed quickly with
limited time for debate. These budget bills slashed the *Canadian
Environmental Assessment Act*, weakened the Canadian Environmental Assessment Agency, significantly cut the *Canadian Environmental
Protection Act*, the *Fisheries Act*, the *Navigable Waters Protection Act*,
and the *Species at Risk Act*. They also cut funding to Parks Canada.
At the same time, the budget made other legislation more industry
friendly and opened up drilling possibilities for oil and gas.

Not all Canadians took this news sitting down. Four women in
Saskatchewan formed the Idle No More movement, a broadly based
Indigenous social and environmental justice movement. Sheelah
McLean, Sylvia McAdam, Jessica Gordon, and Nina Wilson used

Facebook and word of mouth to hold a teach-in in Saskatoon that quickly ignited a Canadian-wide movement that is still a force today. First Nations, Inuit, and Métis Peoples across Canada immediately recognized Bill C-38 for what it was—an attack on Indigenous sovereignty to protect water and nature. Since 2012, Idle No More has helped to organize protests over pipelines, climate change, biodiversity loss, and other critical environmental issues.

But otherwise Saskatchewan politics mirrored federal politics during the Harper years. The 2007 election saw the Saskatchewan Party win 51 percent of the popular vote, and the 2011 election saw that number jump to 64 percent and stay in that range in the 2016 election (62 percent). This is surprising because for most of the twentieth century the province was governed by the centre-left. But since at least 1982, the New Democratic Party has struggled to capture rural votes even though it and its CCF predecessor used to dominate in rural ridings. Howard Leeson, a retired University of Regina professor, suggests in his scholarship that the answer is in the shifting agricultural landscape, in which small family farms have been replaced by larger farms. This is a problem for the New Democratic Party because "larger farms tend to act more like entrepreneurs and businessmen, and to vote accordingly." Essentially, the rural agricultural voter is now a businessperson and thus votes with business interests on the right side of the political spectrum.

The Saskatchewan Party has done a tremendous job of courting this new voter and responding to the economic needs of corporate Saskatchewan—big ag, oil, potash, and uranium. Indeed, the party has campaigned and governed on "corporate populism." As Jim Harding, a retired University of Regina professor, wrote, "the 2009–10 budget was *to keep the SK economy strong*. In 2010–11 it was to be *forward looking and responsible for the people*. In 2011–12 the budget was said to be *building on the economic momentum* and defining *the SK advantage*." These slogans are exactly what business loves. Whereas the first CCF government's slogan was "humanity first," the Saskatchewan Party has shifted that to "profit first." And that is now popular across the province.

For the past dozen years, the Saskatchewan Party government has continued the legacy of unfettered resource development. Oil and gas experienced a boom in southern Saskatchewan with the rise of hydraulic fracturing techniques. Low tax and royalty rates were implemented to attract industry to the province and away from Alberta (and to a lesser extent North Dakota). Former Premier Brad Wall consistently and adamantly rejected a price on carbon and refused to be part of Prime Minister Justin Trudeau's Pan-Canadian Framework on Clean Growth and Climate Change. Indeed, Wall promised to take the federal government to the Supreme Court if necessary. When he stepped down as leader and Scott Moe became premier, this commitment remained in place. The Saskatchewan Party also oversaw the dismantling of the Prairie Farm Rehabilitation Administration lands as well as the Saskatchewan Community Pasture Lands program.

🐦 🐦 🐦

WHEN LORNE FOUND OUT in 2012 that the federal government was going to close the tree nursery near Indian Head, he helped to mount a campaign to keep it open. He had prior experience with tree nursery closures. During his time in office, Lorne oversaw the closure of a provincial tree nursery at Big River. He tried to get Weyerhaeuser, the forestry company, to take the nursery and assume management of it but was unsuccessful. He was successful, however, in helping to save the nursery at Prince Albert, transferred from the provincial government to Pacific Regeneration Technologies in July 1997. Lorne was hoping for another save at the Indian Head Tree Nursery.

The federal government established the nursery in 1901 to help meet the demand and need for trees and shrubs for shelterbelts on the prairies. By 1910, 2 million trees were ordered from the nursery. In 1965, over 9 million trees were distributed, not only to farmers but also to schools, hospitals, churches, cemeteries, and different government agencies. In addition to providing shelter for human structures and crops, the shelterbelts provide habitat for wildlife, including many birds, such as eastern and western kingbirds, mourning doves, and great horned owls. It is obvious why Lorne would be a big supporter of tree nurseries.

But 2015 was the last year for the Shelterbelt Centre at Indian Head. That centre was open for 114 years and provided an estimated 600 million trees to farmers. It provided thirty full-time jobs and thirty seasonal jobs. It was essential to the local economy, and literally thousands of high school students from Indian Head got their first jobs working as summer students at the facility. And then it just closed.

No longer in provincial office, Lorne had to work outside the government to try to keep the Indian Head Tree Nursery up and running. He worked in his capacity both as the reeve of the RM of Indian Head and as a member of the conservation community. Quickly, an informal coalition of farm groups, conservation groups, and municipalities pressed Gerry Ritz, the federal agriculture minister, to stop the closure. There was hope briefly that a non-profit could take over the operation if the federal government no longer wanted the responsibility. It was a "measly 3 million dollars, but the Harper government chose to get rid of it," Lorne explained.

More than 10,000 people mailed in postcards to the Prime Minister to keep the nursery open. (Keep in mind that the RM has a population of 380 people and the town of Indian Head about 2,000 people). The coalition explored the possibility of cost recovery, in which trees could be sold for a dollar to cover the $3 million annual operation. According to the Regina *Leader-Post*, Ritz maintained that "shelterbelts are now a well-established practice across the Prairies, and this change provides a great opportunity for the private sector to step in and deliver the service should the demand exist."

About two months later, the informal coalition became the Western Canada Tree Nursery Coalition. It was composed of six farm groups and two municipalities, including Lorne and the RM of Indian Head and the Town of Indian Head. This group worked with the Agricultural Producers Association of Saskatchewan to sign a formal agreement with a private company to develop a business plan for the nursery. By September, there was a plan in place, but federal funding would be necessary for the transition to take place. In early October, Ritz responded with a hard "no" to this proposal. In a letter to the *Leader-Post*, he said that "our government has been clear that it is ending our involvement in the Prairie Shelterbelt Program by Dec. 31 and that any future tree nursery operations need to be self-sustaining and not based on financial support from the federal government."

Within a few days, a rumour started circulating that the RM of Indian Head had made a deal with the federal government to manage the tree nursery. It was first reported in the Saskatoon *StarPhoenix* as a quotation from the CEO of the Health, Education and Livelihood Project (HELP), a tree nursery charity that operated out of Weyburn. Specifically, it was stated that:

> Earlier this spring, a permission-to-enter agreement was signed with the RM of Indian Head for the seeding and planting of tree crops in 2013 so that future harvestable plants could be available for any new owners of the property or interim lessee pending the completion of the disposal process. AAFC [Agriculture and Agri-Food Canada] also agreed to consider a short-term lease with the RM or another government entity to complete the 2013 fall activities and to take orders for the 2014 tree distribution.

The news came as a shock to Lorne. Even more shocking was that Ritz made vague references to the media, implying that the rumour might be true.

Although this deal offered the community—including Indian Head residents, farmers, and ranchers, as well as conservationists—hope, it was short lived. There was no deal with the rural municipality. "For the minister to say in the media that the RM is managing the [tree] nursery, it's simply totally untrue," Lorne stated to the media. As the *StarPhoenix* reported, he said that he was "befuddled" by Ritz's comments that the rural municipality had agreed to take over management of the tree nursery on an interim basis until new owners could be found. "It's absolutely bizarre," Lorne said.

He had never spoken to Ritz about the issue. No one from Ritz's staff had contacted Lorne or the council members of the RM of Indian Head. Why Ritz would claim that such an exchange had taken place was a mystery. Ralph Goodale, MP for Wascana and then the deputy leader of the Liberals, suggested that maybe Ritz was "spouting empty promises to avoid criticism over shutting down the popular shelterbelt program." Goodale made it clear that Ritz had every intention of seeing the nursery shut down. And that is what happened. After a failed deal with HELP, the nursery completely closed. The land was eventually sold to Carry the Kettle First Nation, which has other aspirations for this part of their homeland.

Of all the issues that Lorne dealt with as reeve, this one was the most difficult. This loss also explains why Lorne, a farmer, keeps a "secret" tree lot on his farm. The Indian Head Tree Nursery was actually part of the Agri-Food Canada Agroforestry Development Centre. The centre was, and still is, a research facility for trees. That includes everything from tree identification to genetics and breeding to insect and disease control. The government closed the shelterbelt program but not the research program. Nevertheless, some of the employees who lost their jobs became deeply suspicious of the provincial and federal governments. At any moment, the government could just close the facility. And in the meantime, the governments of Brad Wall and Stephen Harper controlled the facility and the research. These were governments that had proven themselves to be dismissive of science and resistant to conservation principles.

Thus, a group of concerned employees with expertise in trees decided that they wanted to create their own tree farm for conservation and research purposes. It would be run privately for public benefit. But where could the trees be planted and monitored? None of the employees owned any land. In 2015, Lorne donated about four hectares of his farmland for the establishment of a seed bank for about 100 species of trees and shrubs. Yes, he willingly removed those hectares of farmland from production for the purpose of planting trees.

This might sound crazy. Or sound completely reasonable. I guess it depends on your attitude toward trees, the government, and a farmer's bottom line.

Lorne has shown me the tree lot. We have driven through it on two occasions. It is an amazing assortment of trees and shrubs planted in neat rows. Some are thriving, and some are struggling. Blame the weather. But keep notes, because that is how scientific observation works. If you want to know which trees will be hardy enough to withstand changes in climate and biodiversity loss, then you need to watch them. The tree lot is monitored by some former employees of the Indian Head Tree Nursery and Lorne, who admittedly knows more about birds and farming than trees.

This "secret" tree lot is a statement on so many conservation issues. At a basic level, it is another example of Lorne trying to answer the economic paradox of western development by preserving the integrity, stability, and beauty of his biotic community. But the tree lot is about public distrust of the government. It is about climate change and scientific research. And it is about a farmer whose bottom line cannot be measured in dollars and cents. Lorne's donation of about four hectares protected by a conservation easement is the conservation battleground of the next 100 years. Should we have to rely on the goodwill of farmers and ranchers to donate their time and land to conservation? Can we rely on them? These are some of the most important questions facing society as biodiversity hangs in the balance.

🐦 🐦 🐦

NOT TIRED OF LOSING BATTLES or enduring infuriating political clashes, Lorne helped Nature Saskatchewan to lead the charge on the greater sage grouse habitat protection order from the federal government in 2013. This is an important legal case in setting a precedent, and I always teach it in my environmental policy courses at the University of Toronto. I did not realize that Lorne was involved until Stephen Hazell, at Nature Canada, mentioned it to me in a phone conversation. I had called Hazell to discuss the Rafferty-Alameda project, but the conversation wandered to Lorne's other conservation battles.

The shocking truth is that birds on the prairies are declining at an alarming rate. The 2018 Living Planet Report by WWF-Canada indicates that grassland birds "have seen their numbers plunge on average by sixty-nine percent since 1970." The federal government, through the *Species at Risk Act* and the *Canada-U.S. Migratory Bird Act*, does have some responsibility for grassland birds. This is a good thing since the province basically has no legislation to protect birds and their habitat. Of the fifteen species listed on the provincial *Wildlife Act* (which has no habitat protections), six are birds. One of these birds is the greater sage grouse.

It is the largest of the North American grouse species. It requires large patches of upland habitat with patchy shrub cover. It is very dependent on silver sagebrush for food and shelter. And like some other bird species, individuals return to the same mating sites and reuse other familiar areas for nesting and rearing each year. Indeed, offspring return to the areas in which they were reared to live and nest. Although the sage grouse is highly adapted to prairie life, it is sensitive to habitat disturbance, degradation, and loss. For example, it does not nest near elevated structures such as power poles. Nor does it engage in mating rituals near loud industrial activities such as oil drilling and extraction. Needless to say, over the past few decades, the greater sage grouse in Canada has been reduced to remnant populations on the prairies. The bird is already extirpated from British Columbia and five U.S. states. Experts believe that it might become extirpated from Canada within the next decade.

The federal *Species at Risk Act* (SARA) does not apply to provincial lands, but the law does include an "emergency order" clause by which the federal government can take action to protect a species on provincial lands when the province is deemed to be failing at such protection. This is a rarely invoked clause. But it is not surprising that the first use of the emergency order was to protect a prairie species in Saskatchewan and Alberta, two provinces with weak wildlife acts and little habitat protection. In 2013, an emergency protection order was invoked for the greater sage grouse. The federal government offered immediate protection to the bird under *SARA* on non-private lands (all provincial and federal lands). In doing so, it signalled to Canada and the world that Saskatchewan was failing to protect the habitat of this species.

Hazell acknowledges that Nature Canada, a national environmental group, pushed hard for the emergency order for the sage grouse. But he also admits that it was shrouded in controversy and possibly a mistake. Specifically, he remembers that the order was created around Christmas in 2013, but in the fall "we [at Nature Canada] had heard that they [the federal government] were thinking about it." Nature Canada met with the federal Ministry of Environment and suggested initially that the government issue a draft order to "test the waters." From Nature Canada's perspective, "we had a good relationship with ranchers, and . . . we were concerned . . . [that] ranchers don't like government. That is a cultural thing." Hazell was hoping that floating a draft order would provide a low-stakes way to get some feedback and then finalize a sensible version of an emergency order. However, that is not what the federal government opted to do. It just issued an order that "was very poorly considered."

However, since Nature Canada had pushed for the order, Hazell says, "we had to wear it afterwards. With a lot of unhappy ranchers." The order does identify critical habitat for grouse and offers some protections for it. Namely, it is illegal to destroy or move sagebrush plants in critical habitat areas. The order also prohibits building fences and roads in some areas and making noise that exceeds certain thresholds. But keep in mind that private lands are not included in these provisions. It is true that large grazing lands in the area are almost all Crown lease (public) lands. However, it should be made clear where the government draws the line (unlike in Ontario and the United States, where the law extends to private property for the protection of critically endangered species).

Lorne worked with Nature Saskatchewan (he was its conservation director in 2013) and pushed for the emergency order as well. He recalls that Ecojustice, the environmental law charity, approached Saskatchewan and Alberta conservation groups saying that "this is a for-sure win, but we need local buy in." Nature Saskatchewan said okay. But Lorne recalls being warned by two separate friends in the provincial Ministry of Environment to "back off." This left him uncertain about how to proceed. He asked the board of Nature Saskatchewan "should we step down or hold our ground and do what is right?" The board said "we will do what is right." They opted to protect the biotic community. Ecojustice went to court on behalf of the environmental groups that supported the emergency order. As Lorne remembers it, "we won. It was appealed. We won."

It wasn't that simple. As with most "wins" in the conservation world, there were "losses" just around the corner. Once the emergency order and its regulations on land use were in place, the federal government "was very skilful in saying to the public 'you gotta blame the bird watchers and tree huggers for this.'" Lorne—and the conservation community—felt betrayed by the federal government. Adding salt to the wound, Nature Saskatchewan had been doing habitat stewardship work in the province for a number of years through federal habitat stewardship funds, and "we lost that funding." Essentially, the Harper government punished Nature Saskatchewan for standing up for the sage grouse and pushing for the emergency order. Like the Rafferty-Alameda case, Lorne knows that "we did the right thing," but somehow that still meant losing.

In terms of the bird itself, Lorne believes that the order hasn't done anything. That is debatable. It did at least bring national attention to the plight of the sage grouse and the failure of the Saskatchewan government to protect habitat for it. It also set a precedent for the federal government to use the emergency order again in the future (which it has only one other time, for the western chorus frog in Quebec). And it led to increased funding for the bird from Alberta, including a new captive breeding program at the Calgary Zoo. Finally, and most importantly, sage grouse numbers are up a bit in Saskatchewan and Alberta. Scientists can't say for sure what impact the habitat protections had on the sage grouse since better weather conditions have turned things around somewhat. In 2014, there were only six males in Saskatchewan, in 2016 that number climbed to 33 males, and in 2018 the number dropped back down to 16. In Alberta, there were 14 males in 2012 and 27 males in 2020. Although not robust, this might be the slow progress needed to prevent their extinction. Only time—and protected habitat—will tell.

THE SASKATCHEWAN PARTY, however, cannot take credit for saving the sage grouse or for championing any kind of conservation issue in the province. The party's significant popularity at election polls does not necessarily mean that over 60 percent of the public supports its stance on public lands and conservation. In fact, I would argue, most people in Saskatchewan are not aware of the party's handling of these issues. These types of discussion tend to happen quietly without a lot of media attention or fanfare. One clear example is public land. Jim Harding provides the numbers on land sales: in 2008–09, the Saskatchewan Party sold nearly $1 billion in Crown land. From 2010 to 2016, it sold another $1.1 billion of Crown land, averaging $184 million a year. The government also accelerated the selling of Crown land after the 2017–18 deficit budget. If Saskatchewan's economy looks strong, then it is because it is being propped up by the sale of public land.

I would argue that this issue remains estranged from the public in part because the term "Crown land" is not clear. The government isn't selling so-called vacant or "empty" parcels of land. What the government does is take land out of *The Wildlife Habitat Protection Act* and sell it to anyone or any corporation that meets the ownership requirements of *The Saskatchewan Farm Security Act* (i.e., Canadian citizens or permanent residents and corporations or membership-based organizations 100 percent Canadian owned are eligible to own farmland). It is selling prime wildlife and conservation habitat. And the new buyer is likely interested only in agriculture or oil and gas or potash. This is why the grasslands are the most endangered ecosystem on Earth. It isn't the weather or even really climate change. It isn't mysterious market forces. It is just government policy on the prairies.

During the dust bowl era, when prairie soil was being lost to the winds, the federal government intervened. In 1935, William Lyon Mackenzie King passed the *Prairie Farm Rehabilitation Act* to preserve grasslands by returning cropped land to grass cover. Doing so would also conserve surface water and soil. In 1939, the Saskatchewan government identified blocks of poor-quality farmland (often abandoned and degraded by settlers) to be transferred to the federal government for the program. These were "reversionary lands" and perhaps doubly so since prior to 1930 there was no provincial land in Saskatchewan (natural resources belonged to the federal government). The province "reversed" some land back to the federal Crown with the understanding that in the future it could be "reversed" again and the land returned to Saskatchewan.

With the newly (re)acquired land, the federal Ministry of Agriculture established community pastures that provided farm families with grazing areas known collectively as PFRA lands. After 1949, the federal government also bought lands in Saskatchewan to supplement the PFRA lands. These are "non-reversionary" lands. The federal government owns those lands outright. Among the prairie provinces, there were eighty-five community pastures operated by the Prairie Farm Rehabilitation Administration.

That was just over 900,000 hectares of land, of which 73 percent was native grassland and another 16 percent seeded grassland. Pastures varied in size between 2,000 hectares and 45,000 hectares. Each was managed by a resident manager employed under the PFRA program. All patrons—cattlemen/women wanting to graze their herds on them—paid a service fee subsidized by the federal government, which also paid maintenance costs of as well as municipal taxes on the lands.

For decades, it worked that way. PFRA lands provided quality fee-for-service grazing and habitat for native grassland and native species, such as burrowing owls. Then, in 2011, the federal minister of agriculture, Gerry Ritz, suggested that major changes to the PFRA program were being considered. Less than a year later, in March 2012, Stephen Harper's government ended the PFRA program through a staged multi-year phase-out of the pasture system. At the time, almost 170,000 hectares of federal Crown lands were slated to be given "back" to Saskatchewan since those were reversionary lands.

Why did the Harper government end the PFRA lands and return them to Saskatchewan? It was part of Bill C-38, the omnibus bill that, as stated, cut environmental programs, from the *Fisheries Act* to the *Environmental Assessment Act*. In a broad sense, it was about neo-liberalism and, to some extent, devolution of responsibility from the federal government to the provinces. It was the Harper government's desire to reduce government spending and remove the government from as many policy areas as possible. That is what Harper referred to as "open federalism." And potentially it was a way to clear the path for resource development. Harper gutted federal environmental assessments and handed over lands to provinces.

When I asked Lorne why he thought the PFRA program ended, he said that he believed it was "a vendetta against civil servants." He vividly remembered Minister Ritz calling PFRA managers "wanna-be cowboys riding around on quads." The Conservative federal government was no longer willing to fund a Liberal Party program staffed, in its eyes, by Saskatchewan NDP and centre-left appointees. To Lorne, the closure was a political decision and "a horrible one."

To be clear, there is a lot at stake with the PFRA lands. According to Lorne, some of these pastures represent "the largest remnants of native prairie remaining in the world and are important for environmental, agricultural, recreational, and heritage reasons." This is not just about grazing cattle, also important for both agriculture and biodiversity. Katherine Arbuthnot, the assistant dean at Campion College, and Brian Sterenberg, a professor of chemistry and biochemistry at the University of Regina, argued in a 2013 op-ed published by the Saskatoon *StarPhoenix* that urban residents should care about the PFRA lands too. The reasons are varied:

The pastures provide recreation opportunities such as hunting and bird watching, inspiration to painters and photographers, and habitat for endangered prairie species such as the swift fox, burrowing owl and piping plover. And well-managed grasslands sequester carbon more efficiently and securely than do expensive carbon capture and storage technologies, even if the latter were fully developed. The PFRA pasture system is internationally renowned as one of the best examples of multi-purpose land management, providing both sustainable economic benefit and environmental conservation. Research on these pastures also shows that the management practices developed over the past 80 years has resulted in higher levels of biodiversity and soil quality than in comparable privately-owned lands—factors that may become increasingly important with the advent of climate change.

What is more, with the loss of PFRA lands, the province also lost PFRA employees. The pasture managers were stewards of the land. They were "cowboys" who spent their whole lives on the land and knew it better than anyone else. They had a type of local knowledge that can be gained only from paying close attention to the landscape and watching over it through decades. Wallace Stegner, whose family homesteaded in the early 1900s at what became part of the Battle Creek PFRA pasture in southwestern Saskatchewan, said that local knowledge of the land "comes from working in it in all weathers, making a living from it, suffering from its catastrophes, loving its mornings or evenings or hot noons, valuing it for the profound investment of labor and feeling that you, your parents and grandparents, your all-but-unknown ancestors have put into it." Cutting the PFRA program means that these knowledge holders no longer work for the government. They no longer manage the land on behalf of the Canadian public. This is a devastating and irreplaceable loss.

This is a loss that Lorne and his friend Trevor Herriot understand well. Indeed, Herriot published *Towards a Prairie Atonement* in 2016 based in part upon extensive research on the PFRA lands in south-eastern Saskatchewan taken from the Métis people by the federal government in the 1930s. In Ste. Madeleine, Manitoba, the Métis people had farmed and stewarded the land for generations. Then one afternoon the government told them that they were going to be relocated since their land was needed for community pastures. The Métis were the first knowledge holders to be severed from the land almost eighty years ago. Herriot does not want to see another generation of knowledge holders lost to federal policy. In fact, he would like to find a way to bring the history—good and bad—of the PFRA lands to light and create a path forward that encourages reconciliation and a new way of stewardship based upon "sharing without taking."

In 2012, Herriot and Lorne formed the Public Pastures—Public Interest group to fight the sale of these lands. The overarching aim of the group is to "help Saskatchewan people and their elected representatives safeguard the wellbeing and legacy of the province's publicly-owned grasslands." The group grew out of two public forums, the first on November 23, 2012, in Regina and the second on March 1, 2013, in Saskatoon. Based upon public input, six key principles were adopted for the group:

1. Keep ownership of the PFRA pastures in the public domain.
2. Maintain livestock grazing as a priority.
3. Utilize professional pasture managers.
4. Preserve the natural landscapes and ecological integrity of the pastures.
5. Protect the cultural and historical significance of these heritage rangelands.
6. Recognize and sustain the investment in the public benefits provided by publicly owned community pastures.

These principles, shared by many members of the agricultural community and the conservation community, are close to Lorne's heart. Lorne has always been an advocate for public lands and deeply tied to conservation of the ecological integrity of the prairie landscape.

Not long after forming as an advocacy group, Public Pastures—
Public Interest found that things were really coming apart at the
seams. The provincial government decided to make some changes to
The Wildlife Habitat Protection Act. Yes, the same Act that got Lorne
into politics with the political right in 1981. It was Grant Devine's
legislation, and now a different right-wing government wanted to
make changes. Specifically, it decided to "rank" land under provincial protection in southern Saskatchewan according to its ecological
value. If land was determined to have "high" ecological value, then
it would remain protected in the Act; if land was considered to have
"medium" ecological value, then the government could sell it with a
conservation easement attached; and if land was found to have "low"
ecological value, then the government would sell it outright with no
strings attached.

How can land have low ecological value? Ecology is a branch of
scientific study that deals with how organisms relate to each other and
their physical surroundings. Ecological value is the level of benefits
that the space, water, minerals, biota, and all other factors that make
up natural ecosystems provide to support native life forms. This can
be a difficult thing to communicate to the public. However, if you
think about a landscape in its natural state, its ecology would be how
the soil, rain, wind, snow, and sunshine interact with each other and
the living organisms on the landscape, such as plants, birds, insects,
mammals, and humans. Together all those factors should produce a
healthy living environment for all parts of the community. It should
be a biotic community. And if it functions, it should be beautiful.

Exactly how the Brad Wall government assessed "ecological value"
remains unclear to the public because it has never been explained.
However, according to scientists at the Ministry of Environment,
they used CLEAT, the Crown Land Ecological Assessment Tool. This
involved taking all Crown land, scientifically determining the ecological value of the parcels, and then ranking them from most valuable to least valuable. Politicians then decided the "cut points" on the
list among high, medium, and low value. By 2014, they determined
that almost 700,000 hectares had high ecological value and would

be retained under WHPA protection; 500,000 hectares had moderate ecological value and could be eligible for sale with the protection of a Crown conservation easement; and just over 200,000 hectares had low ecological value and could be available for sale without restrictions. One piece of land put up for sale as low ecological value was immediately purchased by the Nature Conservancy of Canada and is now known as Hole in the Wall. It is a great biodiversity site, with 907 hectares of native grassland, but it is just not great habitat for "economically important" species such as deer.

I think that this ranking system is suggestive of the government's overall approach to land in the province. Land is nothing but economic "value" to a government in need of funds to offset a slumping and unreliable oil industry. The problem with seeing only the economic value, as Leopold said, is that "we abuse land because we regard it as a commodity belonging to us. When we see land as a community to which we belong, we may begin to use it with love and respect." To Lorne and Herriot, and the people behind Public Pastures—Public Interest, land is a community, and indeed these programs had always been informally called "community" pasture programs. Where ranchers and conservationists saw an important community, the government saw only revenue. Thus, despite pressure from some conservation groups, Crown land was being pulled from *The Wildlife Habitat Protection Act* and sold through online auctions. It was happening fast. And with little media attention.

The election of Justin Trudeau in 2015 offered a glimmer of hope to PFRA and WHPA land supporters, such as Public Pastures—Public Interest. At that point, about twenty of the sixty-two pastures had been transferred to patron groups of ranchers that previously accessed the lands. Nature Saskatchewan, with Jordan Ignatiuk as its executive director and Lorne as its conservation director, asked Trudeau to put an "immediate pause" on the transfer of the lands. This request went unanswered. But Lorne thinks that pressure from conservation groups was effective in getting the province to agree not to sell the pastures or allow them to be divided. He adds that this wasn't obvious or easy for the provincial government. Apparently,

Lyle Stewart, the Saskatchewan minister of agriculture, got a phone call from some investors in Alberta who wanted to buy all of the pastures that had been transferred to Saskatchewan. Lorne said of Stewart "to his credit, he said no."

With the PFRA and WHPA shock still reverberating, the 2017 provincial budget included a complete cut of the Saskatchewan Pastures Program. This program had been operated by the province since 1922 and provided fee-for-service grazing similar to the PFRA program. There had been rumours, dating back to 2012, that cuts to the Saskatchewan Pastures Program were in the works. And the provincial government had met with groups in the agricultural community to discuss options. It announced a plan to phase out the program by 2020, including all fifty-one provincial pastures (roughly 325,000 hectares of land).

This means that in the eight-year span between the phase-out of PFRA lands in 2012 and the Saskatchewan Pastures Program in 2020, the landscape in Saskatchewan changed quickly. And the problems are only being compounded by the government's decision to rank lands "ecologically" and sell those deemed to be of "low ecological value." It is hard to keep up, and conservationists are worried that native grasslands will soon be in the hands of private owners and often plowed under for profit.

One place of hope is in southwestern Saskatchewan. Behind the scenes, conservation groups worked on a deal between the federal and provincial governments to preserve some contiguous patches of native grass. There were three pastures of particular interest: Govenlock, Nashlyn, and Battle Creek. It was there that negotiations happened between Ottawa and Saskatchewan. The basic deal is that the federal government got complete title to those community pastures, about 80,000 hectares in total of contiguous native prairie. In return, the province got the remaining federal lands in the scattered PFRA program (not all lands in the program were reversionary and thus returned to the province). As we learned in the Rafferty-Alameda case, some PFRA land was purchased by the federal government and technically is federal land. It was never slated to be "returned" to

Saskatchewan because it did not belong to the province. Numerous sections of PFRA land are actually parcels of provincial land mixed with federal land.

According to Stephen Hazell, Lorne was the key guy from Nature Saskatchewan working on the deal as well as the larger arrangement on the stewardship of transferred PFRA lands. The lobby included Nature Canada, Public Pastures—Public Interest, and Canadian Parks and Wilderness Society. Hazell said that "we have gone through all sorts of lobbying and everything we could do to get Agriculture Canada to recognize its responsibilities for biodiversity in agricultural landscapes." From his perspective, biodiversity has been completely left out of the picture. No one in federal or provincial governments has been attuned to the biological value of the land and the importance of protecting biodiversity.

Hazell became increasingly frustrated during our interview. His voice started picking up volume and speed as he explained his fear of the land going to the province: "Here we have about 80,000 acres of mainly native prairie in Saskatchewan being turned over to a government that has said that it is not going to spend a cent on it. And that its intention was to sell or lease it." If the land didn't remain federal, Hazell warned, "there are no guarantees that any of this land is going to be conserved for biodiversity." That is what propelled him to work with Lorne and others to ensure that the three pastures remained federal. The process and formalization of that agreement were very slow.

Hazell suspected that the slowness had something to do with the Canadian Wildlife Service. "It is a failed organization," he told me. "Ever since the Brian Mulroney [budget] cuts in 1986 . . . they have just not been able to get up off the mat." But if things work out the way that they should, the Wildlife Service will have three important community pastures, and the rest will be transferred to Saskatchewan. That would be impressive and important. The lag is that the service "is an ineffective player in Ottawa." The office is in Edmonton, and Hazell is concerned that it is struggling to get attention in Ottawa.

But all the blame doesn't fall on the Canadian Wildlife Service. The Saskatchewan government needs to take some responsibility for the slowness of the transition. Hazell is quick to point out that "the government of Saskatchewan does not care about the environment. At all. Period." He said this to me from his home in Ottawa. "They just don't care. They are moving to dump their own community pastures. The fact that native prairie is important for biodiversity and carbon storage . . . is just not relevant to them."

Feeling apologetic, Hazell shifted his tone a bit and tried to understand or sympathize with the situation in Saskatchewan:

> A part of me thinks . . . [that] one speculation to offer is that Canadians have always undervalued the prairie and grassland. Canadians don't really see the value in it. They see value in landscapes that have lots of bumps. Like the Rockies are important to protect. But why? They are just rock and ice. You know, for people who actually care about nature, the grasslands are just as important, or actually way more important, than Banff National Park. But it is not something that has gelled in the public's mind. And I think we are biased in favour of trees. Most of the decision makers, we grew up, like I did, in [the] eastern temperate forest. That is my ecological home. I love forested environments.

Conservationists like Lorne and Herriot know better. They know how important the grasslands are to biodiversity. They are fighting—alongside farmers, ranchers, birders, environmentalists, conservationists, and neighbours—for their home and a land community that they love. And their community won a victory in 2021. The new federal area is called the Prairie Pasture Conservation Area and is now under the jurisdiction of Environment and Climate Change Canada (as opposed to Agriculture and Agri-Food Canada, which oversaw the PFRA lands).

The Prairie Pasture Conservation Area is 80,00 hectares of pasture representing some of "the most ecologically significant grasslands in Canada," according to the federal government. I refer those who prefer forests and oceans to what Wallace Stegner said about conserving prairie wilderness: "Save a piece of country like that intact and it does not matter in the slightest that only a few people every year will go into it. That is precisely its value. Roads would be a desecration, crowds would ruin it."

I HAVE NEVER SEEN a wild whooping crane. Chances are you haven't either. The last known whooping crane nest in the U.S. prairie region was in Iowa in 1894. Saskatchewan's last known whooping crane nest was recorded in 1929 near Luck Lake. By 1941, it was estimated that only fifteen birds made the 4,000-kilometre migration from northern Canada to Texas. Whooping cranes are one of the rarest birds in the wild. In fact, these massive birds have teetered on the brink of extinction for the past 100 years.

They are the tallest birds in North America, standing at about 150 centimetres. They easily weigh seven kilograms and have a red patch across the forehead and black legs to match a black mustache. The whooping crane diet consists of insects, plant tubers, crabs, reptiles, and some small mammals. A female will produce two eggs each spring, but often only a single offspring matures. This is because of "inter-sibling aggression" that seems to be related to food scarcity.

Like every other bird native to Saskatchewan, whooping cranes are threatened by habitat loss. Specifically, they have lost their prime wetland habitat across their native range from northern Canada to their wintering grounds in Texas. Then there is the issue of illegal shooting and the disturbance of nesting sites. Similar to passenger pigeons on the prairies, whooping cranes were almost hunted out of existence by the first European settlers.

Believe it or not, whooping cranes have made a bit of a comeback. On the Whooping Crane Conservation Association Facebook page, it was announced that "this morning October 17, 2018 the WCCA was able to confirm an amazing sight. One hundred and fifty-one Whooping Cranes seen together on the staging grounds in Saskatchewan."

Lorne isn't on Facebook, but when I told him the news it made his heart dance. By all accounts, these birds should be extinct.

The 1916 Migratory Bird Treaty made killing the birds in either the United States or Canada illegal. That was the first step in a long road to recovery. Thousands of people—from university researchers to government scientists to private landowners to schoolchildren— were involved with whooping crane conservation in the twentieth century. Even forest firefighters played their role when they discovered a nest in Wood Buffalo National Park in 1954 while fighting a fire.

In 1967, the United States listed the whooping crane as an endangered species. That year the American and Canadian governments collaborated on a "species bank" program by which a captive flock of whoopers was established in Maryland by taking one of the two spring eggs out of the wild and raising it in captivity. The program at the Patuxent Wildlife Research Center in Maryland was successful. In 1976, the program took surplus eggs to the nests of greater sandhill cranes in Idaho. The cranes were able to hatch and rear the whooping cranes. They were also able to teach them a migration route to New Mexico. Unfortunately, in a loss to the conservation community, which had worked so hard, the sandhill-raised whooping cranes never paired or had offspring because they were imprinted on sandhill cranes.

I asked Lorne how a prairie farmer became interested in whooping cranes. Saskatchewan is the only province that they migrate through from Texas to the summer grounds in Wood Buffalo National Park in northern Alberta and the Northwest Territories. Because the whoopers migrate through Saskatchewan, the province has been a stronghold. Indeed, whoopers are the logo for the Saskatchewan Wildlife Federation. It was just a natural fit for Lorne. But it was really Fred Bard at the Museum of Natural History who got Lorne interested in the birds. Bard was a member of the Whooping Crane Conservation Association, which officially formed in 1961 in the United States but had a "Canadian Council" section. The association held its annual meeting in Regina in 1972 at the museum. The three-day event brought together important members of the bird community from across North America, including Stuart Houston, Fred Lahrman, and Lorne Scott.

At the 1974 annual meeting in Denver, Lorne received an honorary lifetime membership in the Whooping Crane Conservation Association. In 1985, he was elected as a trustee of the organization. In 1987, he received another award from it, an Honour Award for his efforts in preserving endangered wildlife in North America. Then in 2003, Lorne received the Jerome J. Pratt Whooping Crane Award from the association. It is "a lifetime achievement award given to an individual or organization who, through exceptional achievement and dedicated service, have contributed significantly to the conservation and/or collective knowledge of the Whooping Crane." Lorne wasn't a researcher, and he wasn't handling the birds or keeping watch over them in captivity, but he worked to educate people and lobby governments in Canada, federal and provincial, to protect habitat for whooping cranes.

From 2004 to 2011, Lorne served as a trustee of the Whooping Crane Conservation Association. From 2011 to 2012, he was its president. During this period, he arranged for George Archibald to speak at a conference in Regina. Archibald is a legend in the whooping crane world. Originally from Nova Scotia, he earned a PhD from Cornell University and then pioneered methods to raise cranes in captivity. He appeared on the *Tonight Show with Johnny Carson* in 1982 to discuss the cranes. Archibald won hundreds of awards and accolades for his work, including the prestigious MacArthur Fellowship (unofficially known as a "Genius Grant"). During his visit to Regina in 2012, he also travelled with Lorne to the last known nest in the province as well as to the location of the last hunting deaths of cranes. Although there was not much media attention on the event, birders in the province rallied around the visit. The fact that Lorne was able to arrange everything is a testament to how important cranes are and how important he is in crane circles.

Lorne once wrote that "over the years the Whooping Crane has become a symbol of conservation and its fate is in our hands. If we fail, this symbol will be lost forever, but if we succeed a great milestone in the field of conservation will have been achieved." At the end of 2018, there were 849 known whooping cranes on the Earth. Of them, 163 were in captivity. In the wild, 505 were in the Aransas—Wood Buffalo migratory flock. The remaining cranes were part of three reintroduced populations: the eastern migratory flock (Florida to Wisconsin), the Louisiana non-migratory flock, and the Florida non-migratory flock.

The Patuxent Wildlife Research Center, where breeding of whooping cranes has taken place for over fifty years, was forced to end its breeding program because of budget cuts by the Donald Trump administration. The seventy-five birds held in captivity were moved to the International Crane Foundation and the Calgary Zoo for continued research and breeding. The International Crane Foundation is headquartered in Wisconsin, and its land holdings neighbour those of the Aldo Leopold Foundation. The land that Leopold's family once lived on is now a staging ground for migratory sandhill cranes. In November 2017, a group of conservationists gathered on those grounds in Wisconsin and were treated to the sight of 4,000 sandhill cranes and—to their surprise—three wild whooping cranes. Two of those birds, identified by cameras able to read the bird band ID numbers, were Leola and Quill, raised at the International Crane Foundation headquarters in 2015. It was a homecoming.

His work with whooping cranes reminds Lorne that "it has been a slow battle. But conservation does work." Specifically, he told me that generating awareness of the cranes has helped and enabled conservationists to lobby governments successfully. In Canada, the cranes' summer grounds are a nationally protected area, and in the United States the cranes' winter grounds are a nationally protected area. Wood Buffalo National Park came into formal existence in Canada in 1922. The cranes' more extensive summer range, a 17,000 square kilometre wetland complex including the park, was created in 1982. It is owned by the federal government and administered by Parks Canada. It is a World Heritage Site, an International Biological Programme Site, and a National Park. It is also the cranes' best chance at survival. It is their only remaining nesting site in the wild.

There are introduced populations that breed in Wisconsin and Louisiana, but it is not yet certain that either population will become self-sustaining.

IF ANYTHING, the 2010s highlighted that Lorne is a doer. He is a farmer, a politician, a naturalist and birder, a volunteer, and a meeting goer. He is a letter writer and a media spokesperson. He is a get-off-your-butt-and-go-save-it person. Lorne has spent the better part of the past decade doing what he does best: fighting for the biotic community. If Wendell Berry really does think that land use and the people who confront it are the "relevant people today," then Lorne must be the most relevant person in all of Saskatchewan. He has challenged land use and abuse in all its forms. And more than Berry, or even Stegner, Lorne is concerned about wildlife as it relates to land. The fate of the sage grouse and whooping crane hangs in the balance. More like Leopold than anyone else in this sense, Lorne is trying to protect the entire community all at once. Only together can the land be healthy.

CHAPTER 8

FARMING AND THE FUTURE OF CONSERVATION

The thought of what was here once and is gone forever
will not leave me as long as I live.
It is as though I walk knee-deep in its absence.

—WENDELL BERRY

Farming is central to Lorne Scott's identity. In July 2018, Lorne gave my editor Karen Clark, my husband, and me a full tour of his land. My husband is from Chicago and had never really been to a working farm in his life. Thus, he wanted to tag along and take some photos. Driving south of Indian Head, deep into canola fields, you come across an island of trees and some native grassland. The bird boxes on fence posts and the "wildlife conservation easement" signs next to the "no hunting" signs guide the way.

Pulling into the farm, I was immediately reminded of what Aldo Leopold said in his essay "The Farmer as Conservationist": "The landscape of any farm is the owner's portrait of himself." Some might look at Lorne's farm and see it as wasted potential or just old-fashioned. But Lorne and his farm are so much more than that. His farm is a mix of well-kept plots and wildness. It is quiet and unassuming and yet full of surprises. It is small and doesn't produce as much as surrounding farms, but what it does produce is high quality. Lorne's farm is like an island of hope. It is a refuge for wildlife and wilderness. It is timeless.

Stepping out of Lorne's old van, the first thing that I noticed was a number of purple martin bird boxes. I had never seen a baby bird up close, so I asked Lorne if he could show me one. Teasing me, he asked what kind of prairie girl I am if I haven't seen a baby bird! He took a bird box down and let me hold a week-old bird in my hand. Karen took another bird. We were squealing. Karen remarked that they looked like dinosaurs. And there were dozens of the little birds—the boxes were stuffed. Each baby bird had a silver bracelet that Lorne had placed around its ankle. They seemed to be so helpless and vulnerable. I was relieved to know that they had Lorne watching over them.

Around the back of his home, the eaves have become home to a family of little brown myotis bats. Scientists and students have come out from the University of Regina to investigate them. Across North America, bats are not doing well, and it is rare to have these ones living at his home. Admittedly, I have a soft spot for bats since they were the first species that I studied in relationship to landowner values. My argument was basically that, if landowners were willing to help bats, then they'd help any species. I found a handful of landowners in Indiana who built bat boxes and placed them on their land. But Lorne was really the first person whom I came across that allowed the bats to literally live under his roof.

His barns and sheds are neatly organized and full of equipment, tools, spare parts, wood, and bird boxes. You could wander around all day exploring the buildings and the obscurities that they contain. His tool shed is exceptionally organized. And a very personal and revealing place. On the wall hangs a list of all his farm equipment and the last date of repair or service. It is handwritten and looks more like code than English. But Lorne knows exactly what it says. And it is exactly how his dad kept track of details. There are also two photographs pinned up beside the list. The first is of his close friend Fred Lahrman, who passed away in 2003. The other is a photo of his partner, Leona Gendron, who passed away in 2012. These photos provide the non-insulated shed with warmth.

In another shed, I walk past an old tricycle, similar to the one that I had as a child in 1984, to the back of the building, where I can see orange and white. I find lawn signs and posters from when Lorne ran for the New Democratic Party in the 1990s. They are covered in dust but still in pretty good condition. He obviously cannot bring himself to throw them out, even though they serve no other purpose. Actually, many things inside the barn don't seem to have a clear purpose.

His farm home is over 100 years old but with some modern additions—an indoor bathroom, for instance. On the back of the front door hangs a poster of a cowboy that reads "keep your city out of my country." Below that is an old poster from the Saskatchewan Firearms Community that says "Register Your Guns" and then "Australians did . . . and look what happened to them." The poster depicts a trash dump full of guns and a machine destroying them—in reference to the million guns that the government destroyed there after the introduction of a gun registry. Before I conducted research for this book, these posters surprised me, but now they seem to reflect some of Lorne's principled beliefs.

Inside his home, the walls are covered with wildlife photos and a few paintings by Fred Lahrman. There are antlers and wildlife figurines. There are hundreds of photos around the rooms and a refrigerator plastered with pictures of his grandchildren and their school artwork. On his bulletin board are notes and business cards. I see two buttons from his campaign days, also orange and white. "I am with Lorne" they both read, and one says "the spirit of Saskatchewan" under his name, whereas the other reads "turning challenge into opportunity." Whoever wrote those slogans must have known Lorne well.

When I visited the farm in July 2018, I hadn't yet met Stuart Houston, but I had heard Lorne mention his name. I saw a signed letter framed on the wall. It was from Houston congratulating Lorne on being named minister of environment and resource management. The end of the letter reads thus:

> Since you tell people publicly that I am your mentor, I am going to offer a little one-time fatherly advice. So far you have retained your honesty and integrity, and we are confident that a cabinet position and power will not corrupt

our Lorne. But you must be realistic and plan very care-fully. The demands of your time will be much greater, and you will have to do some ruthless budgeting of time and money. Both items that most humans have an infinite capacity to fritter away. (1) Time: carve out some time for Adam and Heidi. If you take a trip, use your air miles and/or your extra salary and take one of them with you. (2) Money: now you can afford to take 10% off the top and squirrel it away, before it ever enters your bank account. This will give you a cushion when you quit politics, and meanwhile keep your lifestyle humble. Please don't lose your natural, likeable common touch. Continue to be a good listener. It always seems incongruous for a[n] NDP legislator to drive an ostentatious car or build an ostenta-tious home. Just do your best. That is all anyone can ask. You have a lot of good friends pulling for you.

This strikes me as excellent advice. And, insofar as I can tell, Lorne heeded it.

♪ ♪ ♪

LORNE SHOWED US his farm equipment, which my husband mis-takenly thought was a display of antiques in the yard. Lorne uses the same farm equipment that his dad did. Not just the same model but literally the same equipment. He showed us his old combines and the even older ones that he keeps around for spare parts since we all know that "they don't make them like they used to." He farms with this old equipment not out of frugality but out of principle. However, he doesn't have any farm debt, basically unheard of these days. All his equipment is already paid for in full. Apparently, when Jared Clarke first visited Lorne's farm, he too mistakenly thought that Lorne col-lected antique equipment. He was shocked to find out that Lorne didn't just use that equipment—they were his *only* equipment.

For the most part, Lorne still practises the summerfallow method, which requires little or no fertilizer. Summerfallow is when a farmer intentionally leaves cropland out of production for a season so that the soil can rest. The idea is to conserve moisture and allow for nutrient replenishment for future productivity. Most farmers no longer practise summerfallowing because it leaves a field exposed, and soil can blow away. However, this isn't a problem for Lorne because he has land with many bluffs. This is another benefit of keeping his farm more natural and wildlife friendly.

Lorne uses herbicides but not insecticides on his crops. On many farms, "people are going to spray, then combine, then eat" is his description of farming. He explains that "society thinks that the government has okayed all these chemicals. They think if it is on the shelf to eat then it must be safe. Yet, when someone gets cancer, you hear people say it is probably all the chemicals they eat." This gives me pause. I had Hodgkin's lymphoma, cancer of the immune system, in 2017–18. When I tell people this, a number of them ask me if I think that "glyphosate" is to blame. That is the active ingredient in Monsanto's Roundup. And it is what Canadian farmers spray on their crops before harvesting them. An American, Dewayne Johnson, was just awarded $289 million U.S. in his lawsuit against Monsanto. Johnson is dying of non-Hodgkin's lymphoma, deemed to have been caused by exposure to Roundup. There are about 400 similar court cases pending against Monsanto in the United States.

It can be difficult to find quality affordable organic food in Saskatchewan. It is perhaps even more challenging to grow it. The total acreage in organic production is steadily growing, but it is still small compared with corporate mechanized agriculture. I have visited only one organic farm in the province, the Morrissette farm in the Qu'Appelle Valley. The farm is adjacent to Standing Buffalo First Nation land but continually struggles with other neighbours over chemical use. It is nearly impossible to maintain the integrity of an organic farm when every land manager nearby sprays chemicals. But for the reasons that Lorne mentioned, there is a growing market for organic food both in Saskatchewan and globally. People in Saskatchewan— almost sixty years after Rachel Carson wrote *Silent Spring*—are finally starting to make a connection among chemicals, their food, and their health.

For Lorne, the decision to refrain from using pesticides is about protecting wildlife as much as people. He reads articles about bees and how farm chemicals are killing them. He reads a lot, mostly wildlife magazines and the Regina *Leader-Post* and *Western Producer*. It is good to know that there is attention given to this topic. I asked Lorne if chemicals are killing birds in Saskatchewan. He quickly answered "yes" and then, after a few seconds, said "but the plow and the bulldozer were worse than the chemicals." This is probably true from a snapshot perspective, but in the long run we really don't know the cumulative impacts of spraying chemicals.

Looking at other farms in the area, I was surprised that Lorne can farm without using many chemicals. It doesn't seem possible to compete. I wondered how he made any money. I know from prior conversations with him that farming through the 1970s and 1980s this way was very difficult. Virtually every other farmer in the province was adopting new methods and buying new machines. Lorne was still trying to make a go of farming in the "old way." He farms four quarters of land next to his brother, who still farms their father's land. Staring at the modern farm across his field, I asked Lorne "so do people around here think you two are crazy?" "We are not progressive" is how Lorne replied.

It was tough to eke out an existence. Lorne admitted that his family always relied on "off-the-farm income" to get by. His wife worked in Regina in the 1980s, and he received some income from his time as SWF president. But he also pointed out that other families had to work off the farm because of increasing debt from their new equipment and dependence on chemicals. Basically, no matter what they did, it quickly became difficult to maintain a family farm in the era of corporate farming.

In fact, there is a huge debate in the prairie farm community over whether agriculture, specifically non-family corporate agriculture, can be environmentally sustainable. Some farmers see the mechanization of farming and new technology with genetically modified foods and plant fertilizers as absolutely necessary to compete in the international market and feed the world's population. Others, such as Lorne, reject this approach. Mechanization is criticized for creating farmers' dependence on credit and, subsequently, farm debt. Moreover, as farms become bigger operations through mechanization, rural depopulation increases and rural services decrease. This is an untenable combination.

Lorne acknowledges that Saskatchewan is now dominated by corporate farms. He points out that "it is hard to be principled when you are a corporate farm." Such farms do not prioritize nature, family, or community. The purpose of a corporate farm is profit and economic returns to its investors. This is a big problem for nature. Farmers and ranchers are the most important conservationists because they are the ones who manage the land. If we replace them with corporations, then habitat doesn't stand a chance.

For example, unlike corporate farms, Lorne's farm has a conservation easement in place that covers about 80 hectares (of his roughly 300-hectare farm). That is a legal easement. But before that, when Lorne first started farming in 1975, he had about thirty hectares of natural area on his farm that he never touched: aspen poplar and willow bluffs, sloughs, and some grassland. He wrote for the *Purple Martin Capital News* that, "during the evenings, weekends and holidays spent working on the farm, I was in close contact with nature. While many thousands of acres of natural habitat are being destroyed annually, we hope to maintain our natural areas for many years to come." When conservation easements became legal tools in the province, Lorne put the land in an easement.

The strategic placement of his easements means that no big farm equipment such as a combine will ever fit on his land. It will always have to be farmed using small equipment. That might warm your heart or seem a bit obnoxious to you. But for Lorne being a farmer means being a conservationist. He cannot separate the two. On the farm is where he observes nature. Where he lives in nature. He admitted that "few other occupations can provide one with a closer contact with nature than farming." This has remained true for Lorne since his childhood and is a main reason that he has stayed on the farm.

As we said our goodbyes and chatted in the kitchen, I noticed a handwritten list of dates and bird names hanging on the wall next to the table. At first, I didn't really know what it was, but looking more closely at it I was reminded of Leopold, who noted in *A Sand County Almanac* that "on our farm we measure the amplitude of our spring by two yardsticks: the number of pine planted and the number of geese that stop. Our record is 642 geese counted on 11 April 1946." Lorne's list of birds hanging on the kitchen wall is his yardstick for spring—the first bird that Lorne sees is noted. He started keeping these lists in 1962.

Lorne wrote a piece for the *Purple Martin Capital News* about "spring on the prairies" in which he noted that "flocks of Canada geese which nest on the prairies are the first [waterfowl] to arrive. Alerted by their honking calls, one sees the graceful flock fly in on strong wings from the southeast." He went on to write that "words cannot describe the happiness derived from the beauty and fragrance of the newly-opened crocuses, or from the antics and cooing calls of a flock of whistling swans in preparation for departure on a warm spring evening. Like angels on wings against the lowering sun, the elegant birds become smaller and their voices fainter as they disappear into the distance." Indeed, Lorne is Leopold's farmer as conservationist.

Driving away from his farm back to Indian Head, we pass an area of land where you can see a few large boulders cresting a small hill. Lorne told me that he loves to sit there in the evening to listen and watch. He has been living on the farm for several years, and this was the first time that I really thought about what that meant. I asked him, without judgment, "do you spend a lot of time alone?" He admitted that he does. And he said that people ask him that a lot and sometimes follow up with a less than polite question: "How do you stand it out here? You must be lonely." He told me, and I believed him, "I have never thought of it that way."

Lorne isn't lonely because he is part of a large community, one that includes land, wildlife, and people. Wendell Berry, a farmer, environmentalist, and writer in Kentucky, is similar. According to Wallace Stegner, Berry's "natural move is not inward toward transcendental consciousness, but outward toward membership, toward family and community and human cohesion." That sounds like Lorne. Nature is connection for him, not connection to himself but connection to others. Unlike early conservation philosophers, such as Henry David Thoreau and Ralph Waldo Emerson, concerned with learning more about themselves by spending time alone in nature, people such as Leopold, Berry, and Lorne are focused on bolstering their communities through their connections with nature. In a biotic community, in which everything depends on everything else, it is impossible to be alone.

♪ ♪ ♪

THE FIRST BLUEBIRD BOX that Lorne ever hung on a fence post is still there. Empty. Bluebirds haven't been on his farm for the past three summers. Lorne thinks that it has to do with pesticides, but there has been no formal study of why bluebirds are disappearing from the Saskatchewan grasslands. These birds are a North American symbol of love and hope and happiness. Yet all that I can imagine is Lorne checking the boxes, post by post, with love and hope in his heart and finding nothing. And my heart breaks—for the bluebirds, for Lorne, for the grasslands, and for Saskatchewan. This cannot be how the story ends.

But what is the future of conservation on the prairies? This is one of the most pressing questions of our time. In fact, I would argue, biodiversity loss is the single greatest problem facing humanity today. Once a species becomes extinct, it will be lost to the world forever. Right now there are about 1.7 million recorded species on the Earth, with estimates of somewhere between 8 and 9 million in total, perhaps even up to 100 million.

In 2014, Elizabeth Kolbert published *The Sixth Extinction: An Unnatural History*, in which she argues that the Earth is undergoing a mass extinction of species. Unlike the five mass extinctions that have occurred in the Earth's history, the current one is caused by humans. Climate change and habitat loss—both driven by humans—are the main culprits. By the end of the twenty-first century, in less than eighty years, between 20 and 50 percent of all living species on the Earth will become extinct. That is shocking and grim. Kolbert's book won a Pulitzer Prize in 2015.

On top of this mass extinction, we are experiencing "biological annihilation." Perhaps that sounds more shocking and is equally as grim. It means that we are seeing a staggering loss of wildlife—not the extinction of a species but the loss of individuals that comprise a species. For example, where once you would have seen hundreds of frogs or bluebirds, now you see only a handful. There are simply fewer living things on the planet. Fewer bugs, birds, and mammals than ever before. The reasons are related again directly to humans: habitat loss and fragmentation, climate change, pollution, and over-harvesting. According to the World Wildlife Fund Canada, most wildlife in Canada—even species listed on the federal *Species at Risk Act* and supposedly protected—are declining in numbers.

Exactly how the world plans to confront the loss of biological diversity—both total extinction and decline in numbers of once abundant species—is not entirely clear. The immediate future for countries such as Canada that signed the 1992 UN Convention on Biological Diversity is the Aichi Biodiversity Targets agreed to in 2010 in Aichi, Japan. In total, twenty targets were broken into five categories. The most well known was Target 11: "By 2020, at least 17 per cent of terrestrial and inland water, and 10 per cent of coastal and marine areas, especially areas of particular importance for biodiversity and ecosystem services, are conserved through effectively and equitably managed, ecologically representative and well-connected systems of protected areas and other effective area-based conservation measures, and integrated into the wider landscape and seascape." The targets were agreed to by the Canadian government, but since the provinces manage so much land across the country their participation was essential. The target of 17 percent was not achieved in Saskatchewan. Every other province was crawling forward, and the federal government was taking a few leaps here and there, mostly in the North, where Canada controls the land and territorial transfer is not necessary. Saskatchewan was selling the land that it should have been protecting.

The targets push at some important debates in the conservation community and in public discourse writ large. At one level, there is a debate between conserving nature for its own sake and saving nature for our (humanity's) sake. The latter is "new conservation" and suggests that we should prioritize our own welfare over that of other living things. Although supposedly grounded in science, the moral implications are clear: humans matter the most. The priority is not the biotic community but one species placed at its centre.

In this debate, Lorne falls on the side of "nature for its own sake." He is a "traditional conservationist." Lorne and I have talked a lot about his time in public service and as a volunteer and an activist in the conservation community. He thinks that all of it was important and that he was able to implement change both inside and outside the government. I was interested to know what he would do if he were the minister of environment again for a few days or weeks. He thought about his answer and then said that he "would focus on biodiversity. On carbon sequestration. Make sure no more native prairie is broken up on private or public land." In terms of "how" he would achieve those goals, he would zone land for native prairie. Because, well, "we are at that stage. It has to be done." This is akin to mandatory conservation easements for the purpose of absorbing carbon.

Carbon sequestering refers to a process of "capturing" carbon dioxide and storing it long term or indefinitely. It can happen naturally through biological processes such as trees absorbing carbon dioxide in their root systems. It can also happen through artificial or human processes such as scrubbers or machines that can capture carbon dioxide as it is being released and then pump it into the ground to be stored (and not released into the atmosphere, causing climate change). In Saskatchewan, the Boundary Dam Power Station uses carbon capture and storage at one of its six units. (Two other units have been retired because of federal rules on carbon dioxide emissions, and three units continue to emit large amounts of carbon dioxide). Unit 3 is coal fired, and in 2010 it was retrofitted to capture carbon dioxide that is then either stored in deep saline aquifers or used in oilfields in southeastern Saskatchewan to boost oil recovery (this technology is called "enhanced oil recovery" and is possible because when CO_2 mixes with crude oil, CO_2 dissolves into existing unrecovered oil, making it extractable).

Carbon sequestering is a very political "solution." It is what a politician probably should say. It cuts across climate change and biodiversity loss without alienating people. Everyone, regardless of political stripe, can support natural carbon sequestering, the kind that prairie grass provides. Lorne isn't a politician anymore. He isn't the minister of the day. I wondered if he really thinks that native prairie should be kept intact for the purpose of carbon sequestering. "I think that is the easiest way to convince people." I accept that as true. But he admitted that the "main reason is biodiversity. The second reason is carbon." Right. That was the Lorne I know.

Biodiversity was his answer. But why? We have never seen passenger pigeons, and we are getting along just fine without them. Lorne explained that, "at the end of the day, our survival depends on other living things. Whether it is plants or animals." Again I know that wasn't his real answer. That was Lorne the pragmatist speaking. That was Lorne the farmer, trying to convince his neighbours or people at an RM meeting.

That isn't really why Lorne cares about bluebirds. He doesn't care about them because humans depend on a healthy ecosystem in which bluebirds play their small part. I pushed back: "Is that why you care about the meadowlark?" Lorne knows that he can't fool me. He knows that he doesn't have to convince me. I don't need Lorne the politician or Lorne the director of an organization requesting support or donations. I already know Lorne the great steward of the prairies. I have seen his love for both birds and place. He smiled and said that "seeing a meadowlark, ... hearing a meadowlark sing, is ... a value to me, not a monetary value because money can't buy it, but it is of value."

And that is it. His final and true answer. It makes me sad to think that we have come to a point at which it isn't okay to just admit that we value birds because they are birds. Conservationists on the prairies believe that they need all these reasons—carbon sequestering and ecosystem services—to care about the land. It should be okay to just love your home, including all its inhabitants, because it is your home.

People on the prairies do not often talk this way about birds or nature, but Lorne isn't alone in thinking the way that he does. This is a value that people have. This is a value that I have. The year that I started writing this book I chased nature from Anchorage to San Diego, looking for a sunset, an eagle, a sea lion, or a porcupine. I have been in awe of wolf spiders and terrified by grizzly bears. These are the experiences that I value. But it is not a monetary value.

🐦 🐦 🐦

AT ANOTHER LEVEL, in conservation circles, there is a debate between using market-based approaches and using more regulatory approaches. The former approaches are things such as paying land-owners for the ecosystem services that their lands provide to the rest of us. So we might pay landowners not to plow under native prairie. The latter approaches are about using laws and policies to prohibit certain actions. So we could just make it illegal for a landowner to plow under native prairie. In this debate, Lorne agrees with both sides: we need both programs of compensation and laws of conservation. But his life story suggests that we also need stewards who willingly—and not for compensation—protect habitat and wildlife, even when no one is watching them.

"We are a lot worse off than we were in the 1980s," Lorne told me as we sat across from each other at a picnic table outside the Dairy Mart in Indian Head. It was about thirty-three degrees outside, and we were hogging the only shaded table. Lorne continued that "we thought we had these anchors. The PFRA lands. The community pasture lands. We thought, okay, they are there. We don't need to worry about them." And the truth was hard for him to discuss. Those anchors weren't as heavy as conservationists had hoped.

I asked Lorne if losing some species, charismatic and beloved Saskatchewan species such as the burrowing owl and sage grouse, would make a difference in how residents and landowners think about stewardship and conservation. Lorne was blunt: "No. Not at all." As he explained, "most farmers have more than 5,000 acres [2,000 hectares] of land. If a meadowlark goes or the killdeer goes, or whatever, he doesn't care." Despite the heat, I was in a brainstorm-ing and problem-solving mood, so I pushed the conversation in that direction by asking Lorne how that farmer could manage his land differently. I have some well-formed opinions on the topic, but I am not a landowner. I am not managing land with species-at-risk habitat. I wanted to know how farmers could manage the land differently. "They wouldn't" was Lorne's immediate response. Apparently, Lorne wasn't in the same problem-solving mood. Pushing him further, I asked "but what *could* they do?" Lorne started to think. His first response was the restoration of some natural habitat. And then his neighbour could restore some of the wetlands that he had drained. Oh, and he could let some trees grow back. Lorne was on a roll. Full of suggestions.

Reality came crashing back when we got around to discussing how much land his neighbour would need to take out of crop production to make a difference to biodiversity. Lorne guessed that even eight hectares of each quarter could make a huge difference. But the problem is that eight hectares out of production could mean as much as $5,000–$8,000 annual income loss. That would add up quickly.

Lorne quickly changed direction and suggested that "we are probably better off to focus on the people who already have preserved areas and make sure they keep those areas. Compensate them." Okay, but going back to the farmer; let's just say that he is out $50,000 a year. Is there some way to get the public to subsidize that lost income? "Probably not," Lorne said. "The public has no appetite." But we subsidize farming in all kinds of ways. Why not this way? "Yes, I guess." He said that with zero enthusiasm.

And then we came to the real crux of the issue: a farmer with 2,000 hectares of land would be blown away by the fact that Lorne donated four hectares of land for the tree farm. He has 300 hectares and was happy to donate four. Other farmers couldn't fathom that. They likely wouldn't want to restore eight hectares of land for habitat.

So can we rely on the goodwill of farmers and ranchers to donate their time and land to conservation? Should we rely on them? Lorne and I were not the first people on the prairies to ponder this question. Leopold asked it in 1949: "Can a farmer afford to devote land to fencerows for a patch of lady's slippers, a remnant of prairie, or just scenery? Here the [economic] utility shrinks to zero." Leopold thought it possible. He thought that for a farmer who saw the land as more than profit—as a community to which the farmer belonged—stewardship of that community would be desired. But you can see where the issue gets complicated. Not every farmer is Aldo Leopold or Lorne Scott.

What about conservation groups? Can they buy and steward the land? Writing about prairie dogs for the *Purple Martin Capital News* back in 1972, Lorne was hopeful. He acknowledged that, once plentiful in the southwest, prairie dogs were crippled by "man's warfare with guns," and then "the tide of the battle turned when Man started using chemical poisons" to destroy them. He also pointed to the Saskatchewan Natural History Society's thirty-three-year lease on a quarter of land—what amounted to a sixty-five-hectare sanctuary that officially opened in June 1969. Writing from that sanctuary in 1972, Lorne said that he "took a last look over the miles of unspoiled natural prairie" and knew that "the prairie dogs would be here next year and for years to come." Will that strategy work?

Lorne stated the problem clearly: "We will never buy enough. All the conservation groups combined own about a quarter of 1 percent of southern Saskatchewan. And yet our opponents are saying 'you are buying all the land.'" So that leaves private landowners who desire to steward the land. Private stewardship is not uncommon in Saskatchewan. Indeed, in some ways, it is ubiquitous. Everywhere there are regular people who put out bird feeders, leave or plant trees on their lots, grow wildflowers for bees, donate money to conservation organizations, and so on. There are conservation heroes all over Saskatchewan. But without government leadership and clear signals in the form of public policy, it won't be enough. The last conservation laws were passed while Lorne was in politics: *The Wildlife Habitat Protection Act*, conservation easements, *The Wildlife Act*, *The Forest Resources Management Act*. The last major prairie conservation area—the Greater Sand Hills—was placed in protection under the Calvert government in 2005.

It seems that in the future biodiversity loss will increase as habitat disappears on the prairies. Lorne and I seem to be fighting a losing battle. I asked him jokingly "why aren't more people like us?" He replied with laughter that "they must be stupid." I told him that "I am definitely putting that in the book." But we both know the truth: people aren't stupid. If anything, they are really smart about their own self-interest. Self-interest and the mantra of growth have led us down a dangerous path. It was not ignorance that brought us to this moment in history. It was a series of deliberate policies.

To be certain, public apathy has a role to play. As it always has in history. Apathy was how settlers stood by while the government decimated Indigenous populations on the prairies. Apathy was how the last passenger pigeon died in a zoo. Apathy was how the government of Stephen Harper changed a dozen environmental laws in a single budget bill.

The prairies are an ecosystem in crisis while people don't bother to look up from their cellphones. During the 1960s and 1970s, people all over Canada formed advocacy groups and got involved in political campaigns on behalf of the environment. This was true in Saskatchewan. The Waffle movement in the New Democratic Party pushed for a greener agenda. Conservation and wildlife groups, from Nature Saskatchewan to Ducks Unlimited to the Saskatchewan Environmental Society, promoted awareness, educated the public, and called on politicians to enact policies. But since that time, public interest in environmental issues has waned on the prairies.

Admittedly, it is a bit hard for citizens to engage on issues when it is clear that all political parties have bought in to neo-liberalism and the growth paradigm. Opposition to economic development, whether it comes from landowners, Indigenous groups, or environmental organizations, tends to get ignored by the media and politicians. Still, it is difficult to explain or accept or excuse the apathy. Today southern Saskatchewan is essentially a region with permanent environmental degradation. The prairies have already been sacrificed to economic development and intensive waves of settler exploitation: the fur trade, ranching, and farming, then uranium, potash, oil, and natural gas.

If no one notices and no one cares, then perhaps we should just embrace being a sacrifice zone. Why not just use up everything that we can, use all the resources? Saskatchewan can grow food and produce oil, and those somewhere else can worry about conserving biodiversity or fighting climate change. Maybe the western paradox doesn't really exist. Maybe the boomers and wildcatters had it right all along. We should move in, use it all up, and move on. Listening to me ponder this possibility, Lorne replied "if that is the case, if we do that, I might as well be dead. Because this is my whole life."

In *Towards a Prairie Atonement*, Trevor Herriot suggests that the prairies will be haunted forever by "ghosts of abandoned frontiers." They leave scars on the land and shape how we feel as we encounter the landscape. Old farm equipment, dried-up oil wells, rotting cattle fences. They are common on the prairies. They are links to the past and barriers to forgetting. I hope that when Lorne dies his ghost also haunts the prairies—a whisper of hope that can't be hushed. A voice carried by the wind. A gentle presence that won't release us.

CONCLUSION

No story can match a walk beneath skies ringing with longspur and pipit song,
but the right story might remind us why such things still matter today.
—TREVOR HERRIOT

had the opportunity to work on this book as a writer-in-residence at the Wallace Stegner House in Eastend, Saskatchewan. One weekend Lorne Scott was heading to southwestern Saskatchewan, and my husband and I were going to meet up with him for the Ducks Unlimited dinner in Maple Creek. On the previous Friday afternoon, my husband and I decided to take a short car ride and see whether we could find any boundary marker along the forty-ninth parallel. Turning down one road, we found ourselves at the Battle Creek PFRA land. We called the number on the sign to ask for permission to enter the land. Just like the PFRA program itself, the number had been disconnected. So we drove back to Highway 18 and moved westward looking for another road south. We found one and turned down it. Quickly, we were driving on a clear path in a field. We were not the first people to drive down the well-trod road.

After twenty or so minutes, we came to the end of the road at an abandoned farmhouse. There was an eagle's nest on the roof, and two eagles circled above us. My husband snapped some photos, and I stood in the field watching the birds. After getting back into the car and turning around, we quickly ran into trouble; by avoiding a muddy splodge, we blew out a tire on some rocks.

We walked eighteen kilometres back to Highway 18, really a gravel road. For twelve of those kilometres, we were in prairie pasture land, not farmland. We saw lots of hawks, two coyotes, a million Richardson ground squirrels, some pronghorns, geese, swans, and swallows. Despite not seeing a person or car for four hours, we were never alone. The silence was immense, and the wind was unforgiving. But the walk was peaceful. I felt safe. At one point in our journey, I stepped over a hawk feather and made a note of looking up the meaning of that. According to the internet, in many First Nations traditions, a hawk feather symbolizes guardianship, strength, and far-sightedness. Perhaps it was an ironic feather. Or perhaps it was meant to tell me that the animals were guarding us.

The walk gave me lots of time to think about Lorne. I even tried calling him a few times to see if he'd be willing to come and rescue us. The call could "not be completed at this time," or at least that is what was repeated by a machine at the end of each desperate call. I think that Lorne would have been happy to know that we couldn't connect, because it gave me hours of opportunity to connect with nature. To get back to Eastend, we eventually had to rely on the kindness of strangers, whom we could repay only with a meal at Jack's Café.

Lorne grew up near a small town. He spent a lot of time on the land. Walking and watching. I understand now how he knows the animals. How he recognizes the birds. How he can appreciate the stillness and see beauty where others see an "empty" field. The land is what we can *see* under our feet and in front of us toward the horizon, however close or far that might be. But the landscape is more than that. It is cultural and emotional. It is what we *feel* when we walk and open ourselves up to encounters with nature. Lorne lives on the land, but his life is about the landscape.

Walking across the land and experiencing the landscape, I understood fully what Wallace Stegner meant when he said that the prairie "is as good a place as any for wilderness experience to happen; the vanishing prairie is as worth preserving for the wilderness idea as the alpine forest." Lorne has known this all along. He has spent his life trying to preserve not just the land but also the landscape of the prairies.

But it has been an uphill battle. The province has made it difficult for conservationists to even talk about birds, let alone protect them.

I was reminded of Jim Harding's question "how is it that the province of Saskatchewan that brought Medicare to Canada became one of the world's largest exporters of the toxic and radioactive element uranium, used in both nuclear weapons and nuclear power plants?" Indeed, I had a similar question. As I looked around, I kept asking myself how can the birthplace of environmental impact assessments in Canada be the same place where unconstrained resource development is threatening the prairie ecosystem? Our provincial history is short, but it is complex. The prairies gave us coal just as they gave us Lorne. So much contradiction exists that it was palpable on my walk.

In the most remote and rural space that I have ever been in, standing in that pasture, I experienced nature as deeply as I had hiking through Kluane National Park in the Yukon or the Grand Teton Mountains in Wyoming. Those places are protected as national parks. Those places are conserved for biodiversity and the benefit of future generations. But in Saskatchewan, beyond the protection of Grasslands National Park, we are so busy going after oil that we can't see the riches that we already have. Bernard DeVoto's question echoes: can the west defend itself from itself?

🐦 🐦 🐦

THERE IS NO DOUBT that the most significant environmental changes on the prairies were the demise of the bison and the clearing of the plains to make room for settler agriculture. However, the result was not actually the "vanishing" of First Nations and Métis. Indigenous people survived and remain on the prairies, and since the creation of Saskatchewan in 1905 they have been in a near-constant state of negotiations with governments in the hopes of reclaiming their rights and finding their place in an industrialized capitalist system.

We know that settlers took the land and tried to make it their own. But what can we make of settler stewardship since the time of the treaties? It is difficult because we see that, over the past 115 years, the prairies have lived out the drama of the western paradox. After the bison were gone, ranching and farming took root, followed by coal, conventional oil, natural gas, potash, uranium, and now unconventional oil. Searching for a sustainable economy, governments have enabled the overexploitation of the economic base: nature. Each government has simultaneously enhanced the economy and destroyed its base for the benefit of outsiders. There has been too little focus on a sustainable economy in which future residents of Saskatchewan can enjoy nature while making productive and livable homes in the province.

Prior to the 1960s, the province did little for wildlife and land protection. A few parks were created. The most notable one, Prince Albert National Park, was created by the federal government, which forcibly removed Indigenous people from the land in 1927 to create the park. In the north, there were some programs for conservation of fur and fish but only for the sake of future economic development of those resources. The government of Tommy Douglas gave little thought to environmental protection as it sought to put "humanity first." Following the end of the Co-operative Commonwealth Federation and the Douglas era, the 1960s were exceedingly dull from an environmental standpoint. Premiers Lloyd and Thatcher were busy with health care and education woes across the province.

The 1970s ushered in an era of Crown corporations for natural resource development of all kinds—energy, potash, uranium. The economy boomed across Canada and certainly in Saskatchewan. Allan Blakeney was quick on the draw, creating SaskOil, Sask Mining Development Corporation, and the PotashCorp. This was a reclaiming of "private" resources for the "public good" in the province. His government wanted to make sure that the province was getting its fair share of royalties from resources. It was his answer to the western paradox. But without long-term planning, the resources were used less for conservation or even sustainable development than for quick profit. The government ended up reinvesting profits from one resource to assist in the development of other resources. Blakeney himself admits that he gave little thought to the pressing environmental issues of the time. This is ironic because the decade is considered *the* environmental decade for law and policy in both Canada and the United States.

However, Blakeney's government did request an environmental and social impact assessment of the Wintego Dam hydroelectricity project on the Churchill River. This was unique as the first example of such an assessment in Canada. Even more exceptional is that the assessment resulted in a hard no from the Board of Inquiry and a resulting no from the province. Indeed, let the record show that the first project to be assessed by an independent—non-governmental—board chose the environment and people over the economy. The inquiry included immense public input and involvement from many of the province's growing environmental groups. Looking back, what made this unique was that it was among the few times in provincial history when an environmental assessment fully halted industrial development.

The 1980s were a wild ride of government debt and privatization of natural resource development. Early in the decade, *The Wildlife Habitat Protection Act* came into existence, and a program for an endangered species fund was announced. Grant Devine swiftly set in motion the process of privatization by selling off several of Blakeney's Crown corporations. He also established a heavy oil refinery and ushered in corporate agriculture. Devine saw resources in every corner and under every stone. His government went head to head with environmentalists over a dam but eventually saw the project come to fruition. However, his procedural errors forced the federal government to examine environmental assessments closely. The outcome was the *Canadian Environmental Assessment Act*, one of the biggest and most important pieces of environmental legislation ever passed in the nation's history.

In the 1990s, Roy Romanow tried a "third way," but it looked very similar to the neo-liberalism embraced by Devine and Prime Minister Brian Mulroney in the 1980s. His record will always be marked by pro-uranium and anti–climate change policy. However, his government also did more for wildlife and land conservation than any other in Saskatchewan's history. It was a difficult balancing act of trying to move ahead on some issues, such as biodiversity loss, while adamantly opposing action on carbon pricing. At the time, it made sense to a political party cash-strapped and desperate for rural support. A longer view places the 1990s squarely into the "development" and "growth" paradigm of the prairies. Thus, it is a bit amazing that Romanow's minister of environment was able to push through legislation on conservation easements and generate new awareness of species at risk and ecoregions in need of protection.

The 2000s began with Lorne Calvert trying to create new energy and climate policy for the province. He created a wind farm and started an important dialogue on sustainable agriculture. That all came to an end quickly with the election of the Saskatchewan Party in 2006. Since then, natural resource development—an oil boom, major potash and uranium production, and intensive and ever-expanding corporate farming—has been predominant. Indeed, the 2010s were all about land sales and land uses for resource development. No provincial government in Saskatchewan's history has sold more public lands than the governments of Brad Wall and Scott Moe. Like those who opposed Bernard DeVoto on western conservation and land use, recent premiers would have us believe that the prairies are vast and that "taking what our vast land has to offer is simply a Westerner's birthright." One that comes with the ever-present possibility of striking it rich. Wall and Moe have deregulated and privatized the prairies. Full steam ahead.

Looking back from the vantage point of 2023, we can see that environmental protection and conservation on the prairies were uneven and unpredictable. There was consistency in the provincial government's approach to natural resource development. There was also an unquenchable thirst for more and more resources. Over 100 years of digging, plowing, cutting, and drilling to ship raw resources out into the world. Indeed, political leaders in Saskatchewan were so obsessed with *growth* that they forgot the meaning of *conserve*. If anything, they saw it as an antonym to *growth*. *Grow, develop, advance, build, expand, increase, produce*. These words are the mantras of prairie politics. But the word *conserve* does not mean to cease or decrease or decline. Instead, it is synonymous with the words *safeguard, sustain, steward, keep, support, defend,* and *provide sanctuary.*

To be a conservationist is not to be anti-progress or anti-development. You can value a bird because it is a bird. That does not make you anti-growth. You can see native grass as valuable: an "empty" field has value even if it is not monetary value. That does not make you anti-Saskatchewan. If anything, the concept of conservation is the answer to the western paradox. Serving the biotic community is how we can create genuine long-term prosperity on the prairies.

Indeed, provincial environmental policy appears to be defined largely by a struggle over resources or, more specifically, a struggle over the meaning of resources. Some people see a river where other people see electricity generation. Some people see native grass where other people see oil and canola. This struggle over meaning was most evident in the 1980s. Devine never saw nature, only economic potential. He thought that was best for the people of the prairies.

Had there been no Grant Devine, there probably would have been no Lorne Scott. I can't resist the pun: Grant was the "devine" intervention in Lorne's life, the critical thing that caused something good to happen. It drove Lorne into politics and changed the course of conservation policy on the prairies. And it is fitting that Lorne, interested more in birds than in politics, really got his start in conservation politics by way of a dam. He joined a long list of conservationists who have mounted campaigns against dams, including Leopold and Stegner. In fact, Leopold considered dams "acts of violence on nature." Conservation is a struggle over meaning.

Lorne's life follows a trajectory different from that of the province. Lorne is Leopold's farmer as conservationist. We cannot forget that Lorne farms his land. That is how he makes a living. His farm, private property producing economic profit, is also stewarded by someone ecologically minded and deeply invested in the health of the land and its creatures. If a farmer can be a conservationist, then anyone can be a conservationist. Indeed, no one has done more for wildlife protection and habitat conservation in Saskatchewan than Lorne.

He carries around business cards that list his name and beside it "Farmer—Naturalist—Conservationist." Lorne has been farming since 1975, and farming is central to his identity. He has been a naturalist since he first learned to identify birds, a skill that eventually landed him a job at the Museum of Natural History and then as the first park naturalist for the Wascana Centre. He has acquired an expansive knowledge of nature and become an expert naturalist. And Lorne is a conservationist who practises conservation methods and promotes conservation values. He has been a conservationist since he was a teenager who built bluebird boxes. He has devoted his entire life to principles of stewardship and community.

These values led Lorne to a career in politics. He claims that "shy people who like to watch birds don't run for office." But he had no choice once Devine announced that his government planned to destroy a precious riparian ecosystem. Throughout his conservation career, Lorne fought not just in battles that he thought he could win. He also fought for things in which he believed. And often that strategy led to losses. He lost the battle against the Rafferty-Alameda project, just as he lost the battle over the tree nursery in Indian Head.

In our last recorded interview at the Dairy Mart in Indian Head, I asked Lorne if he thought that there have been too many losses in his career. "After sixty years of work and not many bright spots, except for geese and cranes, it's ah. . . ." He trailed off. Then he started talking about a woman who gave a talk at a wildlife conference during which she said that "I wasted my whole life because things are a lot worse now than when I started." However, Lorne concluded that "the thing is, things probably would have been way worse."

Thankfully, I had the opportunity to eavesdrop on his reflections regarding this topic on another occasion. When Stephen Hazell retired from Nature Canada in 2019, Lorne forwarded me an email with an attached retirement speech. Maybe Lorne didn't realize that I could see his response email to Stephen. What he wrote in that email is both sad and beautiful. It is a true summation of his feelings about a life in conservation politics:

I often feel as you do, despite a life of dedicated efforts towards wildlife conservation, our victories are vastly outnumbered by our losses. When my grandkids will ask: grandpa, why didn't you save the Burrowing Owls for us to see? Other than hanging my head in shame and whispering, I did the best I could, will be my only response. But we cannot give up. The fact that you will continue your much needed work is a testament to our collective commitment to do the best we can. Happy retirement my friend. We did make a difference!

Like pretty much everyone else in the hard business of protecting land and wildlife, Lorne is a believer in the conservation slogan "we cannot measure our success in gains but in the prevention of losses." If we examine his life in that context, then there are so many successes. Unquestionably, the list would include large sections of intact native prairie, provincial parks, burrowing owls, greater sage grouse, Canada geese, whooping cranes, bluebirds, a four-hectare tree lot, and a 300-hectare family farm, and these are just the things that we know about. For these species and these parts of nature, things would have been way worse had Lorne never come along. He prevented those losses. He protected the integrity of the prairie biotic community.

When Karen Clark and I met with Lorne to discuss the possibility of this book, she asked him what his lasting legacy will be. We were sitting at the bar in the middle of the day in Indian Head. Sipping water, Lorne listed his farm with its conservation easement, his bluebird trail, his work with whooping cranes and bird banding, the Rafferty-Alameda fights, the protection of public lands, and his political career, especially his time as minister. That is a life that you could hang your hat on for sure. He rattled off these things and then said "I cannot imagine there is enough for a book."

Having spent the past few years researching Lorne's life by talking to his friends and colleagues, reading his ministerial papers, tracking down old newspaper articles, and talking to Lorne himself, I would say that his lasting legacy will be the following three things.

THE *CANADIAN ENVIRONMENTAL ASSESSMENT ACT*

The *Canadian Environmental Assessment Act* was a decisive victory. It has echoed across the country and through time. If Lorne and his rag-tag team of friends—farmers, hunters, cowboys, professors, lawyers, birders—hadn't been willing to scrap over the issue, then Canada would be a different place. A worse place.

The Act ensures that the federal government considers environmental factors when pursuing development projects on its Crown lands or on projects for which the federal government has provided funding or permits. This means that dams, pipelines, and roads must go through environmental assessments prior to construction. The Act is not perfect, and often environmental damage is noted yet a project is approved because the benefits outweigh the costs or because the damages can be mitigated. But overall the *Canadian Environmental Assessment Act* ensures that the environment remains part of the conversation. It means that industry does not always get to rule over nature.

Lorne did not create the *Canadian Environmental Assessment Act*. I don't want to overstate his role. But two court cases led directly to the federal government's examination of its assessment process and its creation of the Act in 1992. The first case was Rafferty in Saskatchewan (*Canadian Wildlife Federation Inc. v Canada*), and the second was Oldman River in Alberta (*Friends of the Oldman River Society v Canada*). If we remove Lorne from the storyline, then likely there is no Rafferty court case or no Oldman River case ... and no *Canadian Environmental Assessment Act* with the teeth that it has today.

I cannot overstate the lasting impact of the Act. Thousands of projects have gone through environmental assessments since the Act was passed. However, it is also important to point out the legacy of fighting for something that you know is right. When we look at Lorne's life, this is the pattern that emerges. Sometimes you fight and lose but still win in a sense. That is a hard but important lesson to learn for conservationists everywhere. We should be inspired by the Rafferty case even though Lorne ultimately was unable to save the riparian ecosystem from permanent destruction.

THE PROVINCIAL ACTS

When Wayne Pepper met me for lunch in early December 2018, he told me that *The Wildlife Habitat Protection Act* was the single most important piece of legislation passed in the province for conservation. A few hours later that afternoon, Trevor Herriot told me the same thing. The people who have worked in this field for much of their lives know this truth.

Although Devine's government is credited with creating this Act in 1984, it would not exist without Lorne. He went to the party convention in 1982 and had a resolution passed. And he led a lobby inside and outside the government. Dennis Sherratt in the civil service was also important and played a central role in the Act. As did the minister, Neal Hardy, who actually introduced the legislation. But it was Lorne who really fought for the long-term legal protection of wildlife habitat in the province.

Conservation easements are also possible in the province because of Lorne. The most famous easement is probably Old Man on His Back Prairie and Heritage Conservation Area in southwestern Saskatchewan. As previously mentioned, in the mid-1990s, Peter and Sharon Butala donated over 5,000 hectares of their ranch to the Nature Conservancy of Canada through a conservation easement. Today it is native mixed grassland habitat for bison, (re)introduced there in 2003, as well as other native birds, plants, and mammals. In 2011, a burrowing owl den was found on the property for the first time in over a decade.

Although Old Man on His Back is the largest and most prominent example of an easement, there are thousands of hectares of land in formal easements across the province. The Saskatchewan Wildlife Federation has about 365 hectares in a protected easement. And recently Ducks Unlimited signed its largest ever conservation easement with Jason Young's family outside Viscount, Saskatchewan. The Young family donated 1,250 hectares of land in the pothole region of the province where sandhill cranes are dependent on the habitat. The Youngs have been farming the land for over a century and wanted to ensure that it remains intact in perpetuity.

These types of projects, like the easements on Lorne's farm, are an essential piece of Saskatchewan's conservation story. Ensuring the long-term protection of land is important because the government can decide to move land out of *The Wildlife Habitat Protection Act*. But it cannot touch land in easements. Thus, creating *The Conservation Easement Act* was a way for Lorne to supplement WHPA lands while also making it impossible for the government to remove land from an easement. A future government can change *The Conservation Easement Act* but cannot reverse past easements. Thus, the thousands of hectares in easements will remain so for the distant future. That is a powerful legacy.

Of course, related to conservation easements and other regulations in the province is the Representative Areas Network. The extensive consultations and planning involved in creating protected areas meant that progress was slow, and many areas were added after Lorne left office. But it was under his leadership that staff were reassigned and work began on meeting the commitments made in the Statement of Commitment to Complete Canada's Networks of Protected Areas, signed in 1992. By the time Lorne left office, 5.75 million hectares were included, and by 2015 the number had increased to 6.35 million hectares. The two largest programs contributing lands are *The Wildlife Habitat Protection Act* and the Representative Area Ecological Reserves. This means that collectively more than a third of all lands protected in Saskatchewan have Lorne's fingerprints all over them.

Perhaps more importantly, the reserve system—the processes and institutions—exist because of Lorne. As minister, he was practical, fully supporting use of *The Ecological Reserves Act* to create Representative Area Ecological Reserves. The latter name differentiates them from the other reserves and the regulations spelling out the protections that, for example, allowed traditional use for Indigenous Peoples. That cannot be overstated, for it was critical to obtain First Nations support for large northern protected areas. Although Lorne is a self-declared prairie person, the ecological reserves are one of his most significant contributions to conservation in the boreal forest. Even if he remembers the Representative Areas Network as "an inventory," the real accomplishment was the framework and the large amount of new land protected.

LORNE SCOTT MENTEES

Conservation is like a torch passed from one person to the next. When a flame is shared, it multiplies without extinguishing the source. Stuart Houston, Fred Bard, Ed Kennett, and Fred Lahrman mentored Lorne in the disciplines of bird banding and conservation. Time was the precious gift that they shared as Lorne spent weekends and evenings banding birds, feeding birds, and learning about ecology from these individuals.

He has passed that torch on to individuals interested in birds and the prairie ecosystem. Lorne has spent thousands of hours teaching people how to catch a baby bird and slip a band on its ankle. Working through political channels to see land protected, he has impressed and encouraged younger individuals working within Nature Saskatchewan, the Nature Conservancy of Canada, the North American Bluebird Society, the Whooping Crane Association, and other similar agencies.

Specific individuals to whom I can point as mentees are Heather Wiebe and Jared Clarke. After Wiebe and her husband lost their jobs when the PFRA pasture program closed, they moved to British Columbia. They live in the interior grasslands of the province, similar to where they lived in Saskatchewan (minus the mountains). Wiebe now works on recovering caribou for the province and country. She said that "Lorne's heart beats conservation." So does hers. And, as mentioned, Clarke is a bird bander, the former host of the *Prairie Naturalist* radio show, a teacher, an activist with Friends of Wascana Marsh, and an NDP candidate in 2020 in Lorne's old riding.

Lorne is conservation, and he carries its values everywhere. His passion is infectious. He is the kind of person who would help to lead volunteers picking up cold and weak purple martins from the ground on an unseasonably cold night in May. Along with members of the Regina Natural History Society and museum staff, Lorne held watch over fifty-eight birds overnight in the museum. The team force-fed the birds raw hamburger, hard-boiled egg yolk, and water. The first night two birds died. Another six died the next day. But the team did release fifty healthy birds back into the warmth of a prairie day.

That is the kind of thing that makes people shake their heads and say "crazy environmentalists." And it is the kind of thing that might make you ask "what's the point?" when so many birds died that week. Lorne estimates that mountain bluebirds deserted up to 95 percent of their nests and eggs on bluebird trails and that every purple martin colony in the area lost some birds. In the face of such loss, how does he keep showing up for the birds?

In her 2013 Pulitzer Prize–winning book *The Goldfinch*, Donna Tart's main character answers my question, I think: "And I add my own love to the history of people who have loved beautiful things, and looked out for them, and pulled them from the fire, and sought them when they were lost, and tried to preserve them and save them while passing them along literally from hand to hand, singing out brilliantly from the wreck of time to the next generation of lovers, and the next." Tart suggests that this is how the world saves art. But it was no coincidence that the main artistic work in question was that of a bird, a beautiful yellow goldfinch. Because that love—passed "from hand to hand"—is also how we will save the birds. It is how we will prevent the losses. It is how we will answer Bernard DeVoto and the western paradox. And it is why Lorne Scott keeps showing up for anyone and everyone who wants to learn about nature. His legacy will be the inextinguishable flame of the spirit of conservation.

POSTFACE

In the winter of 2022, members of The Key First Nation in Treaty 4 territory welcomed forty bison back onto their land. The bison came from the Grasslands National Park herd and the Nature Conservancy of Canada's Old Man on His Back herd (two places with Lorne's fingerprints). Parks Canada and the Nature Conservancy have been working with Indigenous groups to restore more bison to their traditional ranges across the prairies. There were once tens of millions of bison roaming the Great Plains.

Although predominantly a Great Lakes people, the Anishinaabe (or Western Saulteaux) lived alongside bison in Manitoba and Saskatchewan. Their Seven Sacred Laws are represented by seven animals, of which the bison is one. It is a symbol of trust and respect for all life. The Key First Nation and bison have a long kinship, and their return brings hope for Saskatchewan, reconciliation, and a new pathway toward conservation policy.

In Western science, we talk about bison as a keystone species. Settlers never fully lived with free-roaming bison, but science shows that a keystone species defines an entire ecosystem by holding it together. We could say that on the plains bison bring the beauty to Aldo

Leopold's biotic community. These are principles that Indigenous people have long known, well before Leopold wrote *A Sand County Almanac*. Their Traditional Knowledge has always centred bison as a gift and always tried to respect the community as sacred. Indeed, the inextinguishable flame of the conservation spirit was first sparked by the Indigenous Peoples who called the Great Plains home.

Members of The Key First Nation are some of my closest neighbours during the summer months when I live near a small lake at the Saskatchewan-Manitoba border. I mention this because, as a boy living on his Saskatchewan homestead, Wallace Stegner claimed that his nearest neighbour was four miles away. He was referring to the closest settlers. Of course, his closest neighbours were the Cree and Nakoda, Lakota, and Dakota, as well as the Métis. It was their traditional land on which his family settled.

It is often said in Canada that "we are all treaty people." To take that seriously, we must—as the Truth and Reconciliation Commission calls us to do—renew our relationships "based on principles of mutual recognition, mutual respect and shared responsibility." Settlers must also create space for the "recognition and integration of Indigenous laws and legal traditions." That is how we will find our way home. That is the only "geography of hope" in which we will find opportunity for a better future.

This means that the book cannot close the way in which it opened. Saskatchewan's conservation story needs new chapters and more storytellers. My hope is that the conservation work undertaken by Lorne Scott will inspire the next generation.

CHRONOLOGY OF LORNE SCOTT

- **Born May 19, 1947,** at Indian Head, Saskatchewan, raised on a farm, and attended a one-room country school.

- **1963,** at the age of fifteen, began building nest boxes for birds. By 1975, had made and set out over 2,000 nest boxes for bluebirds and tree swallows.

- **1967 to 1975,** worked at the Saskatchewan Museum of Natural History in Regina.

- **1968,** obtained a federal bird banding permit. Since then has banded over 40,000 birds, including over 10,000 mountain bluebirds and 20,000 tree swallows.

- **1969,** received the Saskatchewan Natural History Society's Annual Conservation Award for work with bluebirds and young people.

- **1972 to 1976,** wrote a monthly nature column for the *Purple Martin Capital News* published in Griggsville, Illinois.

- **1974,** at Denver, Colorado, received an Honorary Life Membership in the Whooping Crane Conservation Association.

- **1975,** began farming near Indian Head and still resides on the 320-hectare farm.

- **1975 to 1991,** held the position of park naturalist for Wascana Centre Authority in Regina.

- **1978,** received a Order of Merit as an outstanding young citizen.

- **1979,** became a founding member of the North American Bluebird Society.

- **1980 to 1981,** served as a board member of the North American Bluebird Society.

- **1980 to 1982,** served as president of the Saskatchewan Natural History Society.

- **1981,** received the Gordon Lund Memorial Conservation Award from the Saskatchewan Wildlife Federation.

- **1981,** in Toronto, Ontario, received the first annual Governor General's Conservation Award sponsored by the Tourism Industry Association of Canada.

- **1982,** played a key role in the creation of Saskatchewan's Heritage Marsh Program.

- **1982,** started a major lobby to protect critical wildlife habitat on Crown land in Saskatchewan.

- **1982,** received a Conservation Service Award from Ducks Unlimited Canada.

- **1982 to 1985,** served as the provincial habitat chairman for the Saskatchewan Wildlife Federation.

- **1983,** at Portland, Oregon, received the John and Nora Lane Bluebird Conservation Award from the North American Bluebird Society.

- **1985,** elected as a trustee to the Whooping Crane Conservation Association.

- **1985 and 1986,** served as Saskatchewan's director for the Canadian Nature Federation (now Nature Canada).

- **1986 to 1987,** served as president of the Saskatchewan Wildlife Federation.

- **1986 to 1988,** served on World Wildlife Fund Canada's Wild West Steering Committee, focusing on endangered species on the prairies and their habitat.

- **1986 to 1989,** served as director of the Canadian Wildlife Federation.

- **1986 to 1989,** embroiled in the Rafferty-Alameda project controversy.

- **1987,** received the B.M. Melanson Award from the Saskatchewan Outdoor and Environmental Education Association.

- **1987,** received an Honour Award from the Whooping Crane Conservation Association for efforts to preserve endangered wildlife in North America.

- **1987,** during the Centennial of Wildlife Conservation in Canada, helped to host Prince Philip during a visit to Saskatchewan to promote wildlife conservation.

- **1989,** received the Canadian Wildlife Federation's highest honour, the Roland Michener Conservation Award.

- **1989,** featured in *Outdoor Canada* magazine as one of the country's top environmentalists of the year.

- **1990,** received the Canadian Nature Federation's top honour, the Douglas H. Pimlott Conservation Award.

- **1990,** nominated as the NDP candidate for the Indian Head–Wolseley constituency for the upcoming provincial election.

- **1991,** elected as a government member of the Legislative Assembly for Indian Head–Wolseley.

- **1992,** served as a member of the government Environment and Resource Caucus Committee. Helped add 600,000 hectares of Crown land to *The Wildlife Habitat Protection Act*.

- **1992,** appointed a fellow of the Saskatchewan Natural History Society for long-term service and outstanding contributions to conservation.

- **1994,** served as chair of the government Environment and Resource Caucus Committee.

- **1994,** served as president of the Whooping Crane Conservation Association.

- **1994,** received the Canadian Legislator of the Year Award from the Canadian Wildlife Federation.

- **1995,** re-elected as a government MLA for the Indian Head–Milestone constituency.

- **1995 to 1999,** appointed and served as provincial minister of environment and resource management.

- **1996,** at Milwaukee, Wisconsin, received the International Wild Waterfowl Association's Conservation Award.

- **2000 to 2003,** served as executive director of the Saskatchewan Wildlife Federation.

- **2000 to 2003,** served as director of Bird Studies Canada and as director of the Saskatchewan Wetlands Conservation Corporation.

- **2003,** received the Jerome J. Pratt Whooping Crane Award from the Whooping Crane Conservation Association.

- **2003,** became a founding member of the Friends of Wascana Marsh and a board member for 2003 to 2009.

- **2003 to 2018,** served as Saskatchewan Region board member of the Nature Conservancy of Canada.

- **2004 to 2008,** conservation director of Nature Saskatchewan.

- **2004 to 2016,** reeve of the Rural Municipality of Indian Head.

- **2004 to 2010,** chair of the Steering Committee for the Saskatchewan Burrowing Owl Interpretive Centre.

- **2004 to present,** trustee for the Whooping Crane Conservation Association.

- **2004 to present,** director of the Saskatchewan TIP (Turn in Poachers) program.

- **2005,** received a Saskatchewan Centennial Medal.

- **2006,** received an Honorary Life Membership in the Saskatchewan Wildlife Federation.

- **2006,** received the Saskatchewan Lieutenant-Governor's Greenwing Conservation Award sponsored by Ducks Unlimited Canada.

- **2006 to 2009,** Saskatchewan Region chair for the Nature Conservancy of Canada.

- **2006 to 2009,** chair of the Friends of Wascana Marsh.

- **2007,** received the Prairie Conservation Action Plan Conservation Award.

- **2008,** received the Saskatchewan Natural History Society Conservation Award (also received in 1969).

- **2008,** invested as a member of the Order of Canada, the country's highest civilian honour, for a lifetime commitment to wildlife and environmental conservation in Canada.

- **2009,** invested into the Saskatchewan Order of Merit, the province's highest honour for a lifetime working to preserve the natural world and inspiring others to enjoy and care about the future of our natural environment.

- **2009 to 2010,** president of Nature Saskatchewan.

- **2010 to 2012,** president of the Indian Head Natural History Society.

- **2011 to 2012,** president of the Whooping Crane Conservation Association.

- **2011 to present,** conservation director of Nature Saskatchewan.

- **2012,** received a Queen Elizabeth II Diamond Jubilee Medal.

- **2013,** founding member and co-chair of Public Pastures—Public Interest, a lobby group working to retain and preserve the federal PFRA pastures, which contain some of the last and best native grassland in Saskatchewan.

- **2013 to present,** chair of SaskTIP (Turn in Poachers).

- **2014 to present,** chair of St. Andrew's United Church Council in Indian Head.

- **2015,** donated four hectares of farmland for the establishment of a seed bank for ninety species of trees and shrubs.

- **2015 to 2018,** chair of the Friends of Wascana Marsh.

- **2016,** received the Saskatchewan Wildlife Federation Lorne Topley Memorial Award for land stewardship, enhancement, and securement

- **2021 to present,** member of Sask (Key Biodiversity Areas) Committee.

- **2021 to present,** co-chair of the South of the Divide Conservation Action Program.

- **2022,** received a Queen Elizabeth II Platinum Jubilee Medal (Saskatchewan).

- **2023,** President of Nature Saskatchewan (for the third time— the only person to have ever done that).

NOTES ON SOURCES

Research for this book included extensive interviews. I interviewed Lorne Scott formally on five occasions for about an hour each time. He also provided the chronological biography given in the previous section. As an avid lister and record keeper, Lorne also provided copies of all the articles that he has published in various newspapers and magazines as well as copies of newspaper clippings about his life and some of the numerous awards that he has received. Of note are his writings in the now non-existent bird-focused publication *Purple Martin Capital News*. It was published in Griggsville, Illinois, from 1967 to 2004 (its name changed to the *Nature Society News*) and peaked at several thousand subscribers across the United States and Canada. Lorne kept the articles that he wrote and shared them with me. However, other than a few university archives in the United States, it is not possible to find the hard copies of the paper. Thus, I am unable to provide issue numbers and page ranges for Lorne's articles. I also visited his farm on three occasions, and Lorne allowed me to snoop around his home and his barns. As described in the book, he has hundreds of photographs, cards, letters, and mementoes, and they provided a rare glimpse of his life.

I also conducted formal interviews with politicians and conservationists in Saskatchewan. They included three former premiers, Grant Devine, Roy Romanow, and Lorne Calvert, as well as two MLAs who served alongside Lorne in the 1990s, Pat Atkinson and Lynda Haverstock. These interviews, each lasting about an hour, centred on Lorne's time in government. However, the conversations also touched on the province's conservation policy and record. I asked each premier specifically about his environmental legacy. These interviews were crucial, and I have used them throughout the book to support many of the claims about political and policy failures over the past fifty years.

In the conservation world, I spoke with Stephen Hazell (Nature Canada), Jordan Ignatiuk (Nature Saskatchewan), Trevor Herriot, Sharon Butala, Wayne Pepper, Heather Wiebe, Stuart and Mary Houston, and Jared Clarke. These interviews centred on Lorne's life outside politics, especially his work as a birder and conservationist. The individuals interviewed all know Lorne personally—sometimes as a friend and sometimes as a co-worker (and sometimes as both). Personal memories of conservation work were shared willingly, and I have used them throughout the book to paint an accurate picture of Lorne as a conservationist. Since the book is a political biography and not a personal biography, I did not seek interviews with Lorne's siblings (five of them) or children. I have sometimes mentioned details of his personal life but have not focused on them.

Beyond the interviews, information in the book has been drawn from newspaper articles, debates in the Saskatchewan Legislative Assembly (the Hansard record), the Lorne Scott Fonds at the Saskatchewan Archives, and peer-reviewed publications (journal articles and books). There are approximately 600 newspaper articles in Canada that mention Lorne. The majority of them refer to the Rafferty-Alameda controversy, Métis hunting, or bluebirds. I got access to these articles through the Factiva database at the University of Toronto Library. Most of the articles appear in the Regina *Leader-Post*, the Saskatoon *StarPhoenix*, and the *Globe and Mail*. Reading journalists' work is like turning back the clock and setting yourself in the time period in which the events occurred. Their articles helped me to understand the historical context and the general thinking of the time when important events unfolded, such as the creation of new policies.

The debates in the Legislative Assembly from 1991 to 1999, the years that Lorne was an MLA, are open to the public and online on the government's website. These debates were essential to understanding both support for and opposition to the Acts that Lorne introduced, as discussed mainly in Chapters 4 and 5. The Lorne Scott Fonds includes all of Lorne's ministerial papers from 1995 to 1999. When a cabinet minister's tenure ends, all the files in his or her office are collected for the public record and housed in the provincial archives. The files include mostly letters between constituents and Minister Scott. But there are also reports, internal memos, internal data, and schedules of events. Between the Hansard record and the ministerial papers, I was able to get an excellent picture of the four years that Lorne served as minister of environment and resource management.

Finally, the book also draws from the work of other scholars, specifically political scientists, historians, and policy scholars who have written extensively about Saskatchewan politics and natural resource policies. It also includes biographies of Saskatchewan politicians, especially *Fiery Joe* by Kathleen Carlisle and *The Prairie Populist* by John Conway. Other books about Saskatchewan history played a large part in setting the context, such as *Clearing the Plains*, *Frontier Farewell*, and CCF *Colonialism in the North*. Essays and books by Wendell Berry, Aldo Leopold, and Wallace Stegner were invaluable sources of inspiration, and I have used them throughout the book.

PREFACE

This book has been influenced significantly by the writing of Aldo Leopold. My passion for his work was reignited recently by Julianne Lutz Warren's book *Aldo Leopold's Odyssey*, first published in 2006 and republished in 2016. It was while reading her book that I really started to see parallels between Lorne and Leopold. I am sure that without her book my own book would not have been possible.

Other information about Leopold and his wife, Estella Bergere, is from Andrew Gulliford's 2017 article about shepherding in New Mexico.

The idea that "beauty" equates to "ecological function" in Leopold's philosophy comes from J. Baird Callicott's 2022 article on research gaps in Leopold scholarship.

My PhD dissertation, written at Purdue University from 2007 to 2009, was eventually expanded into a book-length manuscript that compares Canadian and American landowners and species-at-risk policies. That book was published in 2014 and entitled *Land, Stewardship, and Legitimacy*.

The quotations from Wallace Stegner are from *Wolf Willow*.

The quotation from Trevor Herriot comes from *Grass, Sky, Song*.

Indigenous names are from Blair Stonechild's entry "Aboriginal Peoples of Saskatchewan" in the Encyclopedia of Saskatchewan.

INTRODUCTION

The opening quotation from Aldo Leopold comes from *A Sand County Almanac*.

On the ecology of the prairies prior to European settlement, I draw from Candace Savage's *Prairie* and Bill Waiser's *A World We Have Lost*.

James Daschuk's book that I refer to repeatedly is *Clearing the Plains*.

Much of the data on the state of the grassland ecosystem comes from the 2018 World Wildlife Fund Canada Living Planet Report.

Bernard DeVoto's book to which I refer often is the 2001 release of a working manuscript written in the 1940s and 1950s. The book, as published with permission from his son by Yale University Press, is *The Western Paradox*. I first heard of DeVoto through Jackson Benson's biography of Wallace Stegner. I learned a great deal more about DeVoto through David Gessner's book *All the Wild that Remains*. Indeed, I am indebted to that book in many ways. It served as an aspirational model for my book, and it helped me to think through the western paradox.

Much of the information regarding different political parties' approaches to natural resources over the past 100 years comes from academic work, as noted below in subsequent chapters. I want to draw particular attention to Jim Harding's *Moving beyond Neo-Liberalism in Saskatchewan* and to Jeremy Rayner and Fraser Needham's article "Saskatchewan."

In the introduction, I claim that Lorne is Saskatchewan's most important naturalist. I would add, though, that there have been many other devoted conservationists in Saskatchewan over the years. There have been ecologist-academics such as Stan Rowe (1918–2004) and George Ledingham (1911–2006) and government employees such as Pat Fargey (Parks Canada) and journalists such as Katie Doke Sawatzky (blogger), Jared Clarke (radio host), and Karen Briere (*Western Producer*). Then there are writers such as Wallace Stegner, Sharon Butala, Candace Savage, and Trevor Herriot. There are activists such as Sheelah McLean, Sylvia McAdam, Jessica Gordon, and Nina Wilson, who launched the Idle No More movement from a teach-in outside Saskatoon. There are also individuals who defy categorization, such as Archibald Belaney (Grey Owl). In terms of politicians, the list is shorter. Peter Prebble is notable for his work on environmental issues, especially energy issues.

Indigenous language group names are drawn from the Government of Canada website.

CHAPTER I
The opening quotation by Wallace Stegner comes from *Wolf Willow*.

There are plenty of excellent books that explore Indigenous history in Saskatchewan. For example, see *The Medicine Line* by Beth LaDow, *Farewell Frontier* by Garrett Wilson, *Clearing the Plains* by James Daschuk, and *Walking in Indian Moccasins* by F. Laurie Barron.

I learned a great deal about Saskatchewan's natural history from Bill Waiser's *A World We Have Lost*. I read his book the same summer that I saw the historical marker about Henry Kelsey beside the highway. Waiser's account of Kelsey's trek through Saskatchewan was very informative.

The information about the name of Indian Head is from the town website, Bill Barry's *Geographic Names of Saskatchewan*, and Arok Wolvengrey's *Cree*.

Throughout the book, I draw from a series of essays that Lorne wrote for the *Purple Martin Capital News*, a magazine published in the 1970s in Illinois. This chapter draws from the March 1975 essay "Prairie Ground Squirrels."

Information about Saskatchewan politicians in the twentieth century comes from political scientists in the province, especially James M. Pitsula's *Keeping Canada British*, Dennis Gruending's *Promises to Keep*, Rayner and Needham's "Saskatchewan," and Birgit Müller's "Still Feeding the World?"

For a thorough overview of Joseph Phelps as minister of Saskatchewan's Department of Natural Resources, see Kathleen Carlisle's *Fiery Joe*.

CHAPTER 2

The opening quotation is from Henry David Thoreau's *The Bluebird Carries the Sky on His Back.*

The information on different waves of environmentalism in Canada comes from my book *The Canadian Environment in Political Context.*

The edited volume *Saskatchewan Premiers of the Twenty-First Century* was immensely valuable in my research. Here I draw from Dianne Lloyd Norton's chapter "Woodrow S. Lloyd."

The information on bluebirds and how they got their colour comes from the Sialis website. Note that this work has been paraphrased from *Myths and Legends of California and the Old Southwest*, compiled and edited by Katharine Berry Judson in 1912 and reprinted in 2008.

Information on bluebirds, including their size, diet, and nesting habits, comes from Margaret Barker and Elissa Wolfson's book *Audubon Birdhouse Book* and Frances Backhouse's article "Bluebird Revival."

The story about Lorne Scott and Stuart Houston got its start by Doug Gilroy in 1964 in "Prairie Wildlife" and was expanded by Lorne Scott in 1972 in "One of My Favorite Birds."

The book about Saskatchewan birds to which Houston contributed was *Birds of Saskatchewan* published in 2019.

Information on the museum's history is from an unpublished essay by former museum director Ron Borden, "An Institution that Matters," shared with me in PDF from a current staff member. Other museum information is drawn from the website archives, also shared with me personally.

While writing this book, I learned a lot about Allan Blakeney, especially from his memoirs, *An Honourable Calling*, and from Dennis Gruending's essay "Allan E. Blakeney."

For background on *The Saskatchewan Environmental Assessment Act*, see Marie-Ann Bowden's article "Environmental Assessment Reform in Saskatchewan."

For a history of uranium mining in Canada and Saskatchewan, see Jim Harding's book *Canada's Deadly Secret*. For more information about Eldorado, see Robert Bothwell's book *Eldorado*. And for information specifically about the public inquiries into uranium mining in Saskatchewan, see Liora Salter, Debra Slaco, and Karin Konstantynowicz's study *Public Inquiries in Canada*.

Chief Justice Edward Bayda called for the inquiry into uranium mining, and that is why it is known as the Bayda Inquiry. The final report, as well as the Saskatchewan government response, were published, though it is difficult to track down copies. An analysis of the inquiry is available in Jim Harding's *Canada's Deadly Secret* as well as in "Bibliography on Saskatchewan Uranium Inquiries and the Northern and Global Impact of the Uranium Industry" by Jim Harding, Beryl Forgay, and Mary Gianoli.

This chapter draws from two of Lorne Scott's essays. In "Looking Back on 1975," Lorne comments on being a park naturalist, and in "Bits and Pieces" he writes a eulogy to his van.

CHAPTER 3

The opening quotation is from Wendell Berry's essay "Compromise, Hell!"

The quotation about Grant Devine appointing himself minister of agriculture comes from Deborah Sproat in "Devine the Ag Minister."

Perhaps an important backstory on the Souris River is that in the 1940s the International Joint Commission conducted a formal review of the Souris River to decide an apportionment scheme for sharing the flow among Saskatchewan, North Dakota, and Manitoba. At the request of Tommy Douglas, the commission met in the late 1950s to re-examine Saskatchewan's share of the water because Douglas wanted to build a dam on the river for a coal-powered energy station. An agreement was struck between the federal government and the provincial government by which the province was allowed to retain as much as 50 percent of the water of the Souris River. The Boundary Dam Power Station was built in 1959.

For information on the Souris River and the Rafferty-Alameda project, I draw from W.J. Stolte's essay "The Hydrology and Impacts of the Rafferty-Alameda Project."

Information on the Rafferty-Alameda case, especially the details of the court proceedings and a timeline of events, comes mainly from two books on the topic. The first is *Against the Flow* by George N. Hood, one of Grant Devine's inside guys and a main driver of the project from 1986 to 1991. The second is *Dams of Contention* by Bill Redekop, a writer and journalist with the *Winnipeg Free Press*. Hood's book was written in 1994 and drew primarily from his own experience working on the project as vice-president of the Souris Basin Development Authority (the Crown corporation responsible for the dams). Hood knew all the main players in the story personally and was involved in many, if not all, high-level meetings and discussions on the dams from 1986 to 1991. Redekop's book was published in 2012 and drew from personal interviews with various individuals, court records, newspaper articles, and government documents. Both books have made important contributions to our understanding of the Rafferty-Alameda controversy and the early history of Canada's *Environmental Assessment Act*.

This chapter also draws from Stephen Hazell's book *Canada v. The Environment*. The first few chapters of that book deal specifically with Rafferty-Alameda because Hazell was involved as legal counsel to the environmentalists who brought the legal suit against the project and because any understanding of the *Canadian Environmental Assessment Act* must start with Rafferty-Alameda. Importantly, the Hood, Redekop, and Hazell books mention Lorne by name. He is not portrayed as a main player in the larger Rafferty-Alameda controversy, but he was an important—even critical—player in Saskatchewan and got the legal ball rolling.

It is perhaps worth mentioning that Don Wilkinson's lawyer was my father, Wilson Olive. I did not learn this tidbit until 2012 when I researched the Rafferty-Alameda project for a case study to teach in my environmental policy course.

Lucien Bouchard resigned as the federal minister of environment over issues related to the Meech Lake Accord. That accord involved proposed amendments to the Constitution of Canada that ultimately failed to win support in Manitoba and Newfoundland. Bouchard initially supported the accord. However, after Jean Charest, a former cabinet minister, recommended changes, Bouchard announced his opposition to the accord and his support for Quebec sovereignty. (Charest made recommendations based upon a commission assembled to address New Brunswick's initial concerns about the accord.) Prime Minister Brian Mulroney would not tolerate his cabinet ministers breaking rank on the Meech Lake Accord, so he asked Bouchard to resign. On May 22, 1990, Bouchard formally resigned, ending his friendship with Mulroney and his tenure as the minister of environment.

CHAPTER 4

The opening quotation is from Wallace Stegner's *Where the Bluebird Sings to the Lemonade Springs*.

On Grant Devine's scandal, I drew from D.C. Fraser's *Leader-Post* article "Former Senator, MLA Eric Berntson Dominated Devine Era."

On Roy Romanow's "third way," I drew from David McGrane's chapter "Which Third Way?"

Romanow was quoted on provincial finances in the early 1990s by David Roberts in his article "Premier Reveals Saskatchewan Flirted with Bankruptcy."

The Indian Head–Wolseley riding was created in 1975 when the Qu'Appelle-Wolseley riding was redrawn. But even that riding was actually a combination of the South Qu'Appelle and Wolseley ridings of 1934. Between 1934 and 1975, the Qu'Appelle-Wolseley seat oscillated between Liberal and CCF representation. In 1971, the New Democratic Party won the seat with Terry Hanson. Between 1978 and 1991, the Indian Head–Wolseley seat was held by the Progressive Conservative Party.

The quotation about a close vote in the New Democratic Party comes from James Parker in "Panel Reviewing Uranium Projects Wraps Up after Approving Projects."

The federal provincial assessments of the uranium mines in Saskatchewan can be found in the Canadian Environmental Assessment Agency's "Panel Report."

The quotation about Joe Phelps comes from Kathleen Carlisle in *Fiery Joe*.

The background on climate change and the Kyoto Protocol comes from my book *The Canadian Environment in Political Context*.

In the Lorne Scott Fonds are about 300 pages related to climate change. Mostly they are about the Voluntary Challenge and Registry program created by the federal government. It was essentially a call to industries, organizations, and governments to express their intentions and their means of reducing greenhouse gas emissions. The report can be found in full in the fonds. There are also memos among Lorne Scott, Eldon Lautermilch, and Roy Romanow about Saskatchewan's *voluntary* participation. Finally, there are about fifty letters from Saskatchewan residents to Lorne asking about the government's actions on climate change.

CHAPTER 5
The opening quotation is from Aldo Leopold's *A Sand County Almanac*.

The quotation on cabinet ministers who need to be prairie people is from Roy Romanow's chapter "Forming Shadow Cabinets and Cabinets in Saskatchewan from 1987–2001."

Both Environment and Resource Management were in the same department at the time even though there were overlapping portfolios in Crown Investments Corporations, Energy and Mines, Agriculture and Food, and Northern Affairs. The Department of Environment was created in 1972 separate from the Department of Natural Resources, and the minister and cabinet position remained so until 1987. Then Grant Devine added Public Safety to the Environment portfolio. In 1992, Roy Romanow changed the cabinet position to Environment and Resource Management. That was Lorne's portfolio for almost five years.

Essentially, 3.9 million people visited parks over the course of the year, but that number included repeat visitors, so it is not accurate to say that 3.9 million *different* people visited parks. See the Ministry of Parks, Culture, and Sport's *Annual Report for 2017–18*.

Lorne's comments on forestry are from John Warnock's article "Saskatchewan's Neo-colonial Forest Policy"; Lorne's comments in the Legislative Assembly on May 27 and June 13, 1996; and Sandra Condon's article "Proposed New Forest Management Law in Saskatchewan."

On conservation easements in the United States, see Federico Cheever and Nancy McLaughlin's study "An Introduction to Conservation Easements in the United States."

Lorne's statement in the Legislative Assembly was on April 11, 1997.

For data on easements in the provinces, see Government of Canada, Agriculture and Agri-Food Canada's report *Summary of Canadian Experience with Conservation Easements and Their Potential Application to Agri-Environmental Policy.*

For newspaper articles on Métis hunting, see Randy Burton's articles "Mecca for Métis Hunters," "Gov't Won't Move to Stop Night Hunting," and "Gov't Moves to End Night Hunting"; Bonnie Braden's article "Gov't to Consider Hunting Ban along Manitoba Border"; letters in the Lorne Scott Fonds; and an angry op-ed aimed at Lorne by Cordell Mamer titled "Slaughter Ends Moose Draw."

Today the Federation of Saskatchewan Indian Nations is the Federation of Sovereign Indigenous Nations.

The Northern Saskatchewan Administrative District was created in 1948. It is about half of Saskatchewan's land and almost 5 percent of the population. The forty-five communities in the district are a combination of municipalities, First Nations reserves, and settlements.

For more on Métis hunting rights and Métis rights in general, see Adam Gaudry's 2018 report from the Yellowhead Institute.

For information on *The Wildlife Act*, see Lorne Scott's comments in the Legislative Assembly on April 11, 1997; *The Wildlife Act* 1998, s 5; and my article "Under Threat."

Lorne mentioned to me the idea that Devine traded Grasslands National Park land for federal approval of the Rafferty-Alameda dams. It is also discussed in Bill Redekop's book, especially in regard to Elizabeth May.

CHAPTER 6

The opening quotation is from Adrienne Rich's poem "Natural Resources" in *The Dream of a Common Language*.

The New Democratic Party got 38 percent of the vote and elected candidates to twenty-nine of fifty-eight seats. The newly formed Saskatchewan Party got 39 percent of the vote and twenty-five seats. The Liberal Party, struggling to remain intact as its members left to join the Saskatchewan Party, won 20 percent of the vote and four seats. Romanow remained as premier, but with only twenty-nine seats it was a precarious position and required support from the Liberal Party. If those members chose to vote with the Saskatchewan Party, then together they could match the New Democratic Party's twenty-nine votes.

For a history of guns in Canada, see R. Blake Brown's book *Arming and Disarming.*

For recent gun stats, see Andrew Russell's article "Should Canada Ban Hand Guns?"

On the SWF stance on the registry, see the articles "Wildlife Federation Won't Advocate Gun Law Disobedience" and "Gun Control Act Hurting Hunter Recruitment." Also see Lorne's op-ed "PM Urged to Scrap Gun Registry."

James Daschuk discusses cattle as an ecological disaster briefly in *Clearing the Plains*. The cattle and horses brought to Saskatchewan from Texas also brought diseases such as anthrax, Texas tick fever, brucellosis, and, significantly, bovine tuberculosis. Similar to the way that disease spreads from game elk to wild elk and deer, disease spread from cattle and horses to bison, making even worse the rapid decline of the already disappearing species on the prairies.

On chronic wasting disease, see the Canadian Food Inspection Agency's fact sheet "Chronic Wasting Disease (CWD)." For surveillance program results in Saskatchewan, see the Government of Saskatchewan's CWD surveillance website.

Don McMorris retained that seat through the spring 2016 election, but he formally resigned from the Saskatchewan Party caucus in the summer of 2016 after being charged with impaired driving. He was the minister responsible for Saskatchewan Government Insurance and Saskatchewan Liquor and Gaming Authority at the time.

On the Greater Sand Hills, see the article "Helping Hand for Great Sand Hills."

The quotation from Wallace Stegner is from *Where the Bluebird Sings to the Lemonade Springs*.

The letter from Miles Russell is in Lorne Scott's personal files.

On the Wascana Marsh, see "About Wascana Marsh" and "Our Mission, Vision and Goals" on the Friends of Wascana Marsh website.

On the North American Bluebird Society, see Mary Janetatos's article "A History of the North American Bluebird Society."

The letter from Lynda Haverstock is in Lorne Scott's personal files.

The quotation from Dennis Sherratt on the Order of Merit comes from Trevor Newell's article "Recognition Honours Scott."

The quotation from Peter Carton comes from "Saskatchewan Conservation Leader Appointed to Order of Canada."

CHAPTER 7

The opening quotation is from an interview that I did with Saskatchewan writer and activist Candace Savage.

The quotation from Howard Leeson is from the chapter "The 2007 Election" in his book *Saskatchewan Politics*.

The information on Saskatchewan's budget slogans is from Jim Harding's book *Moving beyond Neo-Liberalism in Saskatchewan*.

For background and information on the Indian Head Tree Nursery, see Lorne Scott's article "Farm Shelterbelts"; Morris Johnson's article "Turn Tree Farm into Success Story"; Bruce Johnstone's articles "Feds Urged to Stop Sell-Off of Tree Nursery," "APAS, McNair Sign Deal," "HELP Says Ritz Rejected Bid," and "RM Reeve Denies Deal to Manage Nursery"; and Gerry Ritz's article "Tree Nursery."

For those unfamiliar with the nuances of local politics in the province, Saskatchewan is divided into rural municipalities (RMs). Today there are 296 RMs in total, but they vary in population—the average being close to 600 people. The RM of Indian Head is the oldest in the province since it was officially incorporated in 1884. It does not technically include the towns/villages of Indian Head, Katepwa South, and Sintaluta, all in the RM, but the rural areas surrounding them. The towns/villages have their own governments: a mayor and council. Thus, the RM of Indian Head 156 is 760 square kilometres and had a population in 2016 of 336 people. In 2004, residents chose Lorne to be the reeve, or president, of their RM. In addition to a reeve, an

RM has a council of six elected members and an administrator. Their work is funded by ratepayer taxes, and they control a small budget that can be used for roads, community events, signage, drainage, and other projects.

For information and background on the PFRA program, see the report by David Phillips titled "PFRA Pastures Transition Study." Also see Trevor Herriot's book *Towards a Prairie Atonement*. In some cases, the lands had been Métis or First Nations lands.

See the Public Pastures—Public Interest report "A Vision for the Future of Saskatchewan Heritage Rangelands."

The op-ed by Katherine Arbuthnot and Brian Sterenberg was titled "Public Community Pastures Matter to Urban Sask."

On ecology, see the article "The Natural Ecological Value of Wilderness" by H. Ken Cordell and co-authors.

For more on the federal-provincial deal on three PFRA lands in the southwest and information on the new Prairie Pastures Conservation Area, see the article by Forrest Hisey, Melissa Heppner, and Andrea Olive titled "Supporting Native Grasslands in Canada."

On whooping cranes, see G.W. Archibald's article "Whooping Crane Update"; Friends of the Wild Whoopers' note on the "Jerome J. Pratt" Conservation Awards; Lorne Scott's article "Whooping Crane Meeting Held in Regina"; the International Crane Foundation's guide "Whooping Crane" and article "Ribbons in the Sky"; and Ramsar Sites Information Service's note on "Whooping Crane Summer Range."

CHAPTER 8

The opening quotation is from Wendell Berry's *The World-Ending Fire*.

On Lorne's land in conservation easements, see his article "Looking Back on 1975."

The quotation about farming and contact with nature is from Lorne Scott's article "Observations from a Tractor Seat."

About spring on the prairies, see Aldo Leopold's book *A Sand County Almanac* and Lorne Scott's article "Spring on the Prairies."

The Wallace Stegner quotation about Wendell Berry is from *Where the Bluebird Sings to the Lemonade Springs*.

On the Roundup case in the United States, see Sam Levin's 2018 article "The Man Who Beat Monsanto."

On "new conservation" versus "traditional conservation," see the article "What Is the Future of Conservation?" by Daniel Doak and co-authors.

The quotation from Aldo Leopold about a farmer's economic utility is from *A Sand County Almanac*.

Lorne's essay on prairie dogs was titled "The Playful Ones."

For more on the concept of "biological annihilation," see the article by Brooke Jarvis titled "The Insect Apocalypse Is Here."

For statistics on Canadian wildlife, see the Living Planet Report by World Wildlife Fund Canada.

CONCLUSION

The opening quotation is from Trevor Herriot's *Towards a Prairie Atonement*.

The observation about DeVoto and those who opposed him comes from David Gessner's book *All the Wild that Remains*.

POSTFACE

In 2020, I was awarded a Social Science and Humanities Research Council Insight Development Grant to study bison reintroduction on the Great Plains as a means of reconciliation. I have spent a great deal of time learning about bison as a cultural keystone species. The news about The Key First Nation is from the Regina *Leader-Post* article "Bison Again Roaming the Plains on The Key First Nation."

I learned about the Seven Sacred Laws in a high school Native Studies class but was recently reminded of them when I took the Indigenous Canada online course through the University of Alberta. I highly recommend this free course to all Canadians.

The reference to the "geography of hope" is from Wallace Stegner in *The Sounds of Mountain Water*.

REFERENCES

Arbuthnot, Katherine, and Brian Sterenberg. "Public Community Pastures Matter to Urban Sask." Saskatoon *StarPhoenix*, March 8, 2013.

Archibald, G.W. "Whooping Crane Update." ICF *Bugle* 14, no. 1 (1988): 4–6.

Backhouse, Frances. "Bluebird Revival." *Canadian Geographic* 106 (1986): 33–38.

Barker, Margaret A., and Elissa Wolfson. *Audubon Birdhouse Book*. Beverly, MA: Voyageur Press, 2013.

Barron, F. Laurie. *Walking in Indian Moccasins: The Native Policies of Tommy Douglas and the CCF*. Vancouver: UBC Press, 1997.

Barry, Bill. *Geographic Names of Saskatchewan*. Regina: Centax Books, 2005.

Benson, Jackson J. *Wallace Stegner: His Life and Work*. Lincoln, NE: Bison Books, 2009.

Berry, Wendell. "Compromise, Hell!" In *The Way of Ignorance*, by Wendell Berry, 20–27. Washington, DC: Shoemaker and Hoard, 2005.

———. *The Unsettling of America: Culture and Agriculture*. Berkeley, CA: Counterpoint, 2015.

"Bison Again Roaming the Plains on The Key First Nation." Regina *Leader-Post*, February 2, 2022. https://leaderpost.com/news/saskatchewan/bison-again-roaming-the-plains-on-the-key-first-nation.

Blakeney, Allan. *An Honourable Calling: Political Memoirs*. Toronto: University of Toronto Press, 2008.

Bothwell, Robert. *Eldorado: Canada's National Uranium Company*. Toronto,: University of Toronto Press, 2011.

Bowden, Marie-Ann. "Environmental Assessment Reform in Saskatchewan: Taking Care of Business." *Journal of Environmental Law and Practice* 21 (2010): 261–77.

Braden, Bonny. "Gov't to Consider Hunting Ban along Manitoba Border." Saskatoon *StarPhoenix*, November 8, 1997.

Brown, R. Blake *Arming and Disarming: A History of Gun Control in Canada*. Toronto: University of Toronto Press, 2013.

Burton, Randy. "Gov't Won't Move to Stop Night Hunting." Saskatoon *StarPhoenix*, November 22, 1997.

———. "Mecca for Métis Hunters." Saskatoon *StarPhoenix*, November 21, 1997, A1.

Callicott, J. Baird. "Three Project Ideas to Fill Research Gaps in Aldo Leopold Scholarship." *Socio-Ecological Practice Research* 4 (2022): 11–16. https://doi.org/10.1007/s42532-021-00102-6.

Carlisle, Kathleen. *Fiery Joe: The Maverick Who Lit Up the West*. Regina: University of Regina Press, 2017.

Carson, Rachel. Silent Spring. Mariner Classics, 2022.

Cheever, Federico, and Nancy A. McLaughlin. "An Introduction to Conservation Easements in the United States: A Simple Concept and a Complicated Mosaic of Law." University of Denver, Digital Commons, 2015. https://papers.ssrn.com/sol3/Papers.cfm?abstract_id=2650024.

Condon, Sandra. "Proposed New Forest Management Law in Saskatchewan." Canadian Press News Wire, March 14, 1996.

Conway, John F. *The Prairie Populist: George Hara Williams and the Untold Story of the* CCF. Regina: University of Regina Press, 2018.

Cordell, H. Ken, Danielle Murphy, Kurt H. Ritters, and J.E. Harvard III. "The Natural Ecological Value of Wilderness." In *The*

Multiple Values of Wilderness, edited by H. Ken Cordell, John C. Bergstrom, and J.M. Bowker, 205–49. Champaign, IL: Venture Publishing, 2005.

Daschuk, James. *Clearing the Plains: Disease, Politics of Starvation, and the Loss of Indigenous Life*. Regina: University of Regina Press, 2019.

DeVoto, Bernard. *The Western Paradox: A Conservation Reader*. New Haven, CT: Yale University Press, 2001.

Doak, Daniel F., Victoria J. Bakker, Bruce Evan Goldstein, and Benjamin Hale. "What Is the Future of Conservation?" *Trends in Ecology and Evolution* 29, no. 2 (2014): 77–81.

Fraser, D.C. "Former Senator, MLA Eric Berntson Dominated Devine Era." Regina *Leader-Post*, September 26, 2018. https://www.pressreader.com/canada/regina-leader-post/20180927/281500752180261.

Friends of the Wascana Marsh. "History." https://www.wascanamarsh.ca/about-us/history.

Friends of the Wild Whoopers. "Jerome J. Pratt—Whooping Crane Conservation Awards." 2014. https://friendsofthewildwhoopers.org/whooping-crane-conservation-awards/.

Gaudry, Adam. "Better Late than Never? Canada's Reluctant Recognition of Métis Rights and Self-Government." The Yellowhead Institute, August 21, 2018. https://yellowheadinstitute.org/2018/08/21/better-late-than-never-canadas-reluctant-recognition-of-metis-rights-and-self-government/.

Gessner, David. *All the Wild that Remains: Edward Abbey, Wallace Stegner, and the American West*. New York: W.W. Norton, 2015.

Gilroy, Doug. "Prairie Wildlife." *Western Producer*, March 12, 1964.

Government of Canada. Agiculture and Agri-Foods Canada. "Summary of Canadian Experience with Conservation Easements and Their Potential Application to Agri-Environmental Policy." 2008. https://publications.gc.ca/collections/collection_2011/agr/A125-17-2011-eng.pdf.

———. Canadian Food Inspection Agency. "Chronic Wasting Disease: What Cervid Producers Should Know." 2021. https://inspection.canada.ca/animal-health/terrestrial-animals/diseases/

reportable/cwd/what-cervid-producers-should-know/eng/
1330189947852/1330190096558.

Government of Saskatchewan. "CWD Surveillance Program Results."
https://www.saskatchewan.ca/residents/environment-public-
health-and-safety/wildlife-issues/fish-and-wildlife-diseases/
chronic-wasting-disease/cwd-map.

———. Ministry of Parks, Culture and Sport. *Annual Report for 2017–18.*
https://www.saskatchewan.ca/government/government-
structure/ministries/parks-culture-and-sport.

Gruending, Dennis. "Allan E. Blakeney." In *Saskatchewan Premiers
of the Twentieth Century,* edited by Gordon Barnhart, 271–316.
Regina: University of Regina Press, 2004.

———. *Promises to Keep: A Political Biography of Allan Blakeney.* Saskatoon: Western Producer Prairie Books, 1990.

Gulliford, Andrew. "Aldo Leopold, Estella Bergere, Mia Casita and
Sheepherding in New Mexico." *Natural Resources Journal* 57,
no. 2 (2017): 395–428.

Harding, Jim. *Canada's Deadly Secret: Saskatchewan Uranium and
the Global Nuclear System.* Halifax and Winnipeg: Fernwood
Publishing, 2007.

———. *Moving beyond Neo-Liberalism in Saskatchewan.* Toronto: Crows-
nest Books, 2018.

Harding, Jim, Beryl Forgay, and Mary Gianoli. "Bibliography on Sas-
katchewan Uranium Inquiries and the Northern and Global
Impact of the Uranium Industry." University of Regina, Prairie
Justice Research, 1988. https://inis.iaea.org/collection/NCL-
CollectionStore/_Public/23/026/23026417.pdf.

Hazell, Stephen. *Canada v. The Environment: Federal Environmental
Assessment 1984–1998.* Toronto: Canadian Environmental
Defence Fund, 1999.

"Helping Hand for Great Sand Hills." *Globe and Mail,* June 16,
2004. https://www.theglobeandmail.com/news/national/
helping-hand-for-great-sand-hills/article25679074/.

Herriot, Trevor. *Grass, Sky, Song: Promise and Peril in the World of
Grassland Birds.* Toronto: HarperCollins, 2009.

————. *Towards a Prairie Atonement*. Regina: University of Regina Press, 2016.

Hisey, Forrest, Melissa Heppner, and Andrea Olive. "Supporting Native Grasslands in Canada: Lessons Learned and Future Management of the Prairie Pastures Conservation Area in Saskatchewan." *Canadian Geographer* 66, no. 4 (2022): 683–95.

Hood, George H. *Against the Flow: Rafferty-Alameda and the Politics of the Environment*. Leaside, ON: Fifth House Publishers, 1994.

Inter-Church Uranium Committee Educational Co-Operative. https://www.icucec.org.

International Crane Foundation. "Ribbons in the Sky." 2017. https://www.savingcranes.org/ribbons-in-the-sky/.

————. "Whooping Crane." https://www.savingcranes.org/species-field-guide/whooping-crane/.

Janetatos, Mary D. "A History of the North American Bluebird Society." 1996. http://www.nabluebirdsociety.org/nabs-history/.

Jarvis, Brooke. "The Insect Apocalypse Is Here." *New York Times*, November 27, 2018. https://www.nytimes.com/2018/11/27/magazine/insect-apocalypse.html.

Johnson, Morris. "Turn Tree Farm into Success Story." Saskatoon *StarPhoenix*, January 29, 2015.

Johnstone, Bruce. "APAS, McNair Sign Deal." Regina *Leader-Post*, June 26, 2013.

————. "Feds Urged to Stop Sell-Off of Tree Nursery." Regina *Leader-Post*, April 23, 2013, D1.

————. "HELP Says Ritz Rejected Bid." Saskatoon *StarPhoenix*, October 8, 2013.

————. "RM Reeve Denies Deal to Manage Nursery." Saskatoon *StarPhoenix*, October 29, 2013, D4.

Judson, Katharine Berry. *Myths and Legends of California and the Old Southwest*. London: Forgotton Books, 2008.

Kolbert, Elizabeth. *The Sixth Extinction: An Unnatural History*. New York: Picador, 2015.

LaDow, Beth. *The Medicine Line: Life and Death on a North American Borderland*. New York: Routledge, 2002.

Leeson, Howard. "The 2007 Election." In *Saskatchewan Politics: Crowding the Centre*, edited by Howard Leeson, 119–41. Regina: Canadian Plains Research Center, 2009.

Leopold, Aldo. *A Sand County Almanac: With Other Essays on Conservation from Round River*. 2nd ed. Oxford: Oxford University Press, 1968.

Levin, Sam. "The Man Who Beat Monsanto." *Guardian*, September 26, 2018. https://www.theguardian.com/business/2018/sep/25 monsanto-dewayne-johnson-cancer-verdict.

Mamer, Cordell. "Slaughter Ends Moose Draw." Saskatoon *StarPhoenix*, April 24, 1997, A5.

McGrane, David. "Which Third Way? A Comparison of the Romanow and Calvert NDP Governments from 1991 to 2007." In *Saskatchewan Politics: Crowding the Centre*, edited by Howard Leeson, 143–64. Regina: Canadian Plains Research Center, 2009.

Müller, Birgit. "Still Feeding the World?" *Canada Anthropology Society* 50, no. 2 (2008): 389–407.

Newell, Trevor. "Recognition Honours Scott." *Regina Sun*, July 6, 2008, 41.

Norton, Dianne Llyod. "Woodrow S. Lloyd." In *Saskatchewan Premiers of the Twentieth Century*, edited by Gordon Barnhart, 213–36. Regina: Canadian Plains Research Center, 2004.

Olive, Andrea. *The Canadian Environment in Political Context*. 2nd ed. Toronto: University of Toronto Press, 2019.

———. *Land, Stewardship, and Legitimacy: Endangered Species Policy in Canada and the US*. Toronto: University of Toronto Press, 2014.

———. "Under Threat: 20 Years since the Saskatchewan *Wildlife Act*." Canadian Centre for Policy Alternatives, 2018. https://www.policyalternatives.ca/UnderThreat.

Parker, James. "Panel Reviewing Uranium Projects Wraps Up after Approving Projects." Saskatoon *StarPhoenix*, November 22, 1997.

Pepper, Wayne. *Conserving the Legacy: Wildlife Conservation in Saskatchewan, 1905–2005*. Regina: Nature Saskatchewan, 2022.

Phillips, Dave. "PFRA Pastures Transition Study." Frogworks Consultants, 2015. https://www.naturesask.ca/rsu_docs/pfra-final-report.pdf.

Pitsula, James. *Keeping Canada British: The Ku Klux Klan in 1920s Saskatchewan*. Vancouver: UBC Press, 2013.

Public Pastures—Public Interest. "A Vision for the Future of Saskatchewan Heritage Rangelands." https://pfrapastureposts.wordpress.com/about/six-principles/.

Ramsar Sites Information Service. "Whooping Crane Summer Range." https://rsis.ramsar.org/ris/240.

Rayner, Jeremy, and Fraser Needham. "Saskatchewan: Change without Direction." *Policy and Society* 28 (2009): 139–50.

Redekop, Bill. *Dams of Contention: The Rafferty-Alameda Story and the Birth of Canadian Environmental Law*. Winnipeg: Heartland, 2012.

Rich, Adrienne. *The Dream of a Common Language: Poetry 1974–1977*. New York: W.W. Norton, 2013.

Ritz, Gerry. "Tree Nursery." Regina *Leader-Post*, October 3, 2013.

Romanow, Roy. "Forming Shadow Cabinets and Cabinets in Saskatchewan from 1987–2001." In *Saskatchewan Politics: Crowding the Centre*, edited by Howard Leeson, 61–76. Regina: Canadian Plains Research Center, 2009.

Russell, Andrew. "Should Canada Ban Hand Guns?" Global News, September 5, 2018. https://globalnews.ca/news/4351811/canada-handgun-ban-danforth-shoting/.

Salter, Liora, Debra Slaco, and Karin Konstantynowicz. Public Inquiries in Canada. Background Study 47. Science Council of Canada, 1981.

"Saskatchewan Conservation Leader Appointed to Order of Canada." *Conservator* 29, no. 3 (2008): 11.

Savage, Candace. *Prairie: A Natural History*. Vancouver: Greystone Books, 2004.

Scott, Lorne. "Bits and Pieces." *Purple Martin Capital News*, July 1976.

——. "Farm Shelterbelts." *Purple Martin Capital News*, January 1975.

——. "Looking Back on 1975." *Purple Martin Capital News*, December 1976.

——. "Observations from a Tractor Seat." *Purple Martin Capital News*, July 1975.

——. "One of My Favorite Birds." *Purple Martin Capital News*, November 1972.

——. "The Playful Ones." *Purple Martin Capital News*, August 1972.

———. "PM Urged to Scrap Gun Registry." *Prince Albert Herald*, December 14, 2002.

———. "Prairie Ground Squirrels." *Purple Martin Capital News*, March 1975.

———. "Whooping Crane Meeting Held in Regina." *Purple Martin Capital News*, October 1972.

Services, S.P. "Federal, Sask. NDP at Odds over Greenhouse Gas Emissions." Saskatoon *StarPhoenix*, October 31, 1997, A11.

Sialis. "How the Bluebird and Coyote Got Their Color." http://www.sialis.org/bluebirdstory.htm.

Smith, Alan R., C. Stuart Houston, and J. Frank Roy. *Birds of Saskatchewan*. Regina: Nature Saskatchewan, 2019.

Sproat, Deborah. "Devine the Ag Minister: 'I Might as Well Take Charge.'" *Western Producer*, January 2, 1986.

Stegner, Wallace. *The Sounds of Mountain Water: The Changing American West*. New York: Penguin Books, 1997.

———. *Where the Bluebird Sings to the Lemonade Springs: Living and Writing in the West*. New York: Modern Library, 2002.

———. *Wolf Willow: A History, a Story, and a Memory of the Last Plains Frontier*. Lincoln: University of Nebraska Press, 1955.

Stolte, W.J. "The Hydrology and Impacts of the Rafferty-Alameda Project." *Canadian Water Resources Journal* 18, no. 3 (1993): 229–45.

Tart, Donna. *The Goldfinch: A Novel*. Boston: Little, Brown, 2013.

Thoreau, Henry David. *The Bluebird Carries the Sky on His Back*. New York: Random House, 1970.

Town of Indian Head. "How Did Indian Head Get Its Name?" https://townofindianhead.com/how-our-town-got-its-name/.

Waiser, Bill. *Saskatchewan: A New History*. Leaside, ON: Fifth House, 2018.

———. *A World We Have Lost: Saskatchewan before 1905*. Leaside, ON: Fifth House, 2016.

Warnock, John. "Saskatchewan's Neo-colonial Forest Policy." *Policy Options*, 2001. http://policyoptions.irpp.org/magazines/political-dissent/saskatchewans-neo-colonial-forestry-policy/.

Warren, Julianne Lutz. *Aldo Leopold's Odyssey*. 10th anniversary ed. Washington DC: Island Press, 2016.

"Wildlife Federation Won't Advocate Gun Law Disobedience." *Moose Jaw Times-Herald*, February 25, 2002.

Wilson, Garrett. *Frontier Farewell: The 1870s and the End of the Old West*. Regina: University of Regina Press, 2014.

Wolvengrey, Arok. *Cree: Words*. Vol. 1. Regina: Canadian Plains Research Center, 2011.

World Wildlife Fund Canada. Living Planet Report. 2018. https://www.worldwildlife.org/pages/living-planet-report-2018.

Wyatt, Mark. "Voluntary Pollution Curbs Useless." Saskatoon *StarPhoenix*, October 3, 1997.

INDEX

Lautermilch, Eldon, 66–67, 96

Leopold, Aldo, xxv, xxxiii, 71, 75,
155; champion of environmental
conservation, 76; coining term
"biotic community," 114, 180;
farmer as conservationist,
147, 154; land as community,
not commodity, 137, 160–61;
opposition to dams, 171; on
trophy hunting, 110–12

Liberal Party of Canada, 13, 20, 56, 100

Lloyd, Woodrow, 12, 168

M

Mackenzie Valley Pipeline, 23

MacMillan Bloedel Limited, 75

MacPherson, Justice Donald, 48

Martin, Paul, 100

May, Elizabeth, 92

McArthur River uranium mine, 61–62

McClean Lake uranium
deposits, 62–63

Métis Nation—Saskatchewan
(MN-S), 81–82, 84

Métis People, 9, 180; as bison hunters,
8; hunting and fishing rights
of, 79–80, 83; severed from
PFRA lands, 135; stakeholders
on resource management, 90

Midwest Joint Venture, proposed
uranium mine, 62

*Migratory Birds Convention
Act* (Canada), 80, 128

Ministry of Environment, 21,
41–43, 85, 89, 97, 129–30

Moe, Scott, government of,
dismantling and sale of
public lands, 123, 170

Monsanto Company, 151

Morrissette organic farm, 151

Muldoon, Justice Francis, 48

Mulroney, Brian, government of,
31, 169; achievements of, 55,
57; cuts to Canadian Wildlife
Service, 139; passage of CEAA, 50

N

Nakoda people, 180

Nakota (Assiniboine) people, 3, 7–8

National Farmers Union, 25

natural gas, as a resource, 131,
162; development of, xxvi, 10;
distribution system for, 54;
exploration for, 93; export markets
for, xxviii; extraction of, 100

natural gas industry, 66, 121, 168;
development of, 33; methane
release reduction in, 101; pipelines,
52, 122, 174; privatization of,
33; royalty rates for, 57, 123

natural resources: development of,
xxviii, 10, 53, 170; exploration
of, 10; extraction of, xxv, 34,
96; government control of,
1; overexploitation of, 168;
ownership of, 132; privatization
of, 13, 75, 169; revenue from, 33,
75; sustainable development, 96

Natural Resources Transfer
Agreement, 79

PHOTO: CHRISTOPHER PETRAKOS

ANDREA OLIVE is a Professor of Political Science and Geography, Geomatics, and Environment at the University of Toronto Mississauga. She has a BA from the University of Calgary, an MA from Dalhousie University, and a PhD in political science from Purdue University. She was born and raised in Regina, Saskatchewan, and still considers the province to be her home. Outside of her research and teaching on wildlife conservation, she is an avid runner, nature enthusiast, and world traveller.

A NOTE ABOUT THE TYPE

THE BODY OF THIS BOOK IS SET IN ARNO PRO, a serif type family created by Robert Slimbach at Adobe intended for professional use. The name refers to the river that runs through Florence, a centre of the Italian Renaissance. Arno is an old-style serif font, drawing inspiration from a variety of 15th and 16th century typefaces. Slimbach has described the design as a combination of the period's Aldine and Venetian styles, with italics inspired by the calligraphy and printing of Ludovico degli Arrighi.

THE ACCENTS ARE SET IN KNOCKOUT, a family of sans serif typefaces inspired by a style of American wood type, which was first introduced in the mid-nineteenth century and remains popular to this day. Because its range of widths exceeds the usual classifications of 'compressed, condensed, narrow, and regular,' Knockout's nine different widths are named after the standards used in professional boxing, from the spindly 'Flyweight' to the gargantuan 'Heavyweight.' (The widest member of the range is named 'Sumo.')